Metal Detecting and Archaeology

'Heritage Matters' Series: Volume Two

DEDICATION

This book is dedicated in loving memory of Olive Smith, a wonderful grandmother who was unwavering in her support and kindness, and who is missed every day

HERITAGE MATTERS

ISSN 1756–4832

SERIES EDITORS

Peter G. Stone
Peter Davis
Chris Whitehead

Heritage Matters is a series of edited and single-authored volumes which addresses the whole range of issues that confront the cultural heritage sector as we face the global challenges of the twenty-first century. The series follows the ethos of the International Centre for Cultural and Heritage Studies (ICCHS) at Newcastle University, where these issues are seen as part of an integrated whole, including both cultural and natural agendas, and thus encompasses challenges faced by all types of museums, art galleries, heritage sites and the organisations and individuals that work with, and are affected by them.

Previously published titles are listed at the back of this book

Metal Detecting and Archaeology

Edited by

Peter Stone and Suzie Thomas

THE BOYDELL PRESS

2009

First published 2009
The Boydell Press, Woodbridge
Paperback edition 2017

ISBN 978 1 84383 415 1 hardback
ISBN 978 1 78327 220 4 paperback

The Boydell Press is an imprint of Boydell & Brewer Ltd
PO Box 9, Woodbridge, Suffolk IP12 3DF, UK
and of Boydell & Brewer Inc.
668 Mt Hope Avenue, Rochester, NY 14620–2731, USA
website: www.boydellandbrewer.com

The publisher has no responsibility for the continued existence or accuracy
of URLs for external or third-party internet websites referred to in this book,
and does not guarantee that any content on such websites is,
or will remain, accurate or appropriate

A CIP record for this book is available
from the British Library

This publication is printed on acid-free paper

Printed and bound in Great Britain by
TJ International Ltd, Padstow, Cornwall

CONTENTS

LIST OF PLATES

(between pages 70 and 71)

ACKNOWLEDGEMENTS

This book stems from a conference organised in June 2005 in Newcastle upon Tyne. The conference followed an approach from the editors to staff from the Portable Antiquities Scheme and Tyne and Wear Museums to bring together both archaeologists and metal detector users, for the first time in the North East of England, to discuss issues of mutual interest. The conference, *Buried Treasure: Building Bridges*, was hosted by the International Centre for Cultural and Heritage Studies at Newcastle University and the Hancock Museum. The Portable Antiquities Scheme and Tyne and Wear Museums, and in particular our conference co-organisers, Philippa Walton and Steve McLean, deserve many thanks for their hard work in bringing the conference to fruition, from their provision of publicity and leaflets through to the friendly encouragement given to local metal detector users to attend the event.

Speakers at the conference included both metal detector users and archaeologists, many of whom have since been able to contribute to this volume. These, along with the speakers who found their work commitments prevented them from contributing, deserve our greatest thanks for providing the springboard for this volume. The authors of the many more chapters in this volume which added breadth and scope beyond what was possible in a regionally focused day conference must also be warmly thanked. Without the contributors' hard work and enthusiasm for the project, this book would not have been possible. Thanks also go to Rupert Redesdale for his Foreword to this volume, and for chairing *Buried Treasure: Building Bridges*.

Many more individuals have been involved directly or indirectly, either by providing access to important information or by just being extremely supportive of the development of the volume. These people are too numerous to name individually, but it is hoped that they know who they are and that their help was greatly appreciated. As ever, Peter would like to thank Genevieve and his family for their perseverance as he worked on yet another book, and Suzie would like to thank her parents in particular for their tireless support at all times. Suzie also thanks the Arts and Humanities Research Council (AHRC) for their support of her research over the past year. Special thanks also go to Catherine Todd, the publications and conference assistant in the International Centre for Cultural and Heritage Studies, and Matthew Champion, our publishing editor.

Finally, Suzie Thomas would like to thank her co-editor and PhD supervisor, Peter Stone, for giving her the opportunity to be part of the development of a volume such as this, and for his many years of (outstanding!) patience and support.

FOREWORD

It is surprising that there are not a large number of books already examining the deep and sometimes bitter battles fought between archaeologists and metal detector users. This enmity is a little like the debate on fox hunting, where the disagreement between the pro and anti lobby was based on issues such as class politics and social divisions as much as on the actual fox hunt.

Traditionally archaeologists distrusted those from outside academia; modern professional archaeologists, while perhaps being less focused within academia, claim ownership of the past as guardians of our valuable and fragile heritage. Metal detector users often have no professional training but have found for future generations some fantastic treasures such as the Ringlemere Cup or the Harrogate Hoard which would have remained lost without their work.

The real problem is that both archaeology and metal detecting is based on hard work with little reward. There are thousands of digs carried out in preparation of development work that are painstakingly excavated, meticulously recorded, and yield nothing or almost nothing of interest. Metal detector users can spend years covering ploughed fields finding little of historical or financial worth. However for both groups there is that dream of finding some long lost treasure. Many archaeologists would protest at this point claiming the context of the site, the historical provenance and the associated information about those living in the past is the only goal; however that protest fails to explain why in almost every archaeological practice in Britain there is a picture on the wall of Indiana Jones about to steal a golden skull from a temple.

That dream of finding an iconic treasure such as a golden skull - but perhaps in a more responsible form, without the question of ownership, massive vandalism and almost total destruction of historical context that is depicted in the film - is what archaeologists and metal detector users share. The hostility comes from a basic distrust between both sides over who controls access to the past.

Archaeologists take the moral high ground, claiming that metal detector users are only interested in the cash value of finds and that massive damage is done to the historical context by removing items that could help decipher the site they came from. Illegal metal detecting, 'nighthawking', has been a constant problem which has caused severe damage to many protected sites around Britain. Even though the majority of metal detecting is done responsibly and legally many archaeologists have long campaigned for its curtailment or banning.

The belief of archaeologists that they are qualified to control access to the past is probably due to the fact that archaeology has become mainly the preserve of professionals. The practice of archaeology, although massively popular on television, is now an increasingly complex and expensive operation and is frequently limited to areas where development is taking place. The idea that archaeology that is not under threat should be preserved for the future is enshrined in planning law and many archaeologists past and present believe that metal detecting is a threat to that heritage and future archaeology.

Metal detector users on the other hand believe that their activity is helping to unearth treasures that due to ploughing would be destroyed and therefore they are far from damaging the historical record but are rather helping to protect it. Deep ploughing over the last few years has done enormous damage to sites and many objects disturbed by ploughing would have been lost without detecting. The formation of the Portable Antiquities Scheme in England and Wales has helped individuals and metal detecting clubs record their finds and there is useful data on find patterns emerging from this work. The view of archaeologists that they should control the access to all archaeological remains is in direct competition with the metal detector users' view that they have a right and freedom to seek out objects on agricultural land avoiding protected sites.

It could be argued that studying the ideological difference between the two groups gives a clear picture of the fault lines that run through the practice of archaeology in Britain and perhaps recent developments show how archaeology will evolve in the near future.

The earliest archaeology was, simply, treasure hunting, the spoils becoming individual collections of interesting objects in private collections. Archaeology was the preserve of the rich who could afford to pay labourers low wages to unearth historical treasures. The pay of modern archaeological practitioners mirrors these early arrangements. The elitist nature of archaeology has moved on from the rich patron funding excavations, through academia, on to private developer funded work. The last group who are now responsible for funding the majority of archaeology do so mainly to meet the requirement of planning laws. The problem is that such digs are viewed by those who fund them as activity that is necessary to clear a site and allow building work to commence. Indeed archaeological work is viewed by many developers in almost exactly the same way toxic waste is: an expensive hindrance that needs professional treatment for quick removal.

Thousands of digs have been undertaken over the last two decades with tens of millions of pounds spent on the process, with, apart from some notable exceptions, very little public involvement or understanding of what has taken place. The generic support for archaeology which has a firm foundation could erode if the general public are not made to feel they have a personal stake in our shared archaeological heritage. Rather than banning metal detecting, more work should be undertaken to draw this large community closer into the archaeological mainstream as a valuable resource.

The reality is that both metal detecting and archaeology are damaging the preserved archaeological record. However, without the constant increase in knowledge of the past that these fragments can give us, what is the purpose of archaeology?

Rupert Redesdale
House of Lords, September 2008

Introduction

SUZIE THOMAS

This book explores the frequently contentious relationship between two very different groups of people: archaeologists and metal detector users. Both groups share a deep and sincere interest in the past but both go about their work with, traditionally, very different methodologies and, some argue, very different aims and objectives. Part of the contentious nature of the relationship can be put down to the unequal academic and social positions of 'professional' archaeologists and those who metal detect as a hobby. The latter are vilified by many professional archaeologists as being a terrible threat to the scientific exploration of the past, whose antics destroy the primary context of artefacts and thus dramatically reduce the value of artefacts recovered in this way to the proper study of the archaeological past. Metal detector users are at best a major nuisance, at worst a group that fosters and propagates the illicit trade in antiquities for its own financial gain to the significant detriment of the archaeological record. On the other side, many metal detector users find the position taken by archaeologists elitist and exclusive, denying those without higher academic qualifications the opportunity to engage in a practical way with their hobby and frequently their life-long burning interest: the discovery of objects from the past.

There is ample historical and contemporary evidence of tensions between the two groups. Some of this stems from earlier campaigns, such as the 1980s STOP campaign ('Stop Taking Our Past'), launched by archaeological organisations against treasure hunting (see Addyman, chapter 5, and Thomas, chapter 14); equally vitriolic accusations have been made against archaeologists by metal detector users at different times (eg Fletcher 1996, 35). No doubt, STOP's 'initial knee-jerk reaction' to metal detecting (Addyman and Brodie 2002, 179) did have an ultimately deleterious effect on the burgeoning relationships between archaeologists and metal detector users. Trevor Austin (chapter 10) echoes the point that in the early years of the metal detecting hobby, attempts by many metal detector users to share information about their finds with local museums and archaeologists were often met with hostility. There is also the very real issue of 'nighthawks' – those metal detector users who operate illegally, displaying the same commercially driven lack of concern for the integrity of the archaeology that they are inadvertently destroying as do *tombaroli*, the tomb-robbers of Italy, or *huaqeros*, the South American 'archaeological bandits' (Brodie 2002, 1).

Given such entrenched and contradictory standpoints it is not surprising that those who have tried to work across the groups have often been castigated for letting one or both of the sides down. However, there have been examples of successful cooperation between metal detector users and archaeologists, such as the work in East Anglia in the 1970s under the guidance of Tony Gregory and Barbara Green (Green and Gregory 1978), a local initiative which has been credited with inspiring the later model used by the extremely successful Portable Antiquities Scheme (PAS) (Bland 2005, 442; and see chapter 6). A code of practice for responsible metal detecting in England and Wales was produced in 2006, with the support of both archaeological and metal detecting organisations (CBA *et al* 2006).

This book concentrates on the positive. Aside from inevitable mentions of problems associated with unscrupulous metal detecting in the following chapters as appropriate, it does not focus on nighthawks, illicit trade in antiquities or looting. Instead it follows in the footsteps of these early pioneers of collaboration and sets out to demonstrate the efforts made in the past and being made today to try to encourage cooperation between archaeologists and metal detector users: to show efforts to build bridges between the two warring parties. To this end contributors include not only archaeologists who have directly or indirectly worked with metal detector users, but also representatives from a non-archaeological background: Trevor Austin (chapter 10) is himself a metal detector user; while Peter Spencer (chapter 11) is a numismatist who works regularly with metal detector users and writes for metal detecting magazines. This is done in the understanding that archaeological attempts to discredit, and on occasion illegalise, metal detecting have failed and that there is little likelihood of the hobby disappearing in the future. At the same time there is increasing evidence (see for example Spencer, chapter 11; Simpson, chapter 12; Richards and Naylor, chapter 15) that metal detecting can *and does* contribute to our understanding of the past in a way that traditional archaeology cannot. It seems logical, therefore, to move away from confrontation and towards conciliation in a way acceptable to all involved.

ARCHAEOLOGY AND METAL DETECTING – PRESENT AND PAST

Metal detecting in the UK today is a popular and apparently growing hobby, with many people who take it up apparently continuing to metal detect for years (Thomas, in prep). While many metal detector users are registered through their membership to either or both of the two national representative bodies, the National Council for Metal Detecting (NCMD) and the Federation of Independent Detectorists (FID), there is also a proportion of metal detector users who are not members of either organisation and who are therefore essentially invisible. Both the NCMD and the FID generally do not disclose exact membership numbers, largely because these tend to fluctuate from month to month as memberships lapse and are renewed. Therefore, estimations of the current total number of metal detector users in the UK vary. For example Grove (2005, 5) suggests there are around 30,000 active metal detector users, but Bland (2005, 441) suggests there are more likely to be only some 10,000. Ten years earlier Dobinson and Denison (1995) estimated the number of people metal detecting to be around 30,000 in England alone, with the acknowledgement that an absolute certainty on the figure was impossible. It can be a challenge, too, to establish what is meant by a 'metal detector user' in terms of frequency of metal detecting: some people may metal detect only occasionally, or purchase a metal detector but tire of the hobby after only a few outings, whereas others are avid enthusiasts who may go detecting twice a week or more.

Metal detecting emerged as a result of mine detecting technology developed during and after World War II (Addyman, chapter 5). This technology was, perhaps inevitably, developed into a machine manufactured for public consumption and marketed as a new hobby, at first in the USA; it was then imported to, and later manufactured in, the UK (Atkinson *circa* 1968, np; Beach 1970). In chapter 5 Peter Addyman – as a 'veteran' of many of the interactions between archaeologists and metal detector users, and as an instrumental figure both in the Portable Antiquities Working Group and the Council for British Archaeology (CBA) – provides us with a history of archaeology and metal detecting in the decades before the PAS was implemented. Roger Bland (chapter 6) then describes the development and future of both the PAS and the 1996 *Treasure Act*, both of which were put into practice in 1997, and which are currently the two principal ways in which metal detecting is brought into contact with archaeological and legislative practices in England and Wales.

THE PORTABLE ANTIQUITIES SCHEME

The PAS, initially set up in just six regions of England, remains a nationally important scheme across England and Wales, creating links in all regions with not only metal detector users but also other members of the public who might discover chance finds. At the time of writing, the PAS operates in the whole of England and Wales. There are currently 34 Finds Liaison Officers (FLOs) covering England, with Wales administered through a network of four Trust Liaison personnel, and a Finds Coordinator based in Cardiff. The contributions by Mark Lodwick (chapter 9) and by Philippa Walton and Dot Boughton (chapter 13) provide case studies of the PAS in action in different regions. As Finds Coordinator for Wales, Lodwick is able to present in detail the ways in which delivery of the PAS in Wales contrasts with the English experience. Walton and Boughton, as FLOs for the North East and Cumbria and Lancashire respectively, discuss the issues and challenges faced in their regions, both of which were added to the PAS network at a relatively late stage and neither of which, when compared to other regions – East Anglia, for example (see above) – had an existing tradition of cooperation between archaeologists and metal detector users. As well as its region-specific interactions, the PAS has a central unit which is responsible for specialist advice on finds, for coordinating its activities and, since March 2007, for administering the 1996 *Treasure Act*. While Bland (chapter 6) provides a comprehensive overview of these core activities, Ceinwen Paynton (chapter 17) describes specifically the educational activities of the PAS, including the resources it has provided for use in schools, although the role of Learning Coordinator within the PAS was unfortunately lost in recent cuts to the Scheme (see below).

Annual conferences at the British Museum have demonstrated not only the success that the PAS has had in engaging large numbers of metal detector users through the network of FLOs, but also the research potential of the data collected through the implementation of the Scheme. The 2007 PAS Conference, 'A Decade of Discovery', demonstrated some of the current academic research projects taking advantage of the information collected on the PAS Finds Database (available at: www.findsdatabase. org.uk). A number of examples of the PAS facilitating the discovery of important sites or the collation of additional data to enhance knowledge about a particular period or geographical area are included in this volume. Faye Simpson's account (chapter 12) of a metal detector user who made a chance discovery at Cumwhitton in Cumbria and promptly reported his find to Simpson, who was at the time the FLO for Cumbria and Lancashire, is a case in point. She describes how a telephone call from a member of Kendal Metal Detector Club with an artefact that 'could be something interesting' led to the discovery and excavation of an extremely significant Norse burial site; important information was thus gathered about a previously undocumented area of Scandinavian occupation in the North West of England. Julian Richards and John Naylor (chapter 15), working with metal detected finds to shed light on the Viking and Anglo-Saxon periods through the 'Viking and Anglo-Saxon Landscape and Economy Project' (VASLE), derived information for their research from a number of methods, which not only included working directly with a group of metal detector users in survey work, but also utilised the data stored on the PAS Finds Database. This is another important example of the way in which metal detector users, by collaborating with archaeologists and allowing their finds to be recorded, can make a real and meaningful contribution to the archaeological record. Conversely, however, Tony Pollard (chapter 16) demonstrates that in battlefield archaeology, while metal detecting is a valuable tool, the data from PAS has not necessarily proven useful, in part because of the location of some of his case study battlefield sites (eg in Scotland, where the PAS does not operate), but also because in many cases metal detector users do not seem to be recording certain types of metal artefact through the PAS, such as musket balls. Similarly, at a metal detecting rally in Cambridgeshire in 2007, a number of metal detector users interviewed as part of a wider research project told surveyors that they had found musket balls, but had not thought that they were worth recording with the PAS staff (see Thomas 2007).

As Bland (chapter 6) demonstrates, many Treasure cases (under the 1996 *Treasure Act*) are also brought to light by PAS staff working with finders. Recent increases in the amount of Treasure being declared may be directly connected to the success of PAS (Lammy 2006, 2). The PAS has recently experienced cuts in funding, with Finds Assistants in some regions and its Learning Coordinator already lost, and is under threat from further possible cuts in order to support the London 2012 Olympics, with proposed plans to drop the central unit of the PAS, 'effectively initiating the Scheme's end' (*British Archaeology* 2008, 7). This seems to beggar belief. Given the demonstrable success of the

PAS, especially in the development of trust and the building of relationships between archaeologists and metal detector users, to lose this valuable tool would surely be close to catastrophic.

That is not to say that the PAS is without its critics. There are concerns, for example, that the PAS, by interacting with metal detector users, adds a spurious legitimacy to metal detecting, making it seem comparable to professional archaeological practices, when this is not truly the case (Corbishley *pers comm* 2008). Some see the development of PAS as an apparent concession of the research agenda to what is essentially treasure hunting (Fowler *pers comm* 2006). From the other end of the spectrum, Peter Spencer (chapter 11) argues that the PAS, perhaps in some areas at least, could be doing even more to create links with metal detecting clubs than it currently does.

In 2003/4 the PAS, in partnership with the British Museum and a number of regional museum services, developed the touring exhibition 'Buried Treasure'. The exhibition toured throughout England and Wales in 2004 and 2005, visiting London, Cardiff, Manchester, Newcastle and Norwich, and displayed some of the most significant finds to have been discovered in England and Wales by non-archaeologists, including the Mildenhall Treasure, made famous in a short story by Roald Dahl (Hobbs 2003, 72), and the beautiful torques of the Snettisham Hoard. To coincide with the visit of the touring exhibition to the Hancock Museum in Newcastle, a one-day conference entitled *Buried Treasure: Building Bridges*, co-organised by the International Centre for Cultural and Heritage Studies (ICCHS) at Newcastle University, Tyne and Wear Museums, and the PAS, was held. The conference was intended to look specifically at relationships between archaeologists and metal detector users, and in part, formed the basis for this book (although the scope here is far wider than that of the conference).

The conference ran smoothly and was very instructive, with a surprisingly large number of metal detector users present. However, its announcement on the CBA's online discussion forum, *Britarch* (archives available at: http://www.jiscmail.ac.uk/lists/britarch.html), elicited some rather negative feedback from some of the regular online discussants. Comments included, from one professional archaeologist:

> It might be easier to 'build bridges' if the emphasis of conferences like this was not so unremittingly on the 'treasure' aspect of the whole portable antiquities thing. The question I ask myself, as an archaeologist, is why should I waste a day, the conference fee and a train fare to hear people talk about material culture as 'treasure', a category that archaeology discarded many years ago and which is of no conceivable interest in archaeological terms. (*Britarch* Discussion List 2005)

Another archaeologist, who objected particularly to the conference's title (among other things), remarked that:

> ... something like 'Finding the Past Together: Building Bridges' would ... be far more descriptive of what those gathered on one side of that 'bridge' would prefer to be the message being discussed. Indeed it is the recognition that it is good 'information about' the past and not 'treasures from' the past which is what is needed before that bridge can even be built. Of course it is always far easier to go for the superficial ... From what has been said here, it looks like the conference is yet another of

those fluff propaganda exercises so characteristic of this discussion over the past few years … (*Britarch Discussion List 2005*)

It should be pointed out that not all discussion on this list was negative towards the conference. It was regrettable, nonetheless, that not only did none of the antagonists attend the conference (surely an ideal forum in which to debate their viewpoints?), but when three of the more strongly opinionated online discussants were approached to produce contributions for this book, all three declined to participate. Reasons ranged from not feeling that they were sufficiently informed (!) on the subject to provide a reasonable chapter through to disagreeing with the entire premise of the book. These individuals are, of course, entitled both to their opinion and to their choice not to contribute to the discussion, but it is nonetheless frustrating that people with such obviously strong opinions on the issue of archaeology and metal detecting were not prepared to lend that opinion to the debate being constructed here, leaving it up to this Introduction to alert the reader to their – very strongly held – views.

A number of the actual contributors to the *Buried Treasure: Building Bridges* conference (Bland, Austin, Simpson, Richards, Walton and Boughton) did agree to contribute to this volume. In addition, further authors were invited to participate in order to present a more comprehensive picture of this fascinating relationship in the early 21st century.

Archaeology and metal detecting – the bigger picture

While, owing in part to the ample scope for analysis and case studies provided by the PAS, the majority of the following chapters focus on the situation in England and Wales, wider pictures are also provided by authors commenting on the situation in other countries, in the UK and beyond. It is certainly remarkable, given its relatively small size as a whole, that different systems are in place in the different countries that comprise the United Kingdom. Alan Saville writes about the Treasure Trove system in Scotland (chapter 7), where the Crown exercises its right to lay claim to *all* archaeological discoveries rather than merely, as is the case in the 1996 *Treasure Act*, a relatively narrow selection of categories (see Bland, chapter 6). That such a wide range of finds is expected to be processed and potentially claimed by Scottish museums, without the aid of a regional network such as the PAS, is surely problematic in itself. Declan Hurl (chapter 8) presents yet another situation in Northern Ireland, where, although the 1996 *Treasure Act* is in operation, there is also the *Historic Monuments Act (Northern Ireland)* 1971, under which digging for archaeological objects without a licence is illegal, effectively outlawing most metal detecting. However, as Hurl reveals, this has not stopped nighthawking (discussed below), and channels of communication between archaeologists and metal detector users seem to have started to develop only within the past decade.

Certainly, within the UK, the combination of rich deposits of metal artefacts and the relatively liberal regulations on the activity of metal detecting (in France, for example, unlicensed metal detecting is completely prohibited), has led to the hobby becoming popular with both UK residents and tourists visiting from elsewhere for treasure hunting tours and metal detecting rallies (eg Addyman and Brodie 2002, 180). In order to provide an international context to the situation in the United Kingdom, contributions have been included from different countries and continents. These illustrate both legislative positions and case studies of collaboration. Zbigniew Kobyliński and Piotr Szpanowski (chapter 2) describe the present situation in Poland, introducing the legislation in place, as well as the challenges faced by archaeologists attempting to protect sites as varied in type as medieval cemeteries and battlefield sites related to both World Wars. Treasure hunting, as a threat to the security of archaeological sites in Poland, seems in recent times to have grown dramatically. That the more negative side of metal detecting – nighthawking – seems to be on the increase in Poland is regrettable, and it can only be hoped that clear solutions are found soon. Elize Becker (chapter 3) provides us with an outline of the use of metal detectors in South Africa, where the metal detector has in fact been utilised by archaeologists as a tool for specific areas of research, such as battlefield archaeology and marine archaeology. Non-vocational use of metal detectors in South Africa, as in Poland, seems largely restricted to illicit activity, unfortunately. It is interesting to contrast these two experiences with the situation in England and Wales, where the PAS, although not without its critics, does enable communication between archaeologists and metal detector users, and as a result records information, even if not to the level that many archaeologists would deem acceptable, that would otherwise be lost.

In the USA metal detecting developed as a hobby as early as the 1940s, and, rather like in the UK, there are organised groups of metal detector users, often referred to as 'relic hunters'. The situation varies from state to state: for example, in some areas there is little or no metal in the archaeological record and so metal detecting is not even an issue, although other activities, such as pot-hunting, do occur. In other areas, such as Georgia, Mississippi and Virginia, metal detecting – for example, relating to Civil War artefacts – is more prevalent (Toner 2002). Battlefield archaeology is a field of archaeological research where metal detectors are particularly useful if operated responsibly. John Cornelison and George Smith (chapter 4) explain how cooperation with metal detecting clubs in the south-east of the USA has helped to build relationships, focus research and enhance understanding.

While battlefield archaeology has been researched in the USA for many years, this sub-discipline, remarkably given the sheer amount of evidence for sites of conflict in such a small country, is still relatively new in the UK. That only some of Britain's battlefields and sites relating to times of war are registered with English Heritage or Historic Scotland, and even then only inventoried without statutory protection, also indicates that decision makers have yet to fully comprehend the importance of these finite resources. Tony Pollard (chapter 16) describes the development of battlefield archaeology in the UK vis-a-vis the potential for and, in some cases, the actual use of metal detector users and their skills in surveying historic battle sites. He explains, too, that while metal detectors used appropriately can shed considerable light on the events of a specific battle, the machines, when used in a way considered irresponsible to the archaeological record, can cause irreversible damage. Metal detecting rallies, already a cause of concern for many archaeological observers, have already taken place at the battlefield sites of Marston Moor and Bannockburn.

AREAS OF CONCERN

Metal detecting rallies are a controversial activity, although in the UK they take place legally. Certain measures have been taken at some of these events, which can attract hundreds or even thousands of metal detector users, to try to optimise the quality of recording (eg Thomas 2007), but their presence in the annual calendar of metal detecting events remains contentious. Even more problematic than metal detecting rallies, many of which now have at least some archaeological presence, and regarding which there is now, at least, dialogue between rally organisers and archaeologists, is the issue of nighthawking. It is not unfair to state that, while most metal detector users have a deep interest in history and archaeology, and are more than willing to participate in archaeological projects if invited, there are some who neither take an interest in archaeology nor particularly care about the impact that their actions may have on the archaeological record. Nighthawks operate illegally: for example, they search scheduled (protected) sites, go on private land without permission (trespassing) or fail to declare Treasure finds under the 1996 *Treasure Act*. Dobinson and Denison (1995) drew attention to a number of known instances of nighthawking, notably at the Roman site at Corbridge in Northumberland, where the raids were closely documented by staff in the 1990s; eventually a private security firm was employed to watch the site. Stead (1998) has written in detail about his role in discovering the looting, sale and subsequent retrieval (of at least some of) the Salisbury Hoard. In this volume another notorious incident of nighthawking at Wanborough in the 1980s is also reassessed (Thomas, chapter 14). The looting of Wanborough, while itself deplorable, was not particularly unusual, certainly if early research carried out by the CBA in the 1970s was anything to go by (Thomas, in prep). Yet the site's significance is in the way in which it was then utilised, even exploited, to draw attention to the threat of uncontrolled metal detecting, and the paucity in legislation available to deal with it. Thus a single event had a profound impact, over time and with a lot of determination, on the eventual change in the law and the abolition in England and Wales of the old Treasure Trove common law.

CONCLUSIONS, AND SOME WAYS FORWARD

The development of this book stemmed from an aspiration to bring together the different opinions about metal detecting and archaeology, at a time when this relationship seems to be at a crucial point in its evolution. The relationship is complex, and possibly in England and Wales also exceptional. On a recent visit to Albuquerque, discussions with American colleagues confirmed both the unique nature of the Portable Antiquities Scheme and the envy of at least some archaeologists in countries where such a system does not exist. This uniqueness is reflected particularly in the international chapters of this volume. Certainly, there are critics of working with metal detector users, and perhaps if history had played out differently there would be a much lesser metal detecting presence in Britain today, without the political influence this large and organised group inevitably now has. However, metal detecting is here, it is not going anywhere and to ignore it or to refuse to engage even in basic communication would, perhaps, be unwise. Austin (chapter 10) and Spencer (chapter 11) both warn that archaeologists ignore metal detecting at their peril, as the alternative to working together seems to be the loss of even more information.

In 1983, the late Tony Gregory suggested that the rise of metal detecting represented the failure of archaeology to appeal to audiences outside the middle classes. His views were echoed by Hodder's (1984, 29) conjecture that campaigns such as STOP, which targeted treasure hunting as a major threat to archaeology, added to social divisions between archaeologists and a public whose views were, possibly wrongly, assumed to be the same as those of archaeologists. It would make sense, therefore, to regard the majority of metal detector users not as selfish treasure hunters (while conceding that nighthawking does, regrettably, occur) but as a section of the public with an active interest in the physical past. Many metal detector users have been pursuing their hobby for several decades, and there is a strong tradition and culture associated with the metal detecting hobby, now into its fifth decade in the British context.

During the course of my research into the relationship between archaeologists and metal detector users in England and Wales, I have frequently been asked by friends and colleagues what my conclusions are. Usually I reply that I try to abstain from forming an opinion until absolutely necessary. What is clear, however, is that communication and cooperation are vital, whether it is through the PAS, museums, or more informal channels. Metal detectors, everyone would accept, can in the wrong hands cause great damage to the archaeological heritage. However, the enthusiasm of many metal detector users for their hobby, and their determination to pursue it, should be seen by archaeologists less as a problem and more as an opportunity; at a time of 'the rise and rise of Community Archaeology' (Archibald 2006), here is a community already interacting with archaeology on a regular basis. The metal detector machine itself, as Richards and Naylor (chapter 15) point out, 'is just another type of remote sensing equipment', a perfectly valid tool in archaeology.

For those reading this book who have a metal detecting background, I hope that it will help reinforce the value of sharing information about finds with archaeologists. For archaeologists, hopefully some light has been shed on the complexity of our relationship with metal detecting, and why it is an important one to cultivate.

BIBLIOGRAPHY

Addyman, P, and Brodie, N, 2002 Metal detecting in Britain: catastrophe or compromise? in *Illicit Antiquities: The theft of culture and the extinction of archaeology*, N Brodie and K W Tubb (eds), Routledge, London and New York, 179–84

Archibald, Z, 2006 *Continuing Education*, unpublished lecture delivered at Teaching and Learning in Archaeology conference, Liverpool University, on 21 June 2006

Atkinson, R, *circa* 1968 Antiquities Bill, letter to unknown newspaper, from CBA archival material

Beach, M, 1970 unpublished letter to the CBA, 25 October

Bland, R, 2005 A pragmatic approach to the problem of portable antiquities: the experience of England and Wales, *Antiquity* 79, 440–7

Britarch Discussion List, 2005 Contributions to discussion thread on Britarch online discussion forum (May 2005) re Conference: *Buried Treasure: Building Bridges*, available at http://www.jiscmail.ac.uk/cgi-bin/webadmin?A1=ind0505&L=britarch (11 March 2008)

British Archaeology, 2008 Popular scheme threatened: culture change needed, *British Archaeology* 98, 7

Brodie, N, 2002 Introduction, in *Illicit Antiquities: The theft of culture and the extinction of archaeology*, N Brodie and K W Tubb (eds), Routledge, London and New York, 1–22

CBA *et al*, 2006 *Code of Practice for Responsible Metal Detecting in England and Wales*, available at http://www.finds.org.uk/documents/CofP1.pdf (18 March 2008)

Dobinson, C, and Denison, S, 1995 *Metal Detecting and Archaeology in England*, available at http://www.britarch.ac.uk/detecting/cont.html (5 January 2008)

Fletcher, E, 1996 *Buried British Treasure Hoards*, Greenlight Publishing, Essex

Green, B, and Gregory, T, 1978 An initiative on the use of metal-detectors in Norfolk, *Museums Journal* 4, 161–2

Gregory, T, 1983 The impact of metal detecting on archaeology, *Archaeological Review from Cambridge* 2 (1), 5–8

Grove, B, 2005 *The Treasure Hunter's Handbook*, Piatkus, London

Hobbs, R, 2003 *Treasure: Finding our past*, British Museum Press, London

Hodder, I, 1984 Archaeology in 1984, *Antiquity* 58, 25–32

Lammy, D, 2006 Foreword, *Portable Antiquities Scheme Annual Report 2005/6*, available at http://www.finds.org.uk/documents/report06.pdf (4 January 2008)

Stead, I, 1998 *The Salisbury Hoard*, Tempus, Stroud

Thomas, S, 2007 *Archaeologists and Metal Detector Users: Unlikely bedfellows? The Durobrivae (Water Newton) Metal Detecting Rally*, paper presented at the Society of Historical Archaeology conference, 11 January 2008, Albuquerque, available at http://www.sha.org/about/conferences/documents/ThomasSHApaper.pdf (10 March 2008)

— (in prep) The relationships between archaeologists and metal detector users in England and Wales: Impact of the past and implications for the future, unpublished PhD thesis, International Centre for Cultural and Heritage Studies, Newcastle University

Toner, M, 2002 Civil War relics at heart of battle, in *The Past in Peril*, M Toner (ed), Southeast Archaeological Center, Tallahassee, 76–80

2

Metal Detector Users and Archaeology in Poland: The Current State of Affairs

Zbigniew Kobyliński and Piotr Szpanowski

The legal background of archaeological heritage protection in Poland

The legal basis for the preservation of archaeological heritage in Poland is the *Protection and Care of Historical Monuments Act* of 23 July 2003, which, after almost ten years of debate on various drafts, replaced the former Act of 1962. From the point of view of the protection of archaeological heritage, the Act must be acknowledged as an important contribution to effective preservation, not only maintaining the principles laid down by the previous legal regulations, but also filling gaps and amending errors existing in the 1962 Act. All the provisions of the *Malta Convention* (*European Convention on the Protection of the Archaeological Heritage*) of 1992, ratified by Poland in 1996, are fulfilled by the 2003 Act.

The most important difference between the 2003 Act and its predecessor is the clear formulation of the 'polluter pays' principle. All costs of necessary rescue excavation have now to be covered by the developer, both in the case of sites known previously, and – even more importantly – in the case of previously unknown sites discovered during development. Where archaeological remains are accidentally discovered, any work which could potentially damage the site has to be stopped, the area has to be safeguarded and the respective authorities (usually the provincial inspector of heritage, also referred to on occasion as the 'Monuments Curator') have to be informed immediately. Within five days of receiving such information, the provincial inspector has to make a decision either to allow the development to continue, or to stop it and instigate a rescue excavation at the expense of the developer. The normal maximum interruption of development is no longer than one month but, in exceptional cases, this period can be extended to a maximum of six months. According to a 2004 Decree of the Minister of Culture, the required archaeological work may also include post-excavation activities, such as the conservation of finds, analysis of results, and the preparation of a report.

The main form of protection of monuments in Poland according to the 2003 Act is their inclusion on a Register of Protected Sites. This Register is administered at a provincial level (but with a central record in Warsaw in the 'National Centre for the Study and Documentation of Monuments' – abbreviated in Polish as KOBiDZ). The 2003 Act places the responsibility for the care of archaeological sites with landowners and prohibits any activity which could affect upstanding archaeology or archaeological deposits in the ground. It also provides certain privileges, such as tax rebates for landowners. In extreme circumstances the 2003 Act permits the seizure of property in case of threat of destruction by the owner (although, to date, the authorities have never taken such action). From the general estimated number of *circa* half a million archaeological sites in Poland only about 9000 are included in the Register.

The 2003 Act does, however, retain the concept of state ownership of all archaeological finds. This prevents the dispersion of collections, prohibits the trade in antiquities, and makes creating private collections of archaeological finds illegal. Every activity relating to the archaeological heritage requires the official permission of the respective provincial inspector. Such permission usually details not only the spatial extent of any excavation or fieldwork, but also the excavation methods allowed and the type and level of recording required. In addition, compulsory standards of archaeological fieldwork documentation were set out in the 2004 Ministerial Decree. It can be argued, therefore, that all archaeological excavations in Poland are fully controlled by competent authorities. Moreover, according to the Act, only individuals with a university degree in archaeology and at least 12 months' field practice after graduation may be given permission to lead an archaeological excavation. By implication the Act forbids any amateur search for artefacts, either for commercial or for personal use.

Apart from the Register of Monuments, the other main way that archaeological sites are protected is by their inclusion in local planning documents as conservation zones. The legal basis for this procedure is the 2003 *Spatial Planning and Development Act*. This Act obliges all communes to prepare planning documents that have to be consulted on, at an early stage, with, among others, archaeologists. Once approved by the conservation service and accepted by local authorities, these documents have a legal status and require that, in the defined conservation zones, any changes in land use are discussed with the provincial inspector, who may impose conditions on future land use to mitigate potential threats or demand full excavation of the site at the cost of the developer. This mechanism of archaeological resource management works well, as long as archaeologists are able to provide the necessary information regarding the known or predicted existence of archaeological sites within the conservation zones. This, in turn, requires systematic reconnaissance programmes to be conducted by archaeologists, using all possible means of prospecting, so that reliable maps of archaeological resources can be prepared. This has been achieved by the creation, at the end of the 1970s, of the 'Polish Archaeological Record' (abbreviated in Polish as AZP), which is based on controlled field-walking of the whole country with the results correlated with archival research and excavation results. This database is about 90 per cent complete and is now in the process of being computerised. It must be noted, however, that this 'completion' is at present based on just one reconnaissance, and it is obvious that the results of such a survey are dependent on many changeable factors, such as the land use, vegetation and even the weather. Moreover, ploughing makes archaeological sites visible on the surface only when the uppermost layers are already at least partly destroyed, which means that field-walking must be repeated cyclically, and any database of archaeological resources can never be claimed to be 'completed'.

The 2003 *Protection and Care of Historical Monuments Act* provides many restrictive measures: whoever destroys a monument faces up to a five-year jail sentence, although if the action was unintentional the maximum sentence is two years in jail, or a fine. Anyone who finds an object that may be an archaeological artefact who does not immediately report it also faces a fine. The fine, however, cannot be greater than 20 times the national minimum salary, and this means that in the case of some developmental projects it can be economically advantageous for the developer to pay the fine rather than finance the necessary rescue excavation. Fines may also be issued in the case of an owner of an archaeological site who has not safeguarded it in a proper way: who has, for example, allowed a metal detector user to search for archaeological artefacts, or allowed an archaeological excavation that does not have official permission. Anyone who owns a site and does not inform the conservation service of conditions or activities having a negative effect on the monument, or changes of ownership, is liable to a similar punishment.

There are also some inducements provided by the legal system for protecting the archaeological heritage. According to the 2004 Ministerial Decree, a person who discovers an archaeological site and fulfils the procedure required by law (safeguarding the site and informing the relevant authorities) may be offered a 'diploma' or (in the case of finds having not only scholarly but also economic value) a financial reward, up to as much as 30 times the average salary.

Other legislation includes provisions important for archaeological heritage management. For example, the 1994 *Building Law* requires the permission of the provincial inspector in the event of any building activities which could affect archaeological sites which are either registered or included in the local planning documents; the 1997 *Immovable Properties Act* states that every change or division of ownership of a registered site owned by the State or by communal authorities requires the permission of the provincial inspector; the 1997 *Paid Motorways Act* requires that the construction of a motorway must be preceded by, among other things, an assessment of the impact on archaeological heritage; and the 2001 *Environment Protection Law* extends the same duty to all developments planned on a provincial and national level.

ORGANISATION OF HERITAGE RESOURCE MANAGEMENT

Despite the obvious negative general evaluation of the Communist era in Poland, it must be acknowledged that it was during this period that the framework was laid down for a modern system of cultural property management. The end result of this long process was, however, only to come after the collapse of the Communist system, in 1990, when the State Service for the Protection of Ancient Monuments (abbreviated in Polish as PSOZ) was formed. This service is directed by a Conservator General acting in the name of the Minister of Culture and Arts. The day-to-day protection of the archaeological heritage is in the hands of the provincial inspectors of heritage. Following the administrative reforms of 1999 there are now 16 provinces in Poland, each of which has an office responsible for the protection of sites and monuments. These offices are headed by the inspector, who oversees all matters concerning all types of monuments (palaces, castles, parks, town planning, export of cultural property, etc). In each province the post of Inspector for Archaeological Monuments has also been established.

Unfortunately, as part of an otherwise laudable tendency towards the decentralisation of power in Poland, on 1 October 1996, the structure of a separate, national, conservation service directed by the Conservator General was abolished. The provincial monument conservators became the employees of local government officials, being the organs of political administration. This means that there is no longer a single conservation policy in Poland on a national level, but 16 policies, different in every province. Moreover, these policies are to a large extent created not by experts in the field of heritage conservation but by local politicians.

This decentralisation would perhaps not be so dangerous if the provincial inspectors of archaeological heritage could obtain help in the form of expert knowledge and advice from any central institution specialising in archaeological heritage management. In theory, such a situation exists. Until 1999, at the head of the conservation service was the Conservator General and his deputies, who acted in the name of (and were responsible to) the Minister of Culture. Between 1997 and 1998 one of the deputies of the Conservator General even had the title of Chief State Archaeologist. In 1999 the name of the service lost 'Ancient' from its title and since that time it has been called the Service for the Protection of Monuments (abbreviated as SOZ). This change reflected an important tendency of the State to renounce many of its duties and responsibilities within the general process of deregulation. In the years 1999–2002 the Conservator General was chief of the central office and held a very high position, equal to that of a minister, but this office still had no direct connection to the provincial inspectors. Unfortunately in 2002 the post of the Conservator General became a political one and is now held not by experts in the field of art history, archaeology or architecture, but by politicians from the ruling party.

In this way, at the beginning of the 21st century, the process of deregulation of the state service for the protection of heritage has finally been completed in Poland. The most serious difficulty in the effective protection of the archaeological heritage in Poland lies, therefore, not in the lack of legal instruments, but in the weakness of the conservation service, which is not able to operate the legal provisions in practice.

TREASURE HUNTING AS ONE OF THE THREATS TO THE ARCHAEOLOGICAL HERITAGE IN POLAND

Destruction of archaeological sites by treasure hunters, a phenomenon which was almost unknown, or occurred only sporadically, until the middle of the 1990s, has recently become one of the most serious threats to the archaeological heritage of Poland (Banasiewicz and Ginalski 1997).

The rapid spread of this phenomenon resulted from several factors happening simultaneously: accessibility to cheap electronic metal detectors; a rise in unemployment and the 'pauperisation' of society following the decline of the utopian concept of the 'protective state'; an increase in crime after the collapse of the Communist system due to the deterioration of social respect for the law; and also the activities of some professional archaeologists, especially those working on numismatics and on the Period of the Roman Influence, from several universities in Poland (particularly Warsaw, Cracow and Lublin).

The scale of destruction caused by metal detector users has been estimated by the present authors on the basis of information collected from the provincial inspectors of archaeological heritage in two periods: first in 1999 (Szpanowski 1999), and then almost ten years later, in early 2007. Unfortunately it was not possible to obtain information from all 16 provinces.[1]

A sad conclusion of the review is that only a few regions of Poland seem to be free from the threat of destruction of their archaeological sites by metal detector users: such fortunate areas are located in the region of Toruń (Kujawsko-Pomorskie Province), Płock (northern part of Mazowieckie Province) and Radom (southern part of Mazowieckie Province). All of the other regions have been extensively plundered by detector users. Moreover, according to the information provided by the provincial inspectors, the threat to archaeological sites has either remained the same during the last ten years, or – in some cases – has dramatically intensified (for example, in the regions of Lublin, Chełm Lubelski and Sandomierz, as well as in the regions of the Świętokrzyskie Mountains in central Poland and the Liwiec river valley in eastern Poland).

A few of the most tragic examples illustrate the scale of the plundering of archaeological sites during the last ten years:

a) Cemeteries of the Lusatian Culture (Bronze Age and Early Iron Age)

Brodno in Dolnośląskie Province: totally destroyed by metal detector users.

Charłupia Mała in Łódzkie Province: at least 40 graves have been plundered.

b) Cemeteries of the Roman Influence Period

Radawa in Podkarpackie Province: systematically plundered by detector users.

Mokra in Śląskie Province: plundered by detector users, who were caught when attempting to sell the artefacts to the Institute of Archaeology of the Jagiellonian University in Cracow (Koj 1998; 1999).

Pikule in Lubelskie Province: plundered by detector users (Banasiewicz 1999).

Paprotki in Warmińsko-Mazurskie Province: the only case in Poland where a detector user was caught in the act of detecting, and consequently sentenced by the courts.

c) Early medieval sites

Trepcza in Podkarpackie Province: early medieval stronghold and cemetery with graves furnished with encolpia, plundered by detector users;

Mogielnica in Mazowieckie Province: early medieval settlement, plundered immediately following the publication of a popular paper.

Tum by Łęczyca in Łódzkie Province: early medieval settlement and stronghold, plundered by detector users.

Gródek on the Bug River in Lubelskie Province: stronghold and vast settlements of the early medieval period, plundered by detector users.

Guciów in Lubelskie Province: early medieval cremation barrows, plundered by detector users.

Other early medieval strongholds all over Poland have been plundered by detector users (eg at Czermno, Mokre and Chodlik in Lubelskie Province, as well as at Grodzisk in Mazowieckie Province).

d)   Ruins of medieval and post-medieval castles

Kaleń Drugi in Mazowieckie Province: fortress of the 16th century, plundered by detector users.

Mirów in the Śląskie province: ruins of the 14th-century castle, plundered by detector users.

e)   Medieval and post-medieval battlefields

Maciejowice in Mazowieckie Province: battlefield of the late 18th century, plundered by detector users.

The present situation is so dramatic because the detector users' movement is growing rapidly and nowadays, according to various estimations, numbers between 10,000 and 30,000 people. Another issue, perhaps even more important, is that the archaeological profession, despite quite clear and compulsory legal provisions in Poland protecting archaeological sites from illicit excavation and archaeological finds from becoming part of private collections, is still not able to agree on a uniform strategy in relation to detector users. Indeed, a section of professional archaeologists, including some university professors, support changes in the present law on the protection of historical heritage which would lead to liberalisation, allowing amateurs to search for archaeological artefacts and excavate them from the topsoil of archaeological sites, and private ownership of archaeological finds. One of the first actions of the new director of the National Centre for the Study and Documentation of Monuments in November 2006 was to organise a public debate on the 'required changes in the law', which was dominated by detector users openly confirming their illegal actions and demanding that these be considered as supporting the development of archaeology.

ARGUMENTS IN FAVOUR OF LIBERALISATION OF LAW ON ARCHAEOLOGICAL HERITAGE

The arguments put forward by the archaeological treasure hunters in Poland can be summarised in the following way:

1. An archaeological find without context still has high scientific value and is important for archaeologists: therefore, the detector users help archaeologists in their studies.

2. State ownership of archaeological finds is a Communist idea, taken from the legal system of the Soviet Union, aimed at limiting private ownership in every way possible. This idea is contradictory to the principles of democracy, as it is limiting the freedom of society.

3. Private collecting of antiquities was the origin of academic archaeology and in most countries is still a significant element of the discipline.

4. The restrictive law on the state ownership of archaeological finds is not observed and this situation has led to the emergence of a 'black market' for antiquities, and at the same time, makes it impossible to establish cooperation between archaeologists and detector users – cooperation which (it is claimed) is harmonious in other countries, such as Denmark and England. In countries where the legal system requires the state ownership of antiquities, as, for example, in Sweden, France, or in some states in Germany, these provisions brought more disasters than benefits for archaeology. If the restrictive provisions were changed, the detector users could help archaeologists by informing them, for example, where to excavate. In the present circumstances archaeologists spend much time, money and energy on fruitless searches for interesting sites which are well known to the detector users.

5. In the Polish system of archaeological heritage protection there are no positive incentives for observing the law, and therefore those who have incidentally found archaeological artefacts are not willing to share such information.

These arguments are certainly not new, as similar general opinions have been previously put forward by treasure hunters in other countries. However, what is shocking is the fact that in Poland, a country in which professional archaeology is so highly developed, where every year there are several hundred excavations, where archaeology is taught at 10 universities from which at least 250 students graduate every year, and in which at least 1000 archaeologists work in the profession, the arguments put forward by detector users find support from quite a large group of prominent archaeologists, who are even prepared to support them in writing (Kokowski 1999; Bursche 2000).

THE MOTIVATIONS OF METAL DETECTOR USERS

Metal detector users in Poland are obviously not a uniform group, and at least two different motivations lie behind their activities. The first of these is purely pecuniary: searching for and digging archaeological sites for profit. The other is the desire to possess ancient artefacts, to find them and to collect them. While these two motivations sometimes occur together, as collectors are frequently involved in the exchange and trade of antiquities, it is important to make this general distinction both to understand the reasons for the emergence of the detector users' movement and to develop approaches to the detector users acceptable to professional archaeology. Unfortunately in both cases, it is the archaeological profession which is to a large extent responsible for the emergence of the phenomenon of detectorism in Poland.

Treasure hunting for profit

The searching and digging of archaeological sites for financial reward stems from the pauperisation of society and the search for any activity which can bring profit. This phenomenon can be compared to the situation in Latin America, where archaeological sites are plundered for subsistence (see Brodie and Tubb 2002). A contributing factor is that, with the collapse of the Communist regime, the public have lost their fear of the police, providing the context that allows the destruction of archaeological sites. However, it is obvious that without demand there would be no reason to supply any commodity, and this is particularly true in the case of antiquities. Without collectors, who purchase illicit antiquities and thus create the market, it would be absolutely pointless to excavate barrows and cemeteries for economic reasons. This means that archaeologists and museums purchasing illegally excavated finds are responsible for creating the demand for such antiquities and consequently for the plundering and destruction of archaeological sites. All the ethical codes of professional archaeological societies and associations, such as the European Association of Archaeologists, the Society for American Archaeology or the Archaeological Institute of America, make this point very clear: archaeologists and museums should avoid engaging in any trade of undocumented antiquities. Even by offering professional expertise on chronology or possible cultural provenance of such illegally obtained artefacts, archaeologists can contribute to raising the commercial value of illicit antiquities (see Renfrew 2000). Unfortunately, a section of the archaeological profession in Poland does engage in such activities, arguing that the claim that purchasing finds by archaeologists or by museums creates a market for such illicit antiquities is fatuous, since the market has existed for several hundreds of years independently of any potential activities of museums or archaeologists (Bursche 2000, 46). The code of ethics of the International Council on Museums (ICOM) states clearly, however, that museums should not purchase any artefacts of non-documented provenance. Moreover, by ratification of the *Malta Convention* in 1996 Poland has pledged 'to take such steps as are necessary to ensure that museums and similar institutions whose acquisition policy is under state control do not acquire elements of the archaeological heritage suspected of coming from uncontrolled finds or illicit excavations or unlawfully from official excavations'.

'Amateur archaeology'

More complex is the issue of those detector users who declare themselves 'amateur archaeologists'. First of all, it is necessary to ask if such a thing as 'amateur archaeology' may exist at all. Contemporary archaeology, contrary to 19th-century antiquarianism, is not simply an expert knowledge of antiquities, but a human science, and collecting an artefact is not an end in itself for professional archaeologists in the 21st century. Particular stress must be put on the context in which artefacts were found (eg Tabaczyński 1999). Antiquities without such a context have only very limited value for the discipline of archaeology. Therefore, these detector users, collectors and archaeologists who think that metal artefacts removed by amateurs from archaeological sites without stratigraphic exploration, without documentation of features, without taking into account potential paleobotanical remains, and without due respect for other finds – such as, for example, pottery sherds – can be still called archaeology, are, in our opinion, totally in the dark as to the nature of the modern discipline. This means that there can only be professional archaeology, and amateurs may help by participating in the professional excavations, and not by taking metal artefacts out of the occupation layers of archaeological sites. If professional archaeologists cooperate with people plundering archaeological sites, because thanks to such cooperation they have access to information on Roman coins or brooches, this is not only illegal and unethical, but also places these archaeologists within 19th-century antiquarianism, rather than in contemporary archaeology.

What makes 'amateur archaeologists' plunder archaeological sites, if they really love archaeology and are really interested in prehistory, is a lack of knowledge about archaeology, its methods and its purposes. It is a totally inaccurate image of archaeology created by the archaeologists themselves, presenting publicly only the spectacular, usually metal, finds (eg Rajewski 1970). As a result, there is nothing surprising in the fact that members of the public think that, by bringing a handful of Roman coins excavated illegally from an archaeological site, they really help archaeologists.

This does not mean that professional archaeologists in Poland do not want to cooperate with amateurs, nor that the legal system makes it impossible for such a cooperation to exist, nor that there are not many ways in which a detector user can really help. However, detector users can help only if they understand that archaeologists are not digging holes to find artefacts. The great challenge for the archaeological profession is therefore to educate and inform society about archaeology. The other requirement for detector users to accept, if they really want to help and cooperate, is the state ownership of archaeological finds. As recently demonstrated clearly by Górny and Kościelecki (2003), this law has nothing to do with the Communist regime. It is present in the legal systems of many countries, and in Poland it was postulated from the very beginning of conscious preservation of archaeological heritage (Demetrykiewicz 1886). Private collecting of archaeological finds was, as early as 1907, considered as detrimental both from a conservational and a scientific point of view. Erazm Majewski, initiator of academic archaeology at the university in Warsaw and creator of the first archaeological museum in Poland, said in his 'ten archaeological-prehistoric commandments': 'You shall not covet prehistoric artefacts to decorate your rooms' (Majewski 1907), and, more recently, such eminent archaeologists as, for example, Zdzisław Rajewski, excavator of the famous Biskupin settlement and director of the State Archaeological Museum, have been of the same opinion (Rajewski 1970). Rajewski also demonstrated that the frequently used argument that, if the trade in works of art is allowed, then trade in antiquities should also be allowed is false, as there is a fundamental difference between archaeological finds and pieces of later art: namely that archaeological finds can only be obtained by amateurs by destroying archaeological sites.

Obviously, it is not true that the system of protection of archaeological sites does not include mechanisms encouraging incidental founders to report their discoveries. As already stated at the beginning of this paper, such a person is eligible to receive a 'diploma', and if the discovery is of high value, also a financial reward.

This all means that the arguments put forward above by the metal detector users are false. If such persons are really fond of archaeology, there are no obstacles in establishing cooperation with archaeological institutions. Some forms of such cooperation already exist: local associations of amateurs may participate in professional excavations; they may also organise joint prospection of archaeological sites by using metal detectors before excavation or during the process of excavating a site.

In 2001 the Conservator General issued guidelines for provincial inspectors of archaeological heritage on how to cooperate with metal detector users. On the basis of these guidelines, as well as the 2003 Act, it is possible to issue permissions to metal detector users for prospecting areas where there are no known archaeological sites. Such permissions always include a provision that any discovery of an archaeological site must be reported to the provincial inspector. If metal detector users are not interested in cooperating with such conditions, this means that they in reality are not interested in archaeology, but simply want to possess historical artefacts, and such a desire really makes cooperation impossible.

Finally, another problem, still not resolved in Poland, is how to treat battlefields, especially from the First and Second World Wars. Are these battlefields archaeological sites? Are the finds from such sites to be treated as archaeological finds, with the consequence that they are state property? At present there is no consensus on this matter, even among the inspectors of archaeological heritage.

The future

To reduce the pace of the destruction of archaeological sites by metal detector users, archaeologists have to take two courses of action. First, and most important, is the education of various sectors of society: of the detector users themselves, but also of owners of archaeological sites, of policemen, of local authorities, of members of parliament and so on (Kobyliński 1999). A change in the academic education of students, to include the ethics of archaeology, must play a particularly important role. The education of metal detector users may be a frustrating exercise, but we can note at least one recent success, when a metal detector user started to study archaeology and completely changed his attitude to the plundering of archaeological sites as a result of his education. Positive examples of emerging societies of amateurs, who are ready to accept the law and to cooperate with professional archaeologists, respecting the requirements of contemporary methods of archaeological fieldwork, make us a little more optimistic than ten years ago. The second course of action is the use of all possible administrative, legal and judicial methods to stop the plundering of archaeological sites. One aspect of this may be to control information on the exact location of archaeological sites (eg Jankowska 1999).

Both courses of action require a uniform approach by all archaeologists in Poland to the emerging problems: strict observation of the law (and not criticising it publicly) and strict observation of ethical rules (and not ridiculing them as dogmatic). This means that actually solving the problem of the metal detector users in Poland is in our own hands.

BIBLIOGRAPHY

Banasiewicz, E, 1999 Zniszczenia spowodowane rabunkową działalnością poszukiwaczy zabytków na Lubelszczyźnie i Zamojszczyźnie, in *Wykrywacze metali a archeologia*, W Brzeziński and Z Kobyliński (eds), Warszawa, 55–63

Banasiewicz, E, and Ginalski, J, 1997 'Poszukiwacze skarbów' jako zagrożenie dla dziedzictwa archeologicznego, *Poznańskie Zeszyty Archeologiczno-Konserwatorskie* 6, 42–4

Brodie, N, and Tubb, K W (eds), 2002 *Illicit Antiquities: The theft of culture and the extinction of archaeology*, Routledge, London

Bursche, A, 2000 Złodzieje i paserzy, dogmatycy i moraliści, *Światowit* 2 (43), fasc. B, 43–52

Demetrykiewicz, W, 1886 *Konserwatorstwo dla zabytków archeologicznych*, Kraków

Górny, P, and Kościelecki, P, 2003 Patrimonium non monetae est…, *Światowit* 5 (46), fasc. B, 271–9

Jankowska, D, 1997 ochrona archeologicznych stanowisk pradziejowych w Wielkopolsce – problem konserwatorski, in *Archeologia wielkopolska. Osiągnięcia i problemy ochrony zabytków*, H Kocka-Krenz (ed), Poznań

Kobyliński, Z, 1999 Świat nauki wobec rabusiów starożytności, in *Wykrywacze metali a archeologia*, W Brzeziński and Z Kobyliński (eds), Warszawa, 35–42

Koj, J, 1998 Procedury ścigania za niszczenie i rabowanie zabytków archeologicznych na przykładzie cmentarzyska z okresu wpływów rzymskich w Mokrej, województwo częstochowskie, in *Badania archeologiczne na Górnym Śląsku i ziemiach pogranicznych w 1995 r.*, Katowice, 263–8

— 1999 Casus Mokrej, in *Wykrywacze metali a archeologia*, W Brzeziński and Z Kobyliński (eds), Warszawa, 67–71

Kokowski, A, 1999 Wykrywacze metali – instrument naukowy czy barbarzyńskie narzędzie, in *Wykrywacze metali a archeologia*, W Brzeziński and Z Kobyliński (eds), Warszawa, 19–31

Majewski, E, 1907 *Dziesięcioro przykazań archeologiczno-przedhistorycznych*, Warszawa

Rajewski, Z, 1970 Zagadnienia kolekcjonowania zabytków archeologicznych, in *Ochrona zabytków archeologicznych 1945–1970*, vol 1, Wrocław

Renfrew, C, 2000 *Loot, Legitimacy and Ownership: The ethical crisis in archaeology*, Duckworth, London

Szpanowski, P, 1999 Poszukiwacze skarbów w Polsce: raport o zniszczeniach stanowisk archeologicznych, in *Wykrywacze metali a archeologia*, W Brzeziński and Z Kobyliński (eds), Warszawa, 45–52

Tabaczyński, S, 1999 Przedmowa, in *Wykrywacze metali a archeologia*, W Brzeziński and Z Kobyliński (eds), Warszawa, 7–12

NOTES

1.   In 1999 the information was collected from 11 provinces: from the south-eastern region of Poland (Podkarpackie and Lubelskie provinces), from the south-western region (Śląskie and Dolnośląskie provinces), from the northern region (Zachodniopomorskie, Pomorskie and Warmińsko-Mazurskie provinces), from the eastern region (Podlaskie province), from the western region (Wielkopolskie Province), and from the central region (Łódzkie and Mazowieckie provinces). In 2007 it was possible to obtain information from only 6 provinces (Kujawsko-Pomorskie, Warmińsko-Mazurskie, Mazowieckie, Łódzkie, Świętokrzyskie and Lubelskie), but together this information covers almost all of the territory of Poland, and in the case of four provinces (Lubelskie, Łódzkie, Mazowieckie and Warmińsko-Mazurskie) it has been possible to compare the situation during these two time periods.

3

The Legislative Position of Metal Detector Use at South African Archaeological Sites

ELIZE BECKER

No person may bring any equipment which assists in the detection of metals, archaeological, palaeontological objects and material, or excavation equipment onto an archaeological or palaeontological site or a battlefield, or use similar detection or excavation equipment for the recovery of meteorites, except under the authority of a permit issued by Amafa aKwaZulu-Natali (The KZN Heritage Act, No. 10 of 1997) or South African Heritage Resources Agency. (National Act No. 25 of 1999)

As can be seen from the above quote, legislation regarding the use of metal detectors is very clear. Unfortunately the implementation of the *Heritage Resources Act* is not always straightforward. Problems arise with reference to the ethical – or otherwise – use of metal detectors and with respect to the reason(s) for the use of metal detectors. This chapter discusses the permit application procedures, and their surrounding rationale, for the use of a metal detector in South Africa.

THE UTILISATION OF METAL DETECTORS IN SOUTH AFRICAN ARCHAEOLOGY

The use of metal detectors in South Africa is minimal as metal does not occur at the majority of archaeological sites. Metal detectors are used mainly by archaeologists at battlefield and maritime sites and to help identify areas for excavation at later-period sites.

Battlefield sites include, for example, the Anglo-Zulu War site of Isandlwana, and Spionkop, an Anglo-Boer War battlefield site. Both wars are regarded by historians and archaeologists as highly sensitive and sites are investigated for metal artefacts on a regular basis. Battlefield archaeology is highly specialised and archaeologists rely on the use of metal detectors to determine the battlefield boundaries. Recovered artefacts may help determine the type of military equipment utilised, which assists with identifying the period of the site. Such finds also assist in the understanding of the development of military technology and tactics.

Metal detectors are also used by marine archaeologists to determine the existence

Fig 3.1: Northern view of the Isandlwana Battlefield Site

© Elize Becker

Fig 3.2: Port Edward Sao Joao Shipwreck Site

© Elize Becker

of shipwrecks, or parts of shipwrecks, at sites below the high water mark. This work requires highly specialised equipment and involves specialised techniques. In South Africa, only a few specialists are available to undertake such a study. Archaeologists also use metal detectors to survey beach areas. Survivor camps related to shipwrecks occur at beach areas, and various research projects to determine the locations of survivor camps through the use of metal detectors have been completed. Artefacts found at hilltops where people camped can identify areas that need to be treated as sensitive. These areas are being surveyed intensively to determine whether artefacts that relate to a particular wreck in the water exist at the sites. Beach locations are regularly under threat from beach dwellers who remove exposed shipwreck artefacts from rocky areas: for example, at Port Edward in KwaZulu-Natal.

Metal detectors may also be used at sites relating to the period of the South African Political Struggle, such as that of the Bambatha Rebellion of 1906, which occurred during the British colonisation of South Africa. Local communities refused to pay poll taxes and some were executed during the rebellion. People were buried handcuffed and metal detectors may thus be used to identify the location of the graves. The use of metal detectors at sites related to medical and/or veterinary research – for example, the David Bruce site at Ubombo KwaZulu-Natal, where research on the Tsetse fly was carried out during the 1800s – has also provided significant evidence. Here, where laboratories used metal equipment, metal detectors have provided archaeologists with the probable location of the laboratory buildings and living area and allowed them to determine where test-pit excavations should be located. This may enable the possible reconstruction of the site at some point in the future.

FIG 3.3: DAVID BRUCE HOUSE

© DAVID IRONS

Fig 3.4: David Bruce Site – previous location of the David Bruce Homestead and living area

© Elize Becker

Fig 3.5: Location of the David Bruce Site and the associated Eastern Outlook

© Elize Becker

REASONS FOR PERMIT APPLICATIONS

All archaeologists who wish to use a metal detector must apply for a permit from the National Heritage Agency or *Amafa*, the Provincial Statutory Body at KwaZulu-Natal, before they use such equipment on site. They must provide the Heritage Resource Agency with background information, details of previous work completed, reasons for the new project, a timeframe, and information regarding the supervisor. Metal detectors must be intended to be used as a secondary device and not as a main tool for identifying sensitive areas.

Applications received are reviewed by a professional council and only after an extensive discussion and decision-making process is permission for the use of metal detecting equipment granted, permission which is always subject to restrictions and guidelines imposed by the council. Applicants must include a proposal stating their reasons for wanting to use a metal detector, and the devices must not, as intimated above, replace basic archaeological processes and should only be used to detect a specific phenomenon: a midden area, for example. Researchers are discouraged from relying on metal detectors to determine the exact location of a whole site, as their use does not imply a robust scientific research method, the lack of which is questioned by the scientific research community. Permits issued are project-specific and are only valid for a limited period. An applicant is not allowed to use metal detecting equipment at locations not specified in the application.

It is important to manage and control heritage resources to prevent destruction and illegal removal of artefacts. In the case of metal detectors, it may happen that individuals identify sensitive or important artefacts and remove them from the site without informing the Heritage Agency. The result is that artefacts are removed illegally and transferred to other institutions without a proper record, leaving the National and Provincial Archaeological Record incomplete.

The detection of metal artefacts may actually result in treasure hunting if proper procedures are not followed. Researchers may concentrate on the search for and identification of metal objects and may ignore the normal scientific methods of archaeology. Artefacts, and their archaeological significance, should be recovered in the context of a research question that forms part of a properly planned project. It has been known for researchers to become so eager to identify a site by using a metal detector that they overlook their main responsibility: the utilisation of basic archaeological fieldwork.

Permits are granted only if the applicant agrees to provide the Heritage Agency with regular reports and updates during and after the fieldwork season. The reports provide an indication of the type of data collected and they show whether the data fit with the researcher's proposal. The data can be used to identify a systematic spatial pattern and the possible illegal removal of artefacts. Reports are assessed regularly, which requires specific criteria, for example GPS coordinates, site significance and details of artefacts uncovered during the operation. A description of the methodology used with reference to the type of equipment and other associated methods should provide a clear insight into the project procedures and the outcome of the project. A strategic plan is necessary to determine if the metal detector is used as part of a thorough research plan or not.

THE ETHICAL USE OF METAL DETECTORS

The question of the ethical use of metal detectors should be dealt with in a sensitive manner. Heritage Resource sites, and in particular battlefield sites, are highly sensitive and it is important to prevent individuals from identifying areas with high concentrations of metal objects or isolated artefacts with the aim of removing the objects illegally; graves at fort areas are a good example. In addition, the use of a metal detector may identify other material that is highly sensitive and not necessarily archaeological. The relationship between the researcher and authorities (municipalities, National Ports Authority, National Defence Force) are of extreme importance in preventing the publication of potentially sensitive information.

PROBLEMS

When individuals illegally use metal detectors to identify highly sensitive areas and to gain data for their own personal use they are destroying the ethics of archaeology and history by removing metal artefacts unscientifically, thereby causing the loss of scientific data and information. Personal gain may therefore result in the loss of artefacts for the people and the destruction of research potential. If an individual concentrates only on the location and uncovering of metal artefacts, such action may result in the removal of such artefacts without the associated environment being recorded, and indiscriminate salvaging of metal artefacts destroys the archaeological and historical landscape. It is extremely important that the Heritage Agencies are able to assess and monitor reports received in order to determine if a site is of high significance. Site significance determines methods of heritage management and prevents the destruction of valuable material.

In South Africa, metal detectors are utilised on a minimal basis, but their use is as sensitive as it is anywhere else, and is therefore strictly managed and illegal without regular reports, monitoring and legal documentation. In most circumstances, the use of a metal detector can cause unsystematic fieldwork and disturbs other non-metal objects during the uncovering of metal objects. Such use is highly unethical and should be discouraged by the professional community.

BIBLIOGRAPHY

Amafa aKwaZulu, 1997 *Natali Provincial Heritage Resources Act No 10 of 1997*

Grisell, B, and Randall, L, 1998 Our marine heritage, *Nordic Underwater Archaeology*, May 1999, available online at http://www.abc.se/~pa/publ/griselle.htm (17 January 2007)

Museum Times, 2006 *The Kannah Creek Mystery Deepens*, available online at http://www.wcmuseum.org/news07/jan07news.pdf (17 January 2007)

National Heritage Resources Act (NHRA), 1999 *No 25 of 1999*

The Archaeological Institute of America, 2005 *The Archaeology of Battlefields*, available online at http://www.archaeology.org/online/interviews/scott.html (17 January 2007)

4

Archaeology, Metal Detecting, and the Development of Battlefield Archaeology in the United States

JOHN E CORNELISON JR AND GEORGE S SMITH

INTRODUCTION

Little common ground had been established between archaeologists and metal detecting hobbyists since the development of portable metal detecting equipment and its recreational use, which began in the mid-1940s. It would probably have continued this way if not for a wildfire that consumed the tall grass covering the Little Big Horn Battlefield in eastern Montana, which provided a unique opportunity for an innovative archaeologist and a group of metal detector hobbyists to establish a mutually beneficial working relationship that resulted in the collection of valuable data about the battle that took place on this site over 130 years ago. This chance encounter on the plains of Montana provided the basis for the development of a whole new line of inquiry which came to be known as battlefield archaeology. Projects undertaken on battlefields in the south-east United States by staff of the Southeast Archeological Center employed, modified and improved battlefield archaeology methods to provide new and/or revised interpretations of battles associated with the American Revolution, the War of 1812, the Indian Wars, and the Civil War. The methods employed, the results and interpretation, and the cooperation between archaeological personnel and metal detecting hobbyists associated with these battlefield studies are discussed in this chapter.

While the first working metal detectors were invented in the mid-1830s – even being used by Alexander Graham Bell to search for the assassin's bullet in an American president – their use as a hobby did not truly begin until the end of World War II (Roberts 1999). The demands for bomb detectors during the war led to the production of large numbers of metal detectors, which were sold as surplus following the war. The post-war boom in America led to a population with a new regard for leisure activity, including metal detecting. However, the hobby of metal detecting did not explode until the 1970s, with the use of the microprocessor, printed circuit board and miniaturised transistor. These innovations had the effect of driving the price and weight of metal detectors down, making them more accessible to the public. However, their usefulness as a tool for archaeological inquiry was met with scepticism, which extended to metal detecting hobbyists as well (Scott 2005). It was an uneasy beginning at best.

Metal detectors were used intermittently by American archaeologists from the 1950s to the 1970s, with mixed results. During this period the majority of American archaeologists dismissed these machines as ineffective for archaeology at best and 'the devil's tool' in the worst cases. With very few exceptions, when archaeologists did employ metal detectors the results were so poor it led to the conclusion that a metal detector in the hands of an archaeologist was the same as doing nothing at all. A review of the use of metal detectors by archaeologists shows that, in many cases, they would locate only large targets and then dismiss the machines as ineffective for use on battlefields or other sites, never realising that they were repeating a pattern common in novice metal detector users. It appears that novice users, which include many archaeologists, tend to locate the larger targets and miss bullets and other battle-related items. It became clear that the most accurate data would result from the proficient use of this technology by individuals who could effectively employ and interpret this technology. Archaeologists and metal detector hobbyists had found some common ground.

BATTLEFIELD ARCHAEOLOGY: THE BEGINNINGS

Archaeologists have been using metal detectors for as long as the machines have been available. Unfortunately during much of this time the machines and operators have not been effective for archaeological pursuits. This is clearly evidenced by previous attempts with metal detectors at Chalmette, a War of 1812 battlefield located near New Orleans, Louisiana (Wilson 1963; Birkedal 2005), and the poor results obtained. Such a lack of success prompted many archaeologists to drop metal detectors as an archaeological collection technique. Other archaeologists refuse to use metal detectors because of a concern that it would link them in the public view with the looters who use them, as well as weaken arguments against allowing open detecting on public lands managed by the federal government.

While the use of metal detectors on archaeological sites has been a story of mixed results, the number of successes has grown as archaeologists developed an appropriate methodology. Projects that stand as milestones in the development of the methodology began in 1972, when Dean R Snow (1981) demonstrated the archaeological data potential of battlefield archaeology. In his work for the National Park Service at the Saratoga Battlefield, a Revolutionary War period site dating to 1777, in upstate New York, he discarded traditional archaeological techniques and chose instead to use aerial photographs, magnetometers and soil probes to locate battlefield positions. Although he did not employ metal detecting, his work clearly showed that there was an enormous historical and cultural data potential in the battlefields preserved by the National Park Service. This served to enhance the value of such studies which set the stage for the use of metal detecting as an archaeological research tool.

A year after Snow's pioneering work, Roy S Dickens, Jr (1979) conducted an archaeological investigation at Horseshoe Bend National Military Park in eastern Alabama (the site of a battle that took place between the US Army and the Upper Creek Indian Confederation in March 1814) that included a systematic sweep using metal detectors. During the survey, 11 artefacts that related to the battle were recovered. These include '… lead rifle balls, three iron grape shot, and two iron cut nails' (Dickens 1979, 26). This study demonstrated that acceptable results could be obtained using metal detectors. However, the archaeological literature is virtually devoid of successful metal detecting surveys on battlefields in the decade following Dickens' work.

Arguably the most important archaeological metal detecting took place in 1984, at Little Bighorn Battlefield in eastern Montana, the site of a battle that took place between the US Army and Lakota, Arapaho and Cheyenne forces in 1876. During this survey Douglas Scott and Richard Fox showed the effectiveness of using metal detectors and metal detecting hobbyists to obtain information about battlefields (Scott and Fox 1987). Based on the results of their testing (Fox and Scott 1991), these researchers later described a post-Civil War battlefield pattern. The identification of a pattern began with the determination of individual actions based on the distribution of artefacts with unique signatures or characteristics (eg rifling patterns on bullets, ejector marks, or firing pin marks). These individual patterns were aggregated into unit patterns, which in turn formed the battlefield pattern. In describing the essence of battlefield archaeology, Fox and Scott (1991, 97) write 'tactics prescribe combat behavior. All cultures have combat tactics, some more rigidly defined than others. In the absence of unit tactical disorganisation, signature patterning may reflect prescribed deployment.'

While Scott and Fox (1987) worked on a battlefield where both sides had different weapon types, this was not true of most of the other conflicts that have taken place in what is now the south-eastern United States. One method used to compensate for the lack of unique bullet signatures was illustrated by William B Lees (1992). His study of the Mine Creek Battlefield in eastern Kansas led him to conclude that 'unfired' or 'dropped' bullets provide the best basis for reconstructing troop positions because they mark the precise location of individuals. Concentrations of fired bullets falling behind unit positions, on the other hand, are most likely indirect indicators of lines, and thus these represent a 'ghost' of those positions (Lees 1992, 8).

Between 1992 and 1993, Charles M Haecker and Jeffery G Mauck (1997) conducted research at Palo Alto Battlefield National Historic Site in south-east Texas, the site of the first battle of the 1846–8 Mexican War. This research showed the effectiveness of using historic maps in conjunction with geographic information systems (GIS) to guide the archaeological testing.

Beginning in 1992 and continuing until the present, the Southeast Archeological Center (SEAC) has been conducting battlefield surveys using metal detector hobbyists. During that time methodological innovations have continued. These innovations include aggregating data into cells and producing contour maps of battle activity (Cornelison 1995), creating a stability index for individual battle areas (Cornelison 2006a), using Sivilich (1996) shot calculation formula in conjunction with GIS maps to interpret battlefields (Cornelison and Cooper 2002a), and the application of multiple technologies on the battlefield (Cornelison and Cooper 2002b).

At SEAC, the relationship between archaeologists and metal detector hobbyists began with a chance comment at a highway planning meeting in 1992. The project took place at Chickamauga and Chattanooga National Military in north-west Georgia, the site of a Civil War battle that took place in September 1863. The Park historian indicated that a local group of metal detector hobbyists had approached him on several occasions asking to help the Park with its survey needs. Fortuitously SEAC had just acquired an electronic total station and needed to field test the equipment.

An area inside the western edge of the Chickamauga Battlefield, which had been previously surveyed using both metal detecting and shovel testing, was slated for development. Since the area had been surveyed by an archaeologist it was believed that no significant archaeological resources were present within the corridor. This was therefore selected as a test location for the transit and the metal detecting survey. The survey was conducted during a number of visits between 1992 and 1993 using hobbyists from the Chattanooga Area Relic and Historical Association (CARHA). The CARHA members were overwhelmingly hardworking and knowledgeable, far from the 'devils' that had been described in other professional contexts. They were willing to expend their own time and money to obtain and share information about cultural resources.

The 1992 work demonstrated the usefulness of metal detecting as a research tool but, more importantly, it demonstrated that experience with the equipment made a significant difference in what was located and recovered and that a working relationship between archaeologists and metal detecting hobbyists was not only possible but important to achieving reliable results. The results and interpretation of the data from this and other projects are discussed in the following sections. As a result of the success of this and subsequent studies, the Southeast Archeological Center has developed a 15-year working relationship with metal detecting hobbyists in which virtually every battlefield in the National Park Service south-east region has been at least partially surveyed. During this time a wealth of information was recovered concerning the wars that have been fought in the south-eastern United States. Collection methodology was substantially modified over this time period, allowing for meaningful interpretations of battles where both sides used the same weapons and tactics. Between 1999 and 2003 almost 4000 hours of volunteer time has been logged conducting systematic metal detector projects with an estimated value to the NPS of some US $65,000.

The SEAC has undertaken archaeological survey using volunteer metal detectors on five American Civil War parks (Cornelison 2000; 2005; 2007), on three Revolutionary War battlefields (Cornelison 2006b; Cornelison and Cooper 2002a; Cornelison and Groh 2007), on one Red Stick (Indian) battlefield (Cornelison 2006b), and on one War of 1812 battlefield (Cornelison and Cooper 2002b). The results of the survey of three of these battlefields will follow, to illustrate the results that can be obtained when there is a good relationship between archaeologists and metal detector hobbyists.

Battlefield archaeology in the south-east United States

The Battle of Kings Mountain – Revolutionary War, October 1780

Historical account

The Battle of Kings Mountain was fought on 7 October, 1780, in southern North Carolina. British Colonel Patrick Ferguson was recruiting a militia force to aid the British cause. Ferguson was quite successful at raising troops but some of his actions had inflamed the Overmountain men from the western part of the state, who formed a force of about 1000 men. They tracked Ferguson's similar sized force to Kings Mountain. The British were camped along a large ridge, now known as Battle Ridge. The Overmountain men encircled the base of the ridge and then began to fight up the slopes. The British muskets, firing down slope, could not match the accuracy of the rifles being fired uphill. Once the Americans made the summit, the British were driven back to the east end of the ridge. After a bloody fight some of the Loyalists were allowed to surrender. Ferguson attempted to escape and was shot dead. This battle, the death of Ferguson and the harsh treatment dealt to the Loyalists following the battle, including hangings, effectively ended the British recruiting of militia (Blythe *et al* 1995; Draper 1971).

Survey, results and interpretation

The survey of Kings Mountain battlefield took place over two field seasons. Almost 300 volunteer hours were logged during this project. A total of some 90 acres was surveyed by metal detecting. During this testing, 139 period artefacts were recovered. These artefacts included 81 fired and 54 unfired lead shot from the battle. The locations of these rounds clearly show the location of the assaults up Kings Mountain.

The results of the metal detecting can best be described using five clusters (Fig 4.1). The first and most important cluster is located on the south-west end of the ridge outside the tour loop. At the time of the survey this area was not considered to be part of the battlefield. Using the most accepted interpretation of troop positions, this south-west cluster would represent Sevier's assault (Draper 1971). Continuing north-east up the ridge, another cluster is located to the north, just inside the tour road. This cluster represents the assault of Shelby's men. These two areas are gentle slopes where the top of the ridge can be mounted without much difficulty. It is logical to assume that the assaulting Patriot force would take the easiest route up the ridge and in fact the physical evidence bears this out.

The next cluster, to the north-east, is a linear cluster that runs on the south slope of the ridge from the Centennial Monument to the US Monument. This cluster, consisting of many fired and few dropped shots, represents the firing that McDowell's men were placing on the unfortunate Loyalists. It is a hard climb to the top of the ridge from this side and would be hard to do under fire. The saddle between the two monuments is virtually devoid of shot. This illustrates that once the western end was taken the Loyalists fled to the east end of the ridge and made their stand.

FIG 4.1: RESULTS OF BATTLEFIELD SURVEY OF KINGS MOUNTAIN NATIONAL MILITARY PARK

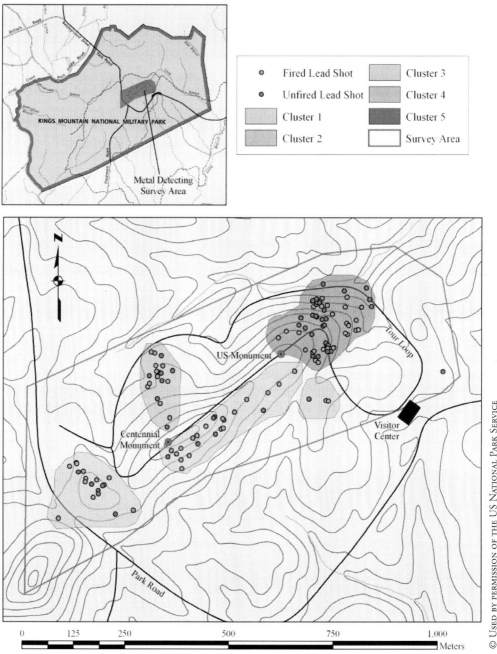

The fourth cluster is important not for what was recovered but for what was not. The flat area due south of the US Monument was the presumed site of the location of Ferguson's wagons. While some shot was collected in this area no evidence of the wagons or their burning was encountered.

The final cluster, located on the eastern end of the ridge, shows the closing of the vice. The troops of William, Cleveland, Chronicle and Winston were putting pressure on the Loyalists as they clung to the top of the ridge. It is interesting to note the absence of shot between the two monuments. This shows that, as tactical stability broke down, there was a quick movement by the Loyalists along the ridge as they sought the perceived safety of those on the western end of the ridge (Draper 1971).

Battle of Cowpens – Revolutionary War, January 1781

Historical account

On 17 January, 1781, a force of approximately 900 Americans, under the command of General Daniel Morgan, defeated a British detachment of 1100 cavalry led by Lieutenant Colonel Banastre Tarleton at the Battle of Cowpens. The battle resulted in the death of 110 British soldiers. Following the British defeat, it has been stated that the Americans buried the British dead in 'wolf pits' – holes dug into the earth to trap wolves attacking cattle grazing in the area – on the field.

Morgan's plan was very simple. He formed his army in three lines perpendicular to Green River Road. The first two lines were militia, with Continentals forming the third. The first two lines were supposed to fire a few volleys and then fall back to the third line. Through a series of fortuitous events, the plan accomplished the desired effect of drawing the Legion into a reckless charge. Fire from the third line broke the cavalry charge and Tarleton withdrew from the battlefield (Bearss 1996).

Survey, results and interpretation

Beginning in 1995, a series of surveys were undertaken in the Park. The aggregated data shows four linear clusters extending across the battlefield on a north-east to south-west alignment (Fig 4.2). This alignment is perpendicular to the route of the Green River Road. The north-western-most linear cluster consists mostly of impacted or fired musket balls. These were large calibre balls representing fire from Continentals, interspersed with fired balls from the Colonial militia. On the northern end of the line are a few small calibre balls that indicate the presence of militia in this area. The majority of the militia retreated from the second Patriot line around the left (north) of Morgan's Continentals (Fleming 1988, 67; Bearss 1996, 31). The documentation is perfectly consistent with the archaeological remains recovered from the north-western-most linear cluster. The militia filed around the Continental left (Bearss 1996, 36) where some joined that line and extended it to the north. Other militia were rallied by Morgan and Pickens and fired on the advancing British as part of 'Morgan's Masterful Manoeuvre' (Bearss 1996).

FIG 4.2: RESULTS OF BATTLEFIELD SURVEY OF COWPENS NATIONAL BATTLEFIELD

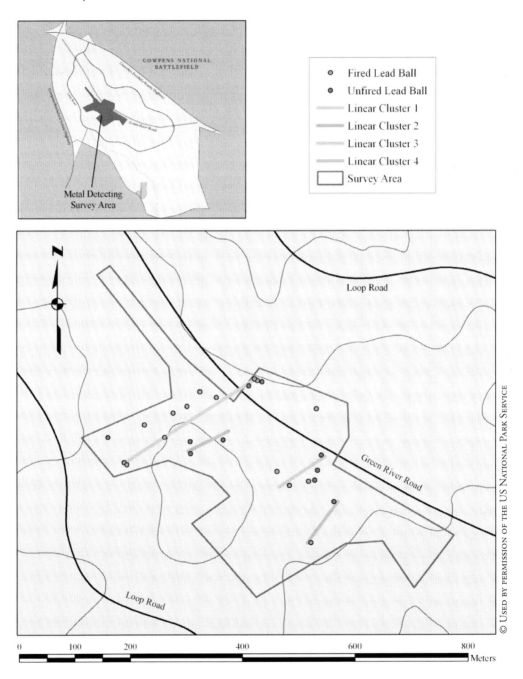

The north-western-most linear cluster consists of 13 lead balls ranging from 0.51 to 0.70 calibre. The smaller calibres are scattered along the length of the line, with a number of balls in the 0.68–0.70 calibre range. Based on the location of this line, the historic documentation and the number and type of balls present, this area probably represents the location of 'Morgan's Masterful Manoeuvre', where Daniel Morgan reformed the retreating Continental line and stopped the British assault.

The musket balls around 0.69 calibre in size could have come from the former Continentals (six month militia), Howard's Continentals or British Regulars. Their location on the western end of the battlefield makes it a near impossibility that these musket balls came from British weapons. The smaller calibre balls had to come from the guns of militia or irregular troops. Since some of Pickens' and the six month militia rejoined Morgan's last line, it is likely that the smaller calibre rounds represent the militia's contribution to the destruction of the British at the last line.

In this cluster, 11 (85 per cent) musket balls were fired and 2 (15 per cent) were unfired, indicating that this location was one in which the combatants received a devastating amount of fire but produced very little return fire. This conclusion is based on the premise that combatants drop balls in locations where they stood and fired. Since only two drops were present in this location, whoever occupied this position did not have time to fire, or they were extremely calm under fire and carefully reloaded. However, given the historic documentation, the former is most likely. The impacting rounds also consist of a range of balls that would be expected from the combined weaponry of Continentals and militia. The location on the western end of the battlefield, the presence of both Colonial and militia weaponry, and the fact that the combatants did not appear to be firing out suggest that this is indeed the location of 'Morgan's Masterful Manoeuvre', where a group of Continentals and militia fired point-blank into the rapidly advancing British (Bearss 1996).

It is interesting to note that a number of the smallest calibres are located to the north of the Green River Road. These balls, no doubt, represent the location where some of the militia reformed on the Continentals' left.

The next linear cluster, to the east, consists of three musket balls with a range of 0.59 to 0.69 calibre. All of these balls were unfired. Because this cluster consists of musket balls with a calibre less than 0.69, which would only be fired by militia at this battle, this location is assumed to be a Colonial position. Based on the location to the east of the final American line along the axis of attack, it is presumed that these balls represent the location of the main Continentals' line, which included some militia prior to the beginning of their retrograde movement. This small number of drops fits the expected pattern, as they were not heavily engaged at the time they began moving westward. This would account for the lack of impacted rounds and limited number of drops that represent stationary troops.

The next linear cluster (third cluster) to the east consists of 7 balls with a range of 0.48 to 0.69 calibre. Four (57 per cent) of these balls are fired and three (43 per cent) are unfired. Two of the unfired balls are 0.69, one is 0.64, and one 0.54 calibre. All of the fired balls are 0.64 and smaller. Because the British were not firing small calibre weapons at this battle, the only source for these balls is the Colonial militia. However, the unfired 0.69 balls in this location on the battlefield suggest that the British occupied this position as well. Based on the historic documentation, only a single location on the battlefield conforms to these conditions. There is a high probability that this is the location where the militia line clashed with the advancing British prior to the militia retiring around the Continental left.

The easternmost linear cluster consists of two balls; one fired 0.62 and one unfired 0.69 musket ball. While the number of balls collected from this area is extremely small, their position is potentially significant. During the Battle of Cowpens, Patriot sharpshooters were advanced 150 yards to the east along Green River Road (Bearss 1996). The positioning of these two balls, a fired ball of a size that would come from a militia weapon and a dropped 0.69 calibre musket ball consistent with what the British regulars were armed with, suggest this may be where the British received fire from the sharpshooters. However, the calibre of the fired musket ball is slightly larger than would be expected to have been fired from a rifle and additional metal detecting is therefore needed in this area to confirm or refute this hypothesis.

Finally, the distances of the linear clusters need to be compared to historic documentation. If the north-western-most linear cluster does indeed represent 'Morgan's Masterful Manoeuvre', the location of the second linear cluster is approximately 50m to the east. Bearss (1996, 36) states in his historical summary of the battle that the British were fired on at a range of 30–40 yards. This distance is not inconsistent with the recorded separation of these two linear clusters.

Pickens' militia, as well as other groups of militia, were stationed 150 yards forward of the Continental line (Bearss 1996, 18). The distance from the second linear cluster to the third is approximately 185m. Again, this distance, while not exact, is very near to the traditionally stated distance.

Lastly, a group of sharpshooters was reportedly positioned 100 yards forward of the militia line. The distance from the third linear cluster to the fourth linear cluster (south-eastern-most) is approximately 50m. The fact that this distance is half of what is expected makes this the weakest of the cluster interpretations. However, the sharpshooters fell back and fired from concealed positions behind trees. This leaves two possibilities. The first is that these balls are simply outliers from the third linear cluster and do not in fact represent the line of skirmishers. The second possibility is that these are the results of sharpshooters firing and falling back. Additional testing should be conducted in this area to confirm or refute this hypothesis.

Battle of Guilford Courthouse – Revolutionary War, March 1781

Historical account

The battle plan for the battle of Guilford Courthouse, which took place in north-west North Carolina, was essentially the same as that of Cowpens. American General Greene arrayed in three lines perpendicular to New Garden Road. The first line consisted of militia, the second of former Continentals, and the third of Continentals. When Cornwallis attacked, the first line quickly collapsed. The second line, however, gave a spirited fight to the British, whose formations were being broken by the heavy vegetation. When the British impacted the third line, their units were coming in uncoordinated attacks rather than, as was the traditional doctrine, *en masse*. The third American line surged forward and appeared to be winning the battle. At the same time the British General Cornwallis arrived on a hill where he could observe the fight taking place below. He ordered his artillery commander to fire grape shot into the crowd (Baker 1992, 69; Buchanan 1997, 379). The artillery fire broke the American attack and Greene ordered a withdrawal. Although Cornwallis won the battle, almost 25 per cent of his soldiers were casualties. This forced Cornwallis to move his army north, where it could rest and resupply. By May, Cornwallis had moved his army to Yorktown, Virginia, where he was forced to surrender before the year's end (Baker 1992; Buchanan 1997).

Survey, results and interpretation

Four archaeological field projects were undertaken at Guilford Courthouse National Military Park between 1995 and 1998. Approximately 34 acres of the park were systematically surveyed using metal detectors. In addition, shovel tests, posthole testing and excavations were undertaken. The majority of the artefacts recovered can reasonably be temporally affiliated with the period the courthouse was in operation. The four surveys have conclusively located the first, second and third battle lines of the Battle of Guilford Courthouse, and study of the surveys, deed records and period maps indicates that the site of Guilford Courthouse has not been correctly interpreted.

Archaeological remains of all three battle lines were collected during the four surveys. The archaeological manifestations of the battle lines consisted of both fired and unfired lead rifle or musket balls (Fig 4.3). Also collected were a number of rifle or musket parts. However, the most illuminating artefacts came from the third line area. Six approximately ¾-inch-diameter iron shot were recovered from this area. This is the only place on the battlefield where this type of artefact was recovered. Their presence on the third line conforms nicely to period battle descriptions of Cornwallis ordering grape shot to be fired into the melee of the third line.

An examination of the metal detecting results shows three heavy concentrations of Revolutionary War artefacts and three smaller areas that consist of relatively fewer Revolutionary War artefacts. The positioning of the Revolutionary War artefacts within the major cluster supports the historic interpretations of the battle for the first and second battle lines and slightly modified third battle line.

The easternmost cluster, A, is located to the south-west of the visitor centre, where the park interpretative signs say the first fine should be located. The line is canted north-west–south-east, suggesting that the battle was oriented slightly more to the north-east than the early historians and park developers believed. However, this slight modification in no way affects the interpretation of the battle.

FIG 4.3: RESULTS OF BATTLEFIELD SURVEY OF GUILFORD COURTHOUSE NATIONAL MILITARY PARK

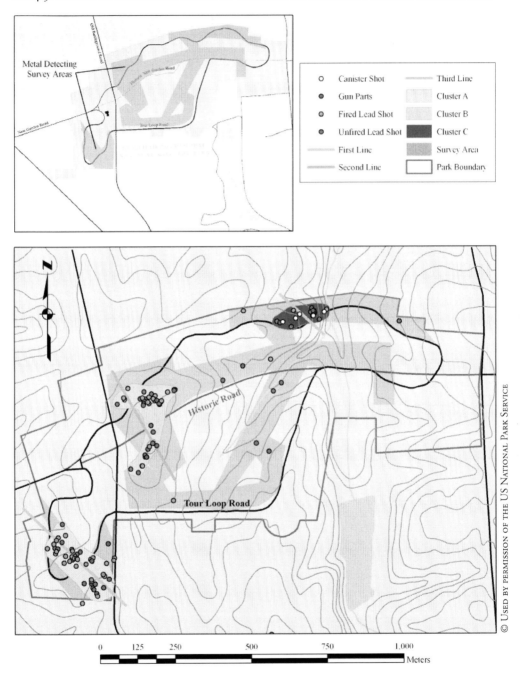

Just to the north-west of the cluster the park boundary juts to the east and crosses New Garden Road. The area to the west of Greenhurst Drive was not available for testing at the time of this survey, but is now a park. However, the tract to the west of the park housing and maintenance buildings was surveyed, with negative results. These results lend credence to the idea that the first battle line was canted more to the north-west.

Cluster A consists of 76 individual items of which 69 per cent are battle related. Of the battle-related objects, 90 per cent are musket balls. Other items include two musket parts and three bags of lead that are attributed to the Revolutionary War era, although they could date to any time period. Previous experience has shown that the majority of the lead on a battlefield is the result of military actions and not the result of post battle deposition (Cornelison and Cooper 2002a; 2002b).

The musket balls from Cluster A range from 0.30 to 0.69 calibre. The two smallest unfired 0.33 and 0.36 as well as the 0.30, 0.36, 0.38, and 0.41 fired are likely to be from militia rifles. Approximately 44.8 per cent of the fired musket balls are 0.64 calibre or larger. Only 26.2 per cent of the unfired were 0.64 or larger. These ratios clearly show the larger calibre British attack in the form of dropped musket balls in proximity to the smaller calibres of the militia.

The second cluster, B, is located in line with the Greene Monument, which commemorates the second line of battle. The cluster is north and south of New Garden Road as well as outside the current park tour loop. Thirty-four per cent of the items collected are battle related. Of the battle-related objects, the majority, 38 (75 per cent), are musket balls. Other objects recovered include four musket parts, seven bags of lead fragments, a piece of eight (Spanish reales) and a hand-carved soapstone bullet mould. The last two items – the piece of eight and the bullet mould – are not strictly battle artefacts, but represent items soldiers would have carried into battle.

The musket balls from Cluster B range from 0.26 to 0.70 calibre. The two smallest unfired 0.26, 0.29 and 0.37, as well as the 0.39 fired, are likely to be from militia rifles. Approximately 16 per cent of the fired musket balls are 0.64 calibre or larger, while 34.1 per cent of the unfired musket balls were 0.64 or larger. The high percentage of large unfired musket balls shows how the former Continentals on the second battle line were armed. The fact that such a small percentage of the fired were large calibre is likely to be the result of two factors. The first factor is that an increasing percentage of the fire coming from the Americans was presumably joined by militia for the first battle line. The second factor relates to the development of the battle as indicated by the distribution of the artefacts in this area. South of New Garden Road the artefact patterns are very linear. However, north of New Garden and south of the tour road the pattern thickens and has an east–west alignment. This is interpreted as the battle moving to the north in what was, at the time of the battle, a heavily wooded area.

The third cluster, C, is located near where the interpretative signs mark the third battle line. The majority of the military artefacts are located to the north of the tour loop on a small rise that corresponds very nicely to the hills drawn on the Tarleton battle map where the third battle line action took place.

Thirty-two per cent of the items collected are battle related. Of the battle-related objects the majority, 55 per cent, are musket balls. Other objects recovered include three musket parts, five bags of lead fragments and, most importantly, six iron canister shot. As important as the presence of these items in this location, however, is their absence from other areas of the park. With over half of the park surveyed and no other battle concentration found, Cluster C is the strongest and most compelling physical evidence that this area was indeed the location of the third battle line. The historical accounts report canister shot being fired in only one part of the battle, when Cornwallis ordered his own artillery to fire into the melee. Had iron canister been located at any of the other battle lines it would not be significant in this location. The fact that it is here and *only here* leaves little room for speculation concerning the location of the third line.

The musket balls from Cluster C range from 0.45 to 0.69 calibre. The smallest round, an unfired 0.45, indicates that the militia support was very low at this point in the battle. Approximately 6 per cent of the fired musket balls are 0.64 calibre or larger. Fifty per cent of the unfired musket balls were 0.64 calibre or larger. The high percentage of large unfired musket balls shows how the Continentals on the third battle line were armed. The low percentage of large calibre projectiles indicates that the British fire was very weak and defused at the point of the battle. Conversely, the American fire was concentrated. Had Cornwallis not ordered the firing of canister his army may have finished the battle in a much worse condition than it did.

Conclusions

The three projects discussed clearly show the information collection possible using a group of dedicated volunteer metal detector hobbyists. Without the relationship that has developed between CARHA and SEAC over the last 15 years this important information may have been lost, and nor would these methodologies have been developed. The relationship has been one of mutual benefit. The volunteers are able to work in places to which they would not otherwise have access and they are able to handle and photograph the artefacts, thus giving them the bragging rights and additional information about material culture.

The archaeologists, meanwhile, have a cadre of hard-working volunteers who are knowledgeable concerning the material culture; each of them is an important resource. They are willing to travel great distances, sometime at large personal expense. In short, we would be unable to do this work without the skills that these volunteers bring.

The four battles discussed are important to American and British history. Without the time volunteered by the metal detector hobbyists, none of this information would have been available to the public. The relationship between the hobbyist and the archaeologist is one that we have a duty to cultivate, while also taking the time to educate the public and bring the cultural resource management issues to light. This relationship allows the metal detector hobbyist to learn that all archaeological collections are not locked away in a vault, Indiana Jones-style. It also helps to dispel the widely held belief that the 'good' artefacts are on the NPS property.

FIG 4.4: IRON CANISTER SHOT FROM GUILFORD COURTHOUSE
AND ARTEFACTS FROM OTHER SURVEYS

BIBLIOGRAPHY

Baker, T E, 1992 *Another Such Victory: The story of the American defeat at Guilford Courthouse that helped win the War for Independence*, Eastern Acorn Press, New York City

Bearss, E C, 1996 *Battle of Cowpens: A documented narrative and troop movement maps*, The Overmountain Press, Johnson City, Tennessee

Birkedal, T, 2005 *The Search for the Lost Riverfront: Historical and archeological investigations at the Chalmette Battlefield, Jean Lafitte National Historical Park and Preserve*, unpublished National Park Service report submitted to the Corps of Engineers, New Orleans District. On file with Jean Lafitte National Historical Park and Preserve, New Orleans, Louisiana

Blythe, R, Carroll, M A, and Moffson, S H, 1995 *Kings Mountain National Military Park: Historic resource study*, National Park Service, Atlanta, Georgia

Buchanan, J, 1997 *The Road to Guilford Courthouse: The American Revolution in the Carolinas*, John Wiley and Sons, Inc, New York

Cornelison, J E, 2000 Archaeology of retreat: systematic metal detector survey and information system analysis at the Battle of Chickamauga, September 1863, in *Archaeological Perspective on the American Civil War*, C R Geier and S R Potter (eds), University of Florida Press, Gainesville

— 2005 *An Archeological Report on a Geophysical Survey and Limited Site Testing: Stones River National Battlefield*, National Park Service, Southeast Archeological Center, Tallahassee, Florida

— 2006a *Victory and Retribution: An archeological survey at Kings Mountain National Military Park, South Carolina*, 38YK 0423, National Park Service, Southeast Archeological Center, Tallahassee, Florida

— 2006b *Final Report of a Metal Detecting Survey of the Palisade Area at Horseshoe Bend National Military Park*, National Park Service, Southeast Archeological Center, Tallahassee, Florida

— 2007 *An Archeological Report on a Metal Detecting Survey and Limited Site Testing at Shiloh National Battlefield, Shiloh, Tennessee*, National Park Service, Southeast Archeological Center, Tallahassee, Florida

Cornelison, J E, and Cooper, T D, 2002a *Battle Lines and Wolf Pits: Archeological testing at Cowpens National Battlefield, South Carolina*, National Park Service, Southeast Archeological Center, Tallahassee, Florida

— 2002b *An Archeological Survey of Chalmette Battlefield at Jean Lafitte National Historical Park and Preserve*, National Park Service, Southeast Archeological Center. Tallahassee, Florida

Cornelison, J E, and Groh, L, 2007 *Battle Lines and Courthouses: Archeological survey and testing at Guilford Courthouse National Military Park, Greensboro, North Carolina*: The 1995, 1997, and 1998 Field Projects, National Park Service, Southeast Archeological Center, Tallahassee, Florida

Dickens, R S, 1979 *Archaeological Investigations at Horseshoe Bend National Military Park, Alabama*, Special Publications of the Alabama Archaeological Society, Number 3, University, Alabama

Draper, L C, 1971 *King's Mountain and Its Heroes*, 1881, Reprint Genealogical Publishing, Baltimore, Maryland

Fox, R A, Jr, and Scott, D D, 1991 The post-Civil War battlefield pattern: an example from the Custer Battlefield, *Historical Archaeology* 259 (2), 92–103

Garza, R L, 2005 *Preliminary Results of the FY05 Archeological Survey at Palo Alto Battlefield National Historic*

Site, report on file at Palo Alto Battlefield NHS, Brownsville, Texas

— 2006 *Preliminary Results of the FY06 Archeological Survey at Palo Alto Battlefield National Historic Site*, report on file at Palo Alto Battlefield NHS, Brownsville, Texas

Haecker, C M, and Mauck, J G, 1997 *On the Prairie of Palo Alto: Historical archaeology of the US–Mexican War Battlefield*, Texas A & M University Press, College Station, Texas

Lees, W B, 1992 *Archaeology and the Interpretation of Civil War Battlefields: The case of Mine Creek, Kansas*, a paper presented at the Southeastern Archeological Conference, Little Rock, Arkansas

— 1994 When the shooting stopped, the war began, in *Look to the Ear: Historical Archaeology and the American Civil War*, C R Geier Jr and S E Winter (eds), University of Tennessee, Knoxville

Roberts, R T, 1999 The history of metal detectors, in *Western and Eastern Treasures*, September 1999, People's Publishing, San Anselmo, CA

Scott, D, 2005 Archaeological Institute of America Website, available at http://www.archaeology.org/online/interviews/scott.html (11 October 2005)

Scott, D D, and Fox, R A, 1987 *Archaeological Insights into the Custer Battle: An assessment of the 1984 field season*, University of Oklahoma Press, Norman

Sivilich, D M, 1996 Analyzing musket balls to interpret a Revolutionary War site, *Historical Archaeology* 30 (2), 101–9

Snow, D R, 1981 Battlefield archeology, *Early Man* 3 (1)

Wilson, R, 1963 *The Search for Jackson's Mud Rampart*, Department of the Interior, National Park Service, Southeast Region, Richmond, Virginia

5

Before the Portable Antiquities Scheme

Peter V Addyman

In the 1970s archaeologists in Britain began to be aware of – and to be alarmed by – a growing use by non-archaeologists of metal detectors to locate archaeological artefacts. The only surprise is that this development took so long.

World War II and its aftermath saw a rapid development of mine- and bomb-detecting technology in response to the need to locate minefields in conflict zones or in defence locations, to clear them afterwards and, especially in post-war Britain, to pinpoint unexploded bombs for disposal. Operators in military bomb disposal units using electromagnetic surveying instruments inevitably became quite used to encountering anomalies that represented artefacts other than mines and bombs, learning to identify them for what they were and to discount them. The more alert operatives very rapidly saw the potential of the 'bomb locaters' and 'Polish mine detectors' of the late 1940s for a range of other uses – for example, for the location of buried pipes by civil engineers and, very soon, for the location of buried ancient metal artefacts (Tite 1972, 32–3). For instance, a Territorial Army contingent from 272 Bomb Disposal Squadron at Green Lane Barracks in Shipley, Yorkshire, was despatched in 1947 for an 'exercise' to 'clear' a field in Abbey Road, Knaresborough, which the officer in charge knew to be the site of a Trinitarian Priory, then under archaeological investigation by a local archaeological group. With remarkable efficiency the squad located first a buried iron five-barred fence section (19th century), then a reasonable selection of medieval and post-medieval ironwork, and finally anomalies that proved to represent the monastery's lavatorium, revealed presumably because of either its electrical resistivity or magnetic susceptibility contrast against the surrounding subsoil. The prehistorian R J C Atkinson, too, had demonstrated the effectiveness of army surplus mine detectors in predictive prospecting of archaeological sites and recommended the use of them in his influential textbook *Field Archaeology* (Atkinson 1953); though the supply of such devices soon dried up, they were anyway anything but user-friendly, and few people followed Atkinson's lead.

Improvements in the wide range of coil-based electromagnetic surveying systems for the location of metal objects came in the late 1960s with the advent of the pulsed induction meter (Colani 1966), overcoming problems of detecting at depth and allowing

FIG 5.1: EARLY METAL DETECTORS MANUFACTURED IN THE
UK IN THE LATE 1960S AND EARLY 1970S

ferrous and non-ferrous metals to be distinguished. It was not long before a range of efficient and effective metal detectors became commercially available (Fig 5.1) and were marketed to a wide public for use in the recovery of lost metal objects and for discovery of ancient artefacts, often implicitly or even explicitly using the lure of the possible discovery of buried treasure. The sophistication and the sensitivity of the devices increased while the price of simpler models came down, resulting on the one hand in serious hobbyists being able to develop remarkably effective search strategies and performance, and on the other in the rapid escalation in the number of users (Dobinson and Denison 1995, 4–6).

At this time there were no constraints in England and Wales on the recovery of archaeological artefacts, the ownership of which, except in cases of Treasure Trove, was presumed to lie with the owner of the land upon which they were found. Detectorists were free to operate on land if they owned it or if they had the landowner's permission, though laws of trespass and theft might apply if they did not. The ancient law of Treasure Trove, in no way originally designed as an archaeological statute, was used to secure finds of gold and silver for the nation, but it was widely recognised as being deficient and inefficient and in the late 1960s the Council for British Archaeology (CBA) had begun consultations aimed at leading to its reform. In these circumstances it is hardly surprising that the relatively sudden placing of powerful, cheap and easy-to-use detecting devices in the hands of a non-archaeologist public caused consternation among archaeologists who were aware that artefacts divorced from their context lose most of their evidential value, whatever their intrinsic interest.

Anecdotal evidence that important finds were being made by detectorists soon began to accumulate and, as statistics on the sale of metal detectors became known, treasure hunting, as it was then popularly known, took on the appearance of yet another threat to add to the many that were at that time besetting the archaeological heritage of the British Isles. Treasure hunting did not feature particularly dominantly in the discussions at Little Barford in 1971 that led to the establishment of the campaigning organisation Rescue, and the Pelican original on the subject (Rahtz 1974) hardly mentions it. Early issues of Rescue's campaigning newspaper *Rescue News* were, however, soon documenting the threat.

> In the Nene Valley, the Roman town of Durobrivae and its suburbs have been the prime target from people hoping to get rich quick by means of metal detectors. Donald Mackreth reports that one American airforce man built up a collection of 2000 objects and has taken them back to the United States. Businessmen often stop at the site and walk over it with metal detectors on their way up or down the Great North Road. The dangers from not only metal detectors but also collectors who walk out over newly ploughed fields is so real that members of the Research Committee are concerned about getting in print details of new discoveries. This leads to a dilemma, for while it is obviously desirable to give information on local sites to the local inhabitants, it is they who make up the major part of what Mackreth calls 'the predators of our past' (Anon 1975).

The same article describes a Dorset junior school carrying out an unofficial excavation aided by metal detectors, 40 holes dug by treasure hunters one weekend at Stansted Castle, Essex, and antiquities for sale in antique shops.

'Surely it is time for this vandalism to stop', *Rescue News* goes on, 'and for archaeological sites to enjoy complete protection in law from the moment of their identification as a site? It would appear that the Department of the Environment is completely unwilling to act in the matter of metal detectors and does not grasp the seriousness of the problem.'

One organisation that did grasp the seriousness of the problem was the CBA. It began to comment on it each year in its Annual Report. The discovery and excavation by treasure hunters of the Aston Rowant (Oxon) hoard of mid-Anglo-Saxon coins, for example, showed the inadequacy of even official archaeology to cope with the problems (CBA 1972, 5–6). The successful treasure hunters at Aston Rowant had reported their find to the British Museum but the County Museum's field staff only eventually heard about it through the Coroner's inquest and initially were denied access to the site. The

CBA commented that amateur and professional 'treasure hunting' had now grown into a continuous menace against which 'official' archaeology seemed powerless and even unwilling to act. It reported archaeological counter action in the field by scattering small metal objects on sites known to be threatened by metal detectors, the posting of overnight watches on sites to deter nocturnal treasure seekers and the introduction of a bye-law by the East Sussex County Council to control the use of metal detectors (CBA 1973, 7). The CBA identified what it saw as a basic legislative deficiency over which it proposed to campaign.

A modest step towards controlling the use of metal detectors on archaeological sites came with the publication in 1977 of a consultation document *Proposals to amend the laws relating to Ancient Monuments* that eventually led to a measure in the *Ancient Monuments and Archaeological Areas Act* 1979 controlling the use of metal detectors on Scheduled Ancient Monuments and Areas of Archaeological Importance. For the CBA, however, which was by now regularly receiving reports of the growth of metal detecting (Burchard *et al* 1975) and damage by treasure hunters to known (though not necessarily scheduled) archaeological sites, this was not a solution to the problem. The number of metal detectors in use in Britain was seen to be enormous, attempts to have them banned seemed to have little chance of success, and thousands of non-scheduled sites remained wide open to looting and damage (CBA 1977, 3–4). The Ancient Monuments Inspectorate of the Department of the Environment, though concerned to apply the new law to sites in its guardianship, and sites which were scheduled, took the view that portable antiquities matters were otherwise largely outside its remit.

The metal detecting hobby, meanwhile, was becoming extremely popular. It developed its own hobby magazines, the pilot issue of *Treasure Hunting* appearing in August 1977. *Coin and Medal News* carried metal detecting articles from about the same date and *The Searcher*, a clone of *Treasure Hunting*, appearing from 1986 onwards. The two magazines registered mass sales that outstripped most archaeological periodicals and earned them in due course a place on the shelves of newsagents, something which no archaeological periodical achieved until the present century. Dramatic finds attracted excited media coverage that inevitably stressed the treasure aspects, featuring heart-warming stories of good fortune smiling on small people and the ever-compelling thought of 'something for nothing'. Attempts by archaeologists to counter these good news stories with complaints about archaeological damage were met with incomprehension by both the media and the public. To the detectorists themselves they seemed to smack of jealousy or chagrin.

Archaeologists were by no means of a single mind as to how to react to the growth of metal detecting, but there was near unanimity that uncontrolled searching with metal detectors represented a threat to the buried evidence for Britain's past. Artefacts are elements of a complex of data on archaeological sites that, studied together and studied systematically, can reveal information about a huge range of activity by people long ago. This is particularly true when archaeological objects remain in stratified archaeological contexts – the layers of deposit that represent human activity over the ages – and have not been disturbed by modern intrusions such as ploughing. Under such circumstances it is a commonplace of archaeology that artefacts recovered in the course of carefully recorded stratigraphic excavation are crucial in defining the date, nature and former use of a site in the past, the social and economic status of its former inhabitants, their conditions of life, even sometimes their religious beliefs, rites and rituals, as well as their burial customs. Holes dug by metal detectorists in these circumstances not only remove the objects, the crucial evidence for understanding the site, but disrupt all the other evidence which, undisturbed, could allow the archaeologist, like the forensic scientist, meticulously to piece together a complex story.

Even objects from a much-cultivated plough soil above such a site have their part to play in defining the areas of former human activity. They are often the evidence which draws attention to the site in the first place. Systematically recorded, they can define its extent and the patterns of activity there in the past and may give a fair hint of its date and nature. It takes little imagination to realise that, once removed without record from the plough soil, they can do none of these things. Without a findspot they pretty well cease to be of much interest to archaeologists at all unless they have exceptional intrinsic qualities.

All of this is common knowledge to archaeologists and easily understood by anyone who has attended a course in archaeology, or participated in an excavation, or even read widely or watched archaeological digs on television. Unfortunately a very large number of detectorists, at least in the early days of the growth of the hobby, had done none of these things. Often they had no more training than it takes to operate a relatively simple and increasingly user-friendly and effective piece of technology. They used their own native wit to work out where objects, ancient or modern, might be found – on beaches, in public parks, along popular paths, in old rubbish tips and, obviously, in known ancient archaeological sites. Many of the latter used to be conveniently and distinctively marked on Ordnance Survey Maps and required no more than simple map-reading skills for their location. Detectorists of a more systematic turn of mind could consult sites and monuments records, public record offices, data banks about archaeology held by museums and local authorities and local archaeological societies, and archives of archaeological air photographs and other such reconnaissance sources. Such knowledge was disseminated by word of mouth, or by the growing experience and expertise of metal detecting clubs, or by *Treasure Hunting* or *The Searcher*, placing information about the location of archaeological sites in the hands of large numbers of people who did not know, or sometimes avowedly did not care (Addyman 1995, 168), about the sensitivity and vulnerability of the archaeological record.

How should the archaeological community react in this situation? The question was vigorously debated, not least in a working party on metal detecting and archaeology set up by the Executive Committee of the Council for British Archaeology under the chairmanship of the distinguished Romanist Dr Graham Webster. Some members of the Working Party felt that an accommodation could be reached with the more responsible metal detector users (CBA 1979, 4), while others felt that total opposition to metal detecting was the only solution. After much discussion, in 1979 the Council for British

Archaeology agreed a statement which in effect declared total war on metal detecting for ancient artefacts. It ran as follows:

> In the view of the Council for British Archaeology, treasure hunting constitutes a great threat to the country's archaeological heritage, and is thus contrary to the national interest. The concept of treasure hunting is totally at variance with the objectives and practices of archaeology in studying and safeguarding our tangible past for the public good of present and future generations. The Council recognises that many users of metal detectors are motivated by a genuine interest in the past and its remains and that they would not knowingly damage those remains. Such people are welcome to join the active membership of British archaeology, but they must accept the methods and disciplines of archaeology.

In 1979 the Council for British Archaeology had 14 regional groups representing 219 archaeological societies, 6 national and 96 regional museums, 7 local government departments and 28 universities and colleges: in total, many tens of thousands of people. It was, and still is, the nearest thing there is to a voice for British archaeology. With no-one dissenting, it thus roundly condemned treasure hunting.

Following the passing of this resolution, the Council joined together with the Museums Association, the Society of Museum Archaeologists, the Association of County Archaeological Officers, RESCUE the Trust for British Archaeology, the Standing Conference of (Archaeological) Unit Managers and the United Kingdom Institute of Conservation to plan an anti-treasure hunting campaign, Stop Taking Our Past, with the acronym STOP.

STOP began a campaign on two fronts, first to inform and educate the public about the threat to the country's archaeological and historic heritage from the indiscriminate use of metal detectors and the resulting despoliation of sites and monuments (CBA 1980, 1) and second to persuade major property-owning and management groups to ban the use of metal detectors on their properties, as the National Trust, the third-largest landowner in the United Kingdom, had already done. An early success was the persuasion of the Home Secretary to approve bye-laws designed to prohibit the use of metal detectors on council-owned properties, and a number of local authorities subsequently brought in such bye-laws. The publicity campaign had the aim of making treasure hunting on archaeological sites seem as socially unacceptable as the collecting of birds' eggs or the taking of rare wild plants; even more so, perhaps, as birds and plants could renew themselves but archaeology, once destroyed, could never be replaced. The message of the campaign was widely implanted and remains in the consciousness of a generation of the public.

At the same time, archaeologists began to realise that the era of open information about archaeological discoveries had gone. Means have been found to restrict – or restrict access to – information about old and new finds in publicly accessible sites and monuments records. At most, only four-figure map references are quoted to prevent the raiding of sites. The practice of publishing aerial photographs of newly discovered sites was seen to be an invitation to treasure hunters, so relatively few have been published in recent years. Only the most obvious archaeological sites are now marked and annotated on Ordnance Survey maps. Detectorists themselves have added to the drift towards secrecy, insisting that records of their finds are kept confidential to protect 'their' sites from being raided by other treasure hunters. The restriction of free access to information has undoubtedly limited archaeological research and will have deterred many from attempting research routines now made intolerably onerous. At a more general level it will have denied us the enjoyment of learning about much recent archaeological discovery. At the same time, however, it has protected many sites that would otherwise have been targets for detectorists.

A second negative effect of the campaign against treasure hunting was the reluctance of archaeologists to add metal detecting to the range of techniques of geophysical prospection commonly used in archaeological field research. Prior knowledge of the likely presence of metal objects can certainly be of benefit in excavating the layers of a stratified site, and the recovery rate of small metal objects and metal waste can be greatly increased by the use of metal detectors. Similarly, objects missed in excavation can be recovered by the systematic monitoring of excavated soil. Although the value of detectors for prospecting and such uses was demonstrated and reported by the Norfolk Museums and Archaeology Service as early as 1984 (Gregory and Rogerson 1984), archaeologists chose to believe that use of the devices gave the impression that they were condoning them. Archaeologists who did try them, myself included, often employing volunteers from the metal detecting fraternity using their own equipment, tended to find that the extra information product was minimal, the routine tedious and time consuming and the results not worth the effort involved. The truth is that metal detectors do have a place in the archaeologists' armoury when circumstances are right, and they have been used to good effect on a number of sites in later years. The routines under which metal detecting surveys can legitimately and usefully be deployed on archaeological sites have recently been clearly set out by English Heritage (English Heritage 2006), which has belatedly begun to be involved in portable antiquities matters, at least as regards Scheduled Ancient Monuments and sites under guardianship; the principles expounded as regards these matters are, however, generally applicable.

By 1980, when the STOP campaign got under way, there were already many thousands, perhaps tens of thousands, of detectorists at work annually in Britain. Many of them were organised in local metal detecting clubs. Conscious that the STOP campaign represented a threat to their hobby, a number of them, 'a representative body of elected volunteers', collaborated in 1981 to form a National Council for Metal Detecting, a kind of counterpoint to the Council for British Archaeology. NCMD saw itself as a democratic forum to discuss problems affecting the hobby and an authoritative voice to counter ill-informed and frequently misleading criticism of the hobby (NCMD 2007). A breakaway organisation, the Federation for Independent Detectorists, followed it in 1982. These organisations and an ever more vociferous *Treasure Hunting* challenged the perceptions of the STOP campaigners and began their own programme of public persuasion and lobbying of government. The National Council for Metal Detecting saw itself as the voice of what it described as responsible metal detectorists, and it soon became clear both to STOP campaigners and to the National Council that there could be at least some common cause in the creation of a Code of Conduct for responsible metal detector users that would identify some of the caveats that archaeologists might like to see. Discussions therefore began, unproductive and combative at first, but more positive later on, between the two Councils. The NCMD Code of Conduct, developed from a much earlier 'Code for Thoughtful Treasure Hunters' published by the British Amateur Treasure Hunters Association in the 1960s, came into being in 1983 and, with subsequent changes, was still in use twenty years on.

While attitudes were struck by the national bodies, the reality on the ground in the 1980s was that increasing numbers of detectorists, many of them increasingly skilful both in identifying sites and in detecting over them, were learning to co-exist with the then-increasing number of professional archaeologists addressing other aspects of the so-called 'Rescue' crisis in archaeology. Similarly, detectorists, frequently discovering objects which baffled them, turned to their local museums and archaeological authorities for help with identifications. It proved very difficult, for example, for the professional finds specialists from the York Archaeological Trust to rebuff friendly enquiring approaches from members of the York Metal Detecting Club, especially as their detecting was producing both individual finds of note and distribution patterns of finds which gave new insights into York's past. The kindly and patient work of the late Christopher Clarke, Finds Officer of the Trust, done largely in his own time at what most professionals would consider the anti-social hours favoured by detector groups – in evenings or weekends and often involving interminable chat in (then) smoke-filled rooms – began to bridge the gulf between tyro and professional. Similar work was under way, but on a far more systematic scale, in Norfolk, where the late Tony Gregory, based at the Norfolk Museums and Archaeology Service, devoted huge amounts of time to liaison with detectorists in this most archaeologically productive area of the British Isles (Gregory and Rogerson 1984). The result was systematic recording of artefacts in due course in their tens of thousands, demonstrating the archaeological dividends that collaboration rather than confrontation could produce.

The Norfolk experience also showed the extent of metal detecting in at least one area of Britain, and the very large number of objects that each year were being recovered from the plough soil of at least one area of intense arable cultivation. The data came as a shock to archaeologists, but was gleefully seized upon by detectorists to demonstrate that they were doing everyone a service in recovering material that, because of intense farming, was now increasingly being riven from its context by deep ploughing and was year after year being turned over in the plough soil and subjected to further erosion. It was suggested that the extensive use of modern chemical fertilisers accelerates chemical erosion of metal artefacts. The practice of metal detecting, therefore, was a timely way of rescuing at least some data about objects that were otherwise doomed.

Not all archaeologists were comfortable with this 'fraternising with the enemy'. After all, it did not solve the problem that the recording of artefacts after they had been divorced from their context or from their findspot meant that most of their data potential was lost. While many objects had an intrinsic interest, and excited archaeologists as much as metal detectorists, sharing this enthusiasm might imply condoning a practice which was anti-archaeological. Besides, it might simply encourage detectorists to go out and find more. Furthermore, it became apparent that some detectorists were inventing false provenances, either to divert other searchers from their secret sites, or to ensure that objects were 'found' on land where they had permission to detect. A false piece of data is in a sense worse than no data at all, for it creates a false positive in the archaeological record. While there is no doubt that most information given by detectorists to archaeological recorders is accurate and true, nevertheless the knowledge that some of it is not places suspicion on everything. Are such records, archaeologists asked, worth the time and effort required to make them?

Archaeologists were taxed, too, during the 1980s, when the incidence of metal detecting probably reached its height, with possibly up to 300,000 people involved at some time or another (Dobinson and Denison 1995, 4), by a series of notorious instances of the illicit removal of demonstrably valuable materials. The repeated raiding of the Wanborough Roman Temple site, north of the Hogsback near Guildford in Surrey, for Iron Age and Roman coins (Hanworth 1995, 173; and see Thomas, chapter 14), and the illicit excavation and export of the Icklingham Roman bronzes (Browning 1995, 145–9) are two well-documented examples, but there is anecdotal evidence of many more instances of what has become known as 'nighthawking'. Despite the hopeful signs that responsible detectorists could and would cooperate with archaeologists to mutual benefit (but how many archaeologists could afford to give the necessary hours, days or weeks of 'free' consultancy to make this work?), there was a clear need for some rationalisation of the situation.

One of the prime objectives of the CBA when it was set up in 1943 was a duty to 'press for legislative change' so that 'all future finds of movable archaeological material be treated as are antiquities coming under the Treasure Trove laws' (Addyman 1995, 166). To give it its due, the CBA tried its best to achieve this over the next 50 years. The Council's Honorary Legal Adviser, the late Charles Sparrow QC, drafted no fewer than 11 versions of one possible bill. Had portable antiquities legislation been reformed in the 1960s or 1970s, the problem of dealing with the advent of mass metal detecting would, arguably, have been much simpler. Britain would have had legislation broadly in accord with that of a number of European countries where archaeological artefacts are assumed to be the common heritage of the nation and treasure hunting using metal detectors is banned. It would also have brought Britain more demonstrably within the terms of the Valetta Convention (Council of Europe 1992; O'Keefe 1993), in so far as the use of metal detectors on archaeological sites is concerned. By the 1980s, the challenge of achieving such legislation was much greater. The CBA's last attempt limited itself to minor rationalisation of the absurd law of Treasure Trove, and did not attempt to deal with treasure hunting; but even this, presented to the House of Lords by Lord Abinger in 1982, was talked out in the House of Commons.

After much badgering from the archaeological community, the Government eventually agreed to look at the issue through a Department of the Environment review on the protection of portable antiquities in general. Its consultation paper came out in

1988; it was full of thoughtful and useful ideas, but led only, after long delay, to rejection by Government in a House of Lords debate in which the Minister, Lord Hesketh, while admitting that the activities of metal detector users may 'fall some way short of the highest scholarly standards', considered that 'it would be unduly cumbersome to set up a bureaucratic machinery to deal with it'. Suggestions that the system operating in Northern Ireland or Scotland, of mandatory reporting of finds, should be extended to England and Wales were described as 'nationalisation of finds', trashing the carefully worked out schemes suggested to the Department of the Environment by the archaeological world (CBA 1989, 9).

In these circumstances, when there appeared to be reluctance by Government to consider even the simplest reform of the Law of Treasure Trove, and no inclination to contemplate any measure to mitigate the wastage of archaeological resource from uncontrolled metal detecting, the CBA decided that some hard facts were needed.

The resultant survey, *Metal Detecting and Archaeology in England* (Dobinson and Denison 1995), produced with the support of English Heritage, provided at last some reliable data and some intelligent evidence-backed guesses at the true situation. Given the almost impossible task of assembling information about an activity when most of the activists were reluctant to cooperate, and of assessing the incidence of illicit nighthawking, by its nature covert, Dobinson and Denison did sufficient to demonstrate that the threat to archaeology constituted by metal detecting was, if anything, far greater than had been guessed.

The CBA report produced estimates of the number of archaeological artefacts annually hoovered up from the soil of Britain that were staggering and it paved the way both for the reform of the law of Treasure Trove achieved by the 1996 *Treasure Act*, and for the Portable Antiquities Scheme. To the new figures for the incidence of metal detecting and the extent of object recovery was added the striking fact that by far the majority of metal detected finds came from areas of the country where the extent of arable cultivation was high. It tended to corroborate the claim of metal detectorists that a large proportion of their finds did indeed come from plough soil. Furthermore, it drew the attention of archaeologists to the horrendous extent of archaeological damage done by the late 20th-century move to intensive agriculture. The removal of hedgerows, the flattening of archaeological landscapes and the deep ploughing of archaeological sites was probably the most destructive single threat to the past of the country in the last quarter of the 20th century (McAvoy and Holyoak 2007), albeit one so general and so insidious that it tended to go either unremarked upon or ignored.

The time was ripe for the change in opinion among archaeologists. The orthodox view became one which saw that metal detecting was with us to stay; that it was, like it or not, recovering huge numbers of objects important to the understanding of Britain's past; that these objects could at least be recorded, even if their contexts by and large could not; and that this was worth doing.

The change in perception gained a first formal expression in a joint statement from the CBA, the Museums Association and the Society of Antiquaries of principles for the protection of portable antiquities, which was issued in 1993. This set out the case for bringing portable antiquities within the law. Widely discussed at the time, it led to the establishment of a Standing Conference on Portable Antiquities, providing a forum at which representatives of all relevant national archaeological bodies and of the National Council for Metal Detecting could meet. The Council for British Archaeology at the same time set up a Portable Antiquities Working Group that met on a regular basis to forward matters. Its work might in due course have led to a new general antiquities statute had it not been overtaken by a separate and independent initiative led by the Surrey Archaeological Society, which was incensed by the Wanborough nighthawking affair, to promote a more limited bill to reform the law of Treasure Trove. This, subsequently passed as the 1996 *Treasure Act*, caused the Standing Conference and the Working Group to give new and innovative thought to the recording of antiquities not covered by the 1996 *Treasure Act*, thus leading to the formation of the Portable Antiquities Scheme. This, though failing to answer the fundamental objection of archaeologists to metal detecting – loss of contextual information – has nevertheless produced for the nation so rich a harvest of information about artefacts – and so great an enrichment of its archaeological collections – that its work must be worthwhile. Its pragmatic approach takes account of human nature and the practicalities of the situation, and, by a considerable order of magnitude, achieves better results than those obtained through the clever and high-minded legislation of our European neighbours.

BIBLIOGRAPHY

Anon, 1975 So who says the crisis is over? *Rescue News* 9, 1–2

Addyman, P V, 1995 Treasure Trove, Treasure Hunting and the Quest for a Portable Antiquities Act, in *Antiquities Trade and Betrayed, Legal Ethical and Conservation Issues*, K W Tubb (ed), Archetype Books, London, 163–72

Atkinson, R J C, 1953 *Field Archaeology*, Methuen, London

Browning, J, 1995 A layman's attempts to precipitate change in domestic and international 'heritage' laws, in *Antiquities Trade and Betrayed, Legal Ethical and Conservation Issues*, K W Tubb (ed), Archetype Books, London, 145–9

Burchard, A, Rance, A, Rudkin, D, and Schadla-Hall, T, 1975 The problem of treasure hunting, *Rescue News* 10, 2–3

CBA, 1972 *Archaeology in Britain 1971–72 Report No. 22 for the year ended 30 June 1972*, London

— 1973 *Archaeology in Britain 1972–73 Council for British Archaeology Report No. 23 for the year ended 30 June 1973*, London

— 1977 *Council for British Archaeology Report No. 27 for the year ended 30 June 1977*, London

— 1979 *Council for British Archaeology Report No. 29 for the year ended 30 June 1979*, London

— 1980 *Council for British Archaeology Report No. 30 for the year ended 30 June 1980*, London

— 1989 *Council for British Archaeology Archaeology in Britain 1989*, London

Colani, C, 1966 A new type of locating device. I – the instrument, *Archaeometry* 9, 3–8

Council of Europe, 1992 *European Convention on the Protection of the Archaeological Heritage* (The Valetta Convention)

Dobinson, C, and Denison, S, 1995 *Metal Detecting and Archaeology in England*, English Heritage and Council for British Archaeology, London and York

Gregory, T, and Rogerson, A J G, 1984 Metal-detecting in archaeological excavation, *Antiquity* 58 (224), 179–84

Hanworth, R, 1995 Treasure Trove: new approaches to antiquities legislation, in *Antiquities Trade and Betrayed, Legal Ethical and Conservation Issues*, K W Tubb (ed), Archetype Books, London, 173–80

McAvoy, F, and Holyoak, V, 2007 Conservation of scheduled monuments in cultivation, *Conservation Bulletin* 54, 27–8

NCMD, 2007 National Council for Metal Detecting, available at http://www.ncmd.co.uk/about%20us.htm (29 November 2007)

O'Keefe, P J, 1993 The European Convention on the Protection of the Archaeological Heritage, *Antiquity* 67, 406–13

Rahtz, P A (ed), 1974 *Rescue Archaeology*, Penguin, Harmondsworth

Tite, M S, 1972 *Methods of Physical Examination in Archaeology*, Seminar Press, London and New York

6

The Development and Future of the *Treasure Act* and Portable Antiquities Scheme

Roger Bland

All countries have legal frameworks and other systems intended to protect objects of archaeological, historical or cultural importance found in their territory by members of the public, either by chance or as a result of deliberate searching. While these approaches vary widely, in most countries – although not in England and Wales – there is a legal requirement to report all objects of archaeological importance and normally the state claims ownership of them; there are mechanisms for paying rewards to the finders and there is usually protection for archaeological sites and controls over the use of metal detectors (Bland 1998). This paper looks at the development of twin mechanisms to deal with this issue in England and Wales, the 1996 *Treasure Act* and Portable Antiquities Scheme, both of which were ten years old in 2007.

Treasure

Treasure Trove

The 1996 *Treasure Act* was the culmination of a long series of unsuccessful attempts to reform the common law of Treasure Trove, which goes back to the mid-19th century. Under the old law, only gold and silver objects whose owners were unknown and which had been deliberately buried with the intention of recovery could be declared Treasure Trove and thus become Crown property. Since 1886 the Government had paid *ex gratia* rewards to finders for declaring finds (Hill 1936).

The final, and successful, attempt to reform the law was started by the Surrey Archaeological Society at the end of the 1980s as a response to the looting of the site at Wanborough (O'Connell and Bird 1994), where a very large hoard of Iron Age coins had been systematically stolen by detector users and great damage done to the Romano-Celtic temple there; subsequent prosecutions failed because of the deficiencies of the common law of Treasure Trove. The 1996 *Treasure Act* was championed with great energy by the Earl of Perth (Palmer 1993; Bland 1996).

Treasure Act

The *Treasure Act* finally passed through Parliament in 1996 and came into effect the following year (Bland 2005). It applies only to objects found since September 1997 and it has effect in England, Wales and Northern Ireland (DCMS 2002a).[1] Under the 1996 *Treasure Act* the following finds are Treasure, provided they were found after 24 September 1997:

a)   objects other than coins at least 300 years old with a minimum precious metal content of 10 per cent

b)   all groups of coins from the same find at least 300 years old (if the coins have a precious metal content of less than 10 per cent then the hoard must consist of at least 10 coins)

c)   objects found in association with Treasure

From 1 January 2003 the Act was extended by Order to include:

d)   groups of prehistoric base-metal objects from the same find

Objects belonging to their original owner or his heirs are excluded, as are unworked natural objects (such as fossils) and wreck.

Rewards and valuations

Any object that a museum wishes to acquire is valued by a committee of independent experts, the Treasure Valuation Committee, and their remit is to determine the full market value of the object in question. The reward is normally divided equally between the finder and landowner. The committee is advised by a panel of valuers drawn from the trade and interested parties can commission their own valuations, which the committee will consider. The reward can be reduced or not paid at all if there is evidence of wrongdoing and once a valuation has been agreed museums have up to four months to raise money. Archaeologists are not eligible for rewards (DCMS 2002a).

In 2001 there was a review of the Act and a report was published in November of that year (DCMS 2001a). This contained over 50 recommendations, many of which required changes to the 1996 *Treasure Act* Code of Practice, which was developed to accompany the 1996 *Treasure Act*. This Code of Practice offers guidelines for the treatment of Treasure in England and Wales, including advice to finders, coroners and museums. The most important recommendation was that the definition of Treasure be extended to include prehistoric base-metal hoards, and an Order implementing this, together with a revision of the Code of Practice, came into effect in January 2003 (DCMS 2002a).

Examples of Treasure cases

So what sorts of finds have been reported under the 1996 *Treasure Act*? Perhaps the most iconic prehistoric find is the middle Bronze Age gold cup found by Cliff Bradshaw with a metal detector at Ringlemere in Kent in 2001 (See Plate 1; DCMS 2003, 14–15; Needham *et al* 2006; Hobbs 2003, 55–9). The cup is only paralleled in Britain by a smaller one found at Rillaton in Cornwall in the early 19th century, and it is an object of outstanding importance. It seems that it had been hit by the plough in the previous season and, in the opinion of the archaeologist who has excavated the site, Keith Parfitt, if it had not been recovered when it was it would have been in several pieces after the next ploughing. The discovery prompted a programme of archaeological work on the site, which revealed that

FIG 6.1: HOARD OF ROMAN VOTIVE OBJECTS FROM NEAR BALDOCK, HERTFORDSHIRE

© PORTABLE ANTIQUITIES SCHEME

the cup was buried in a Bronze Age barrow overlaid by an Anglo-Saxon cemetery.

One of the most important Treasure finds from the Roman period is the temple treasure discovered near Baldock in Hertfordshire (Fig 6.1; DCMS 2004a, 38–43; Jackson and Burleigh 2005). It was found by metal detector user Alan Meek in September 2002 and comprises some 27 gold and silver objects, including gold jewellery, a silver figurine and votive plaques of silver alloy and gold, which have been studied by Ralph Jackson. The finder immediately contacted Gil Burleigh, a local archaeologist, who arrived at the site shortly after the removal of the last pieces of the hoard. As a result it was possible to establish and record the precise circumstances of the find. A programme of fieldwork shed valuable light on the context of the find. Most importantly, 5 of the 19 silver and gold plaques contained the name Senuna (there is one further plaque inscribed with the name of Minerva), a previously unknown Romano-British goddess. It is likely that the silver figurine is a representation of her. Other plaques are inscribed with the names of the worshippers: Cariatia, Celsus, Firmanus, Lucilia. Two complete inscriptions record the same vow: *Servandus Hispani willingly fulfilled his vow to the goddess Se(nuna)*. The hoard can be dated to the later 3rd or 4th century AD and it must have been connected to a temple or shrine of the goddess Senuna.

Perhaps the most important Anglo-Saxon find reported under the 1996 *Treasure Act* is a swivelling seal ring with the name of Baldehild, found by detector user Roy Crawford at Postwick near Norwich, Norfolk, and studied by Leslie Webster (See Plates 2A and

2B; DCMS 2000a, 31–2). The scene on Plate 2B is probably a betrothal scene, while the obverse shows a portrait of her with her name. This is the first example of a swivelling seal ring to be found in Britain. Baldehild is the same name as that of an Anglo-Saxon princess who married Clovis II of France in about AD 648 and then later entered a monastery. We can never know for certain whether the woman named on the ring represents this historical individual, but they are certainly of similar date. A further mystery is why such a high-quality Frankish object came to rest in rural Norfolk, though such a ring might certainly have been a prestige gift, or even a sign to identify the wearer as an emissary of the owner. This object has been acquired by Norwich Castle Museum.

The largest category of items reported as Treasure date from the medieval and post-medieval periods – that is, from the time of the Norman Conquest down to the end of the 17th century. These objects consist largely of jewellery, especially rings and brooches, and many are of limited interest. From the 16th and 17th centuries other artefacts start to appear, such as Tudor silver-gilt dress fittings (Gaimster *et al* 2002) (Figs 6.2A and 6.2B). These objects were hardly known to archaeologists before the 1996 *Treasure Act*, as they are very seldom found in excavations. Since the Act some 100 examples have been recorded and they have been studied by David Gaimster and others. They come in a wide variety of shapes and it is likely that now we are aware of them we will be able to find out more about how they were used by looking at personal and household inventories of the Tudor period.

Under the 1996 *Treasure Act* the number of coin hoards that have been reported has trebled. One of the most important hoards of recent years is the one from Patching in West Sussex, found by two detector users in 1997 (See Plate 3; DNH 1998, no. 18; Abdy 2006). It consists of 23 gold solidi, 27 silver coins, 2 gold rings and 54 pieces of silver scrap. The hoard pushes the date of the latest known hoard of Roman coins from Britain forward by some 40 years from about AD 420 – the latest of the latest hoard known

FIG 6.2A AND 6.2B: 16TH CENTURY SILVER-GILT DRESS FITTINGS FROM WANBOROUGH, WILTSHIRE (4A) AND BRAMPTON, LINCOLNSHIRE (4B)

 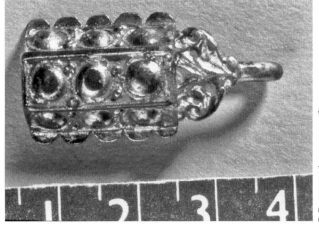

hitherto – to the AD 460s, as it contained a coin of Libius Severus (AD 461–5), besides some 20 other coins that are all later than AD 410. This one find has completely changed the previously held orthodoxy that Roman coins ceased to enter Britain after the reign of Constantine III.

Numbers of Treasure cases

In 1994 it was predicted that the number of cases would be between 100 and 200 a year, but in fact the increase has been much higher than that. Before the Act came into force, about 25 finds were declared Treasure Trove each year. In the first full year of the Act, 1998, this number increased to 201. It remained at that level for the next three years, and then in 2002 it went up by 100 to 300 and each year since it has risen by about 100 cases a year, so that in 2005 the total was 595, in 2006 it was 673 and in 2007, 749 (Fig 6.3).

The increase since 2002 is undoubtedly a result of the development of the Portable Antiquities Scheme and especially the expansion of the Scheme across the whole of England and Wales in 2003, when 21 new Finds Liaison Officers were appointed. Since 2003 there has been an average increase of 154 per cent in the reporting of Treasure. The most significant increases have been in the Isle of Wight and Sussex (1186 and 953 per cent respectively); both areas had a Finds Liaison Officer for the first time in 2003.

Problems

This success has brought problems in its wake. Museums struggle to raise the money to acquire Treasure and about half of all finds are now disclaimed because no museum is able or willing to find the funding. The MLA/V&A Purchase Grant Fund, the Art Fund and the Heritage Lottery Fund are the principal sources of financial support and they have been joined more recently by a new dedicated fund for Treasure from the Headley Trust which is very welcome, but is not likely to exist permanently.

FIG 6.3: TREASURE CASES 1988–2007

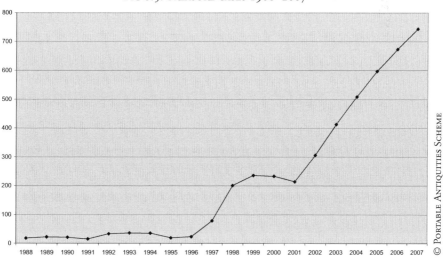

© PORTABLE ANTIQUITIES SCHEME

The system of administration of Treasure is also very complex and consequently the period between the discovery of a find and the payment of a reward is often longer than the one-year target time set out in the Code of Practice. It is therefore essential to do everything possible to make the system work as efficiently as possible. One initiative should lead to some improvement: at present the administration of Treasure cases is divided between the British Museum (and for Wales, the National Museum Wales), which deal with cases up to the coroner's inquest, and the Department for Culture, Media and Sport (DCMS), which deals with cases thereafter (principally the valuation process). In March 2007 the DCMS transferred its responsibilities to the British Museum, which established three posts, two full-time and one part-time, to deal with these responsibilities. Concentrating the whole administration in one place is more efficient and enables us to provide a better service to finders, landowners and museums.

Enforcement

There are also problems of enforcement. Many unreported finds of Treasure have been appearing in trade, on the *eBay* website and elsewhere. There is also a significant problem as regards the looting of sites for antiquities. The Council of British Archaeology's 1995 survey on metal detecting found that over a five-year period, 188 Scheduled Ancient Monuments had been attacked and 37 out of 50 professional archaeological units reported raids on their excavation sites during the same period (Dobinson and Denison 1995). Providing physical protection for the potentially enormous number of sites that could be attacked is always going to be very difficult, given that in most areas the police give such crime low priority, and when prosecutions are brought they are often unsuccessful because courts tend not to regard these offences as serious, although a recent initiative in Kent, where 'nighthawking' (unauthorised metal detecting) is being tackled as part of the wider anti-social behaviour and rural crime agenda, is encouraging.

Another way of tackling the problem is to make it harder for the thieves to sell their finds. At present, it is too easy for the 'nighthawks' to sell their finds to dealers who are happy to purchase such objects without checking that the vendors are acting legally and with the agreement of the landowners. Many items of potential Treasure are openly offered for sale, especially on the *eBay* website. In October 2006 the PAS signed a memorandum of understanding with *eBay* whereby *eBay* will take such items down from its website when notified by PAS and the police. PAS has been systematically monitoring *eBay* since then. *eBay* published comprehensive guidance on buying and selling antiquities on its website for the first time (http://pages.ebay.co.uk/buy/guides/antiquities/), while PAS also developed its own guidance (www.finds.org.uk/treasure/advice.php). During 2007 PAS followed up 144 cases of potential Treasure offered for sale on *eBay*. Although there have not yet been any criminal prosecutions as a result of this monitoring of *eBay*, there have been a number of cases where vendors have voluntarily agreed to report the finds they were selling as Treasure. However, monitoring *eBay* on a daily basis, which is what is needed, is a time-consuming process and potentially lays the Scheme open to expensive legal challenges. More resources are needed in order to pursue this work; these should logically come from *eBay*, which profits from the sale of antiquities on its website.

The Government's accession to the 1970 UNESCO Convention in 2002 (DCMS 2004c) and the Dealing in Cultural Objects (Offences) Act, which came into force on 30 December 2003 (DCMS 2004b), should help to suppress the market in finds illegally recovered from the UK but no prosecutions have been brought under this Act, nor have any been brought under the 1996 *Treasure Act*.

There is definitely a need to make the law enforcement agencies, the police, the Crown Prosecution Service and the Government more aware of the problems caused by the illegal recovery of artefacts from the UK and their sale on the market, and one of the essential tools needed to push this issue higher up the political agenda is an authoritative survey of the extent of the problem. English Heritage, together with its sister heritage agencies in the other countries of the UK, is currently funding a major study on the extent of illegal metal detecting, on a proposal developed by PAS. This study is being undertaken by Oxford Archaeology and it is hoped that the report will be published in 2008. Ultimately the answer must be to raise public awareness on this issue and to educate those who buy and sell such finds on good practice.

PORTABLE ANTIQUITIES SCHEME

The establishment of the Portable Antiquities Scheme

In 1995 the Government recognised that, although the 1996 *Treasure Act* would remove the major anomalies of the old law, the great majority of archaeological finds would remain outside its scope. The Government therefore developed the concept of a voluntary scheme to record all archaeological objects to complement the 1996 *Treasure Act*, with a network of archaeologists around the country to record them. This resulted in *Portable Antiquities: A discussion document* (DNH 1996). This paper made a distinction between the public acquisition of finds, which the 1996 *Treasure Act* addressed, and the recording of finds, which it attempted to tackle. It noted that only a small percentage of objects found by the public are recorded by museums and continued that the failure to record finds made by the public 'represents a considerable loss to the nation's heritage. Once an object has left the ground and lost its provenance, a large part of its archaeological value is lost. The result is a loss of information about the past which is irreplaceable.'

The document set out proposals for a voluntary scheme for the reporting of finds that fall outside the scope of the 1996 *Treasure Act* and sought views. All those who responded agreed that the recording of all archaeological finds was important and that there was a need to improve the current arrangements, and they stressed that this could not be done without additional resources. For the first time there was a consensus among both archaeologists and detector users that a voluntary scheme offered the best way forward (DNH 1997, 40–1).

The Government agreed to fund six pilot schemes through what is now the Museums, Libraries and Archives Council and the first six posts were established in 1997 in Kent, Norfolk, North Lincolnshire, the North West, Yorkshire and the West Midlands. A further six posts started in 1999 with funding from the Heritage Lottery Fund, in Dorset and Somerset, Hampshire, Northamptonshire, Suffolk and Wales (Bland 2005, 272–3). In 2003, thanks to further funding from the HLF, it was possible to extend the Scheme across the whole of England and Wales and there is now a network of 36 Finds Liaison Officers, six Finds Advisers, and five other support posts.

Aims of the Portable Antiquities Scheme

The principal aim of the Scheme is to arrest the large level of archaeological information lost every year by actively recording this material on a systematic basis for public benefit. Our philosophy is that we do not seek to encourage metal detecting but we recognise that it exists and is legal, provided the detector user has the landowner's permission and avoids scheduled sites. We believe it is better to engage with detector users, to encourage them to behave responsibly and report their finds, than to ignore them, as was often the attitude in the past. It is a difficult path to tread and it is easy for PAS to be accused of legitimising the activity, but I do believe very strongly that it is much better to engage actively with these people and to encourage good practice rather than to brush them aside. They will go on detecting regardless and we will all be the losers if we fail to record their finds.

Code of Practice

A long-held aim of the Scheme was to secure agreement on a metal detecting code of practice that would be endorsed by all the key bodies. This was realised in May 2006, when the Code of Practice on Responsible Metal Detecting was published (see Appendix, below). The thinking behind the Code is that education and self-regulation offer the best prospect of progress. The Code aims to minimise damage to the historic environment and ensure that finds are reported. Although it may not go as far as some archaeologists would like, it does go a great deal further than any of the existing metal detecting codes. The Code will also stand as a statement of good practice that can be used by archaeological and government bodies in developing policies that affect metal detecting.

One challenge that remains is to ensure that the good practice encapsulated in the Code is also observed by those who organise and attend large metal detecting rallies. Several of these events are held each year and they can be attended by several hundred metal detector users from all over Britain and from abroad: if the rally is held on a site that is rich in finds, it is extremely difficult to ensure that an adequate record is made of all the objects discovered and the limited resources of the PAS are often stretched to the limit. In the long run, PAS believes that those who profit from such events – the rally organisers – should be prepared to put the resources into ensuring that all finds are properly recorded.

Results of the Portable Antiquities Scheme

A key aim of the project is dissemination of the data and this is done principally through the PAS website, www.finds.org.uk, which hosts the database and much other material and also through a series of Annual Reports (DCMS 1999; 2000b; 2001c; 2002c; Resource 2003; MLA 2004; 2005a; BM 2006), and also through newsletters and guidance, such as advice notes on conservation (MLA 2005b).

As at January 2008 the PAS database contains some 210,000 records describing

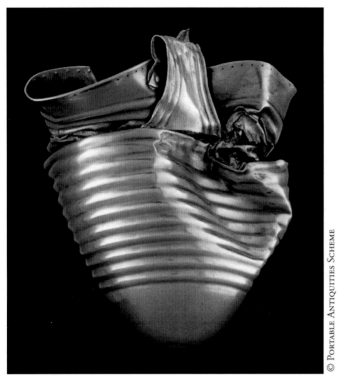

PLATE 1:
Bronze Age gold cup from Ringlemere, Kent

PLATE 2A (TOP) AND 2B (BOTTOM):
Seal matrix of Baldehild
from Postwick, Norfolk

PLATE 3:
Hoard of late Roman gold and silver coins, jewellery and scrap from Patching, West Sussex

PLATE 4:
The Staffordshire Moorlands bowl. PAS database WMID–3FE965

PLATE 5:
Julian Watters, Finds Liaison Officer, taking part in a controlled metal detecting survey of a site
at Braughing, Hertfordshire.'

Plate 6A and Plate 6B:
Two 18th or 19th century manillas found on the Isles of Scilly.
PAS database CORN–327A62 and CORN–31B3A7

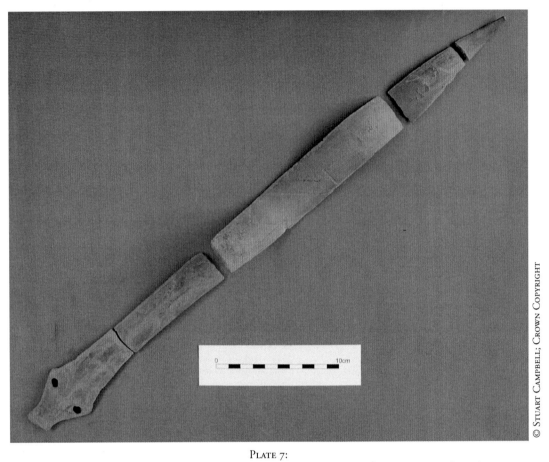

PLATE 7:
Late Bronze Age sword (TT.56/06) of the late second millennium BC from Kinnesswood, Perth and Kinross. One of the blade fragments was recovered when a curator and a member of the Treasure trove Unit staff returned with the detector user to re-examine his findspot of the previous fragments. This sword has been allocated to the collection of Perth Museum and Art Gallery.

317,000 objects with 160,000 images: in 2007, 77,540 archaeological objects were recorded, a 33 per cent increase on the previous year. Figure 6.4 shows the numbers of objects recorded onto the database since it was developed in 1998. Sixty-five users can enter data directly and a hundred users have research access to the database.

In 2007, 6126 finders offered finds for recording: 3910 detector users and 2226 others. Given that it is estimated that there are no more than 10,000 detector users in England and Wales (a figure of 8500 has been suggested) and a significant proportion of them – maybe a quarter – do not find any archaeological objects at all, we are probably being shown finds by over half of all active detector users (Bland 2006a; 2006b; see also Barford 2006a; 2006b).

Findspots

Another key measure of data quality concerns the precision with which findspots are recorded on the database. For the Historic Environment Record (HER) a findspot needs to be recorded to at least a six-figure grid reference (a 100-metre square) if it is to be of use and it has been a key performance measure for the Scheme to record as many findspots as possible to at least this level of detail.

It is not always easy, for various reasons, to persuade those who make their finds available for recording to give precise information about the findspot. It may be that the find was made some time ago and the finder did not keep a record of where it was found, or it may be that finders are unwilling to pass this information on because they are concerned about the use to which such information may be put – either that it may be published and that would encourage other detector users to try to detect on 'their sites', or that archaeologists might approach the landowner and recommend that he or she stops allowing metal detecting on that site.

Fig 6.4: Finds recorded on PAS database, 1998–2007

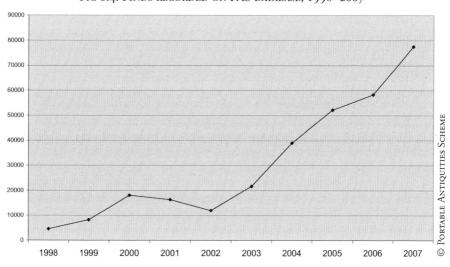

The PAS therefore does not publish findspots of any finds to more than a four-figure grid reference (one square kilometre) on its website and there is provision for findspots to be published even less precisely if they are Treasure finds or if the finder believes that there may be a conservation threat to the site if the findspot is published to four figures.

Overall, the key target of the percentage of findspots recorded to at least a six-figure NGR has improved year on year since 1997–99, when only 56 per cent of findspots were recorded to at least a six-figure grid reference, to 2007, when the figure was 90 per cent.

In 2005 an agreement governing transfer of data from PAS to HERs was concluded and, so far, 52 HERs have signed that agreement, so that the data gathered by the Scheme is now actively contributing to the management of the historic environment. The Arts and Humanities Research Council is funding a PhD studentship which will carry out a detailed study of how PAS data for the Roman period contributes to our knowledge of the historic environment.

Types of objects recorded by PAS and their distribution

The following Figures (6.5–6.11) show the type of information that has been collected by the PAS. Figure 6.5 shows the types of objects that are recorded and demonstrates that metal objects account for about 33 per cent, coins for 36 per cent, lithics for 10 per cent and pottery for 19 per cent. Figure 6.6 illustrates the chronological breakdown of objects recorded, and clearly shows that Roman and medieval finds predominate. Figure 6.7 shows an analysis of the method of discovery of finds recorded by PAS: the majority (68 per cent) are found by detector users (a significant number by detector users using their eyes only); 25 per cent are found by amateur fieldwalkers; and 7 per cent are chance finds. It is also possible to analyse the type of land from which finds are being reported. Cultivated land accounts for 90 per cent of all finds. This is significant because

FIG 6.5: TYPES OF OBJECT ON THE PAS DATABASE

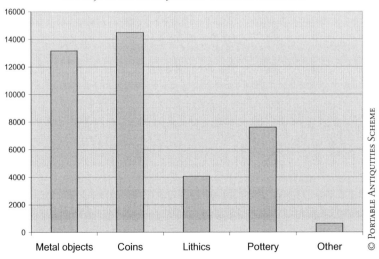

it demonstrates objectively that the great bulk of archaeological objects found by detector users come from cultivated land where, in most cases, the immediate context has already been destroyed by ploughing and where the objects are, in most cases, lying in the topsoil where they are vulnerable to damage by further ploughing. Figure 6.8 looks at the regional breakdown of objects recorded and shows the very great variations. The most productive areas are the East (25 per cent of all finds) and South East (22.7 per cent), while the least productive ones are London (2.5 per cent), Wales (1.6 per cent) and the North, especially the North East (1.4 per cent) and North West (2.6 per cent). Figure 6.9 shows

FIG 6.6: CHRONOLOGICAL BREAKDOWN OF OBJECTS RECORDED ON THE PAS DATABASE

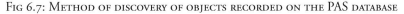

FIG 6.7: METHOD OF DISCOVERY OF OBJECTS RECORDED ON THE PAS DATABASE

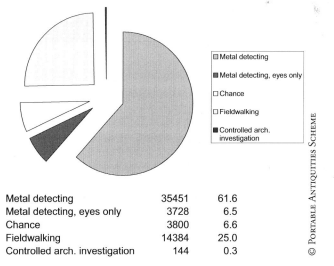

Metal detecting	35451	61.6
Metal detecting, eyes only	3728	6.5
Chance	3800	6.6
Fieldwalking	14384	25.0
Controlled arch. investigation	144	0.3

© PORTABLE ANTIQUITIES SCHEME

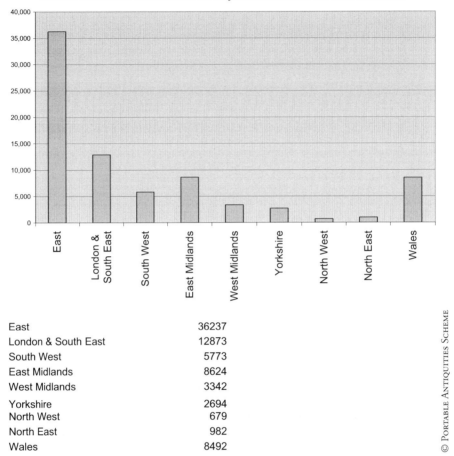

FIG 6.8: REGIONAL BREAKDOWN OF OBJECTS RECORDED ON PAS DATABASE

East	36237
London & South East	12873
South West	5773
East Midlands	8624
West Midlands	3342
Yorkshire	2694
North West	679
North East	982
Wales	8492

the distribution of these findspots across the country. The map shows that the database is undoubtedly a very powerful research tool which is only just starting to be exploited. Its main strength lies in the fact that the data is now truly national, so the database allows us to start looking at the regionality of the distribution of types of artefact in a way that was not possible before. Finally, the PAS database allows us to look more closely at the distribution of finds within particular areas. One example (Fig 6.10) is Greater London, where there has been a part-time Finds Liaison Officer since 2003. The findspots show two concentrations: along the Thames, reflecting the activities of the Thames Mudlarks, and along the south-east border of Greater London, reflecting the existence of arable land there. A second example (Fig 6.11) is the Isle of Wight, which has had a part-time Finds Liaison Officer since 2003, and which has shown itself to be extremely rich in finds. However, here, too, the finds are concentrated in a number of hotspots and much of the island is blank. This is a fascinating pattern which would repay closer study.

Fig 6.9: All findspots recorded on the PAS database

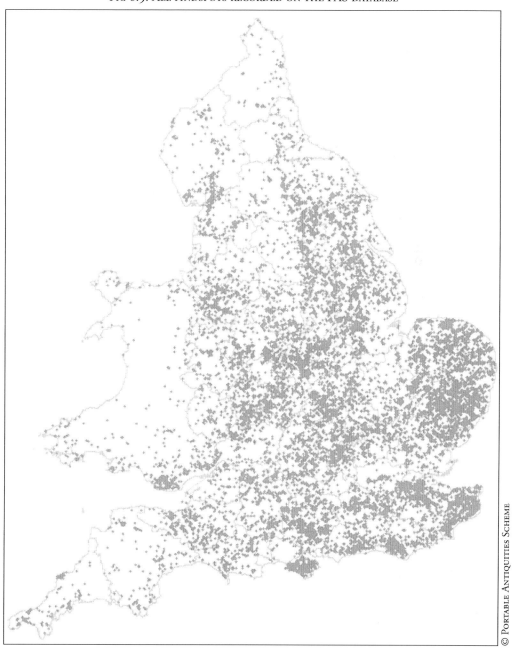

Fig 6.10: Findspots from Greater London on the PAS database

© Portable Antiquities Scheme

Some case studies

Perhaps the most important individual object recorded by the Portable Antiquities Scheme is a small patera known as the Staffordshire Moorlands bowl (PAS database reference WMID-3FE965) (Plate 4). It was found by metal detector users Kevin Blackburn and Julian Lee and reported in 2004. It was studied by Ralph Jackson of the British Museum and Roger Tomlin of Oxford University. Dated to the 2nd century AD, the vessel's decorative design consists of 'Celtic-style' motifs inlaid with coloured enamel. Only two other similar bowls are known to inscribe the names of forts on Hadrian's Wall: the 'Rudge Cup', discovered in Wiltshire in 1725, and the 'Amiens patera', found in Amiens in 1949. The decoration, however, is quite different, as the Rudge and Amiens examples both carry a stylised representation of the wall itself, with crenallated stone turrets. The most important feature of the patera is the inscription, which reads MAIS COGGABATA VXELODVNVM CAMMOGLANNA RIGORE VALI AELI DRACONIS. The first four words refer to forts at the western end of Hadrian's Wall: Bowness, Drumburgh, Stanwix and Castlesteads. The other bowls bear some of the same fort names, but the cup from Staffordshire is the first to include COGGABATA. The rest of the inscription is more enigmatic. Roger Tomlin has interpreted RIGORE VALI as 'along the line of

FIG 6.11: FINDSPOTS FROM ISLE OF WIGHT ON THE PAS DATABASE

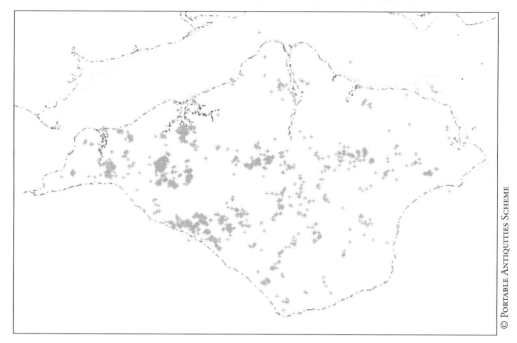

© PORTABLE ANTIQUITIES SCHEME

the Wall'. The last two words, AELI DRACONIS, can be interpreted in two different ways. They could be the names of the owner for whom the bowl was made, Aelius Draco, but another, fascinating, interpretation is that Aeli should be read with Vali and taken as a reference to Hadrian's Wall – Hadrian's full name was Titus Aelius Hadrianus. If that is correct then this would be the earliest contemporary documentary evidence for associating the Wall with Hadrian. The county archaeologist assessed the findspot of the bowl and concluded that it was probably an isolated find and not part of a larger Roman site.

In July 2005 a metal detecting survey took place on the site of a Roman town at Braughing in Hertfordshire (Plate 5). Metal detecting on a Scheduled Ancient Monument is allowed only with the consent of English Heritage; however, the County Archaeological Officer for Hertfordshire was so concerned with reports of illegal detecting on the site that he obtained permission from English Heritage for an organised survey in order to recover some information from the site. The work was undertaken by the Saffron Walden Metal Detecting Club, and the Finds Liaison Officer, Julian Watters, and colleagues mapped findspots using Global Positioning System machines. Finds were recorded from over 180 separate locations and, while much of the material consisted of undatable building materials such as brick and tile, there were also several incomplete Roman brooches, forty Roman coins and a few fragments of Roman puddingstone quern. The full results of the survey are to be published in a forthcoming report.

Two of the more unusual finds recorded by PAS were two copper alloy manillas from the Isles of Scilly (Plates 6A and 6B). Manillas are arm bands made in Birmingham in the 18th and 19th centuries as currency items for trade in West Africa, originally for the slave trade. The first one was found about three feet down by an islander while laying drains on St Agnes in December 2003 and was taken by him to the local museum who, in turn, sought the advice of Anna Tyacke, Finds Liaison Officer in Cornwall. Eighteen months later Anna was holding a Finds Day in Cornwall and a second manilla was brought in which turned out to have been found in 1945, very close to the first one. Both objects are very similar to an example in the Royal Cornwall Museum, also from St Agnes, which is believed to have come from the shipwreck of the *Duoro*, which was *en route* to Africa with a cargo of manillas on board when it was lost with all hands off Crebawethan, Western Rocks, Isles of Scilly, on 27 January 1843.

CONCLUSIONS

One of the main difficulties that the Scheme faces is the problem brought on by its success. Many Finds Liaison Officers have more finds than they are easily able to record and they also face many other pressures on their time to carry out outreach events, give talks, organise opportunities for finders to be involved in archaeology and so on. The funding agreed by the DCMS for 2006–8 allows for continued funding of all the current 46 posts in the Scheme, but not for any expansion, while future funding is subject to the Government's Comprehensive Spending Review.

The impact of the PAS can be judged on more than one level. It can be judged according to its principal aim, namely that of recording archaeological finds made by the public for public benefit. When they were first established, the Portable Antiquities pilot schemes were regarded as a test-bed to judge the merits of a voluntary approach to the recording of those archaeological finds that fall outside the scope of the 1996 *Treasure Act*. Although there have been three independent reviews of the Scheme, in 2000 (Chitty 2001), 2004 (Chitty and Edwards 2004) and 2006 (Edwards 2006), all of which have been positive, there has not been a fundamental evaluation to judge the success of the voluntary approach embedded in the Scheme. Many European countries have legislation requiring the reporting of all archaeological finds and vesting their ownership in the state (Bland 1998), as indeed do Scotland and Northern Ireland, so England and Wales would seem to be out of step with the rest of Europe. To what extent, therefore, can the twin-track approach of the 1996 *Treasure Act* and PAS be judged to be successful on their own terms?

The number of objects reported as Treasure and recorded by the PAS from England and Wales can be compared with the numbers of finds being reported as Treasure Trove in Scotland (Normand 2003). All ownerless objects are deemed to be Treasure Trove in Scotland, so in scope of finds that are reported it matches the PAS; the 1996 *Treasure Act* of course is much narrower.

Clearly such a comparison can only offer a very impressionistic picture. Scotland is smaller in land area than England and Wales and much more thinly populated. The

Table i. Finds reported as Treasure Trove in Scotland compared
with Treasure and PAS finds from England and Wales

	Scotland	Treasure cases: England and Wales	PAS finds: England and Wales
1995	78	20	-
1996	197	24	-
1997	265	79	-
1998	278	201	4589
1999	324	236	8205
2000	248	233	18106
2001	284	214	16368
2002	330	306	11995
2003	343	413	21665
2004	308	520	39023
2005	299	595	52223
2006	236	673	58307
2007	225	749	77540

amount of arable land – which as we have seen, accounts for 90 per cent of all findspots recorded by PAS – is very much less (only 12.5 per cent of Scotland is classed as arable land). No doubt there are many fewer metal detector users in Scotland than in England and Wales (for example, 8 metal detecting clubs are known in Scotland, as against 173 in England and Wales). However, even after taking all these factors into account the Scottish data would hardly seem to lend support to the view that a legal duty to report all finds should be introduced into England and Wales, and the numbers of finds reported as Treasure Trove in Scotland is actually static, if not declining. I have little doubt that if such a comparison were to be repeated with other European countries (and in most countries the relevant information is very difficult to find), a similar pattern would emerge.

The definition of Treasure in the 1996 *Treasure Act* certainly does not include all objects of archaeological importance, as it is still rooted in the Treasure Trove concept that gold and silver should belong to the King. There are obvious attractions in the Scottish definition of Treasure Trove, whereby only those objects deemed to be of archaeological importance are claimed by the state. However, such a definition also requires the mandatory reporting of all finds and that is where the system does not seem to work so well. If there were a mandatory requirement to report all finds in England and Wales, finders would have to be given some kind of documentation to prove that they had reported a find and this would be a very bureaucratic and expensive system to operate (see Barford 2006a; 2006b; Bland 2006a; 2006b). The evidence from Scotland suggests that it is unlikely that the requirement to report finds on its own would lead to an increased rate of reporting: that is surely most likely to come from changing the climate of opinion so that there is a common understanding of the need to report finds, the long-term aim of PAS. The 595 Treasure cases and 80,000 other finds reported to the PAS in 2005–6 clearly represent only a proportion of all the objects being found, but if we want to increase that number this is most likely to come through education (Bland 2006a; 2006b).

Perhaps the real significance of the Scheme is that it is a unique initiative in the way that it adds to our collective knowledge of the past through a project that is founded on public involvement and participation, rather than through a research project conceived and executed by professionals. It would probably be true to say that there is no parallel to this initiative in the rest of Europe and there is increasing interest in it from other countries. The PAS can measure in a demonstrable way that it is helping to foster growing public interest in the past. It has established a mechanism to harness that interest through the recording of finds made by the public and the publishing of the results for all to see.

Appendix

Code of Practice for Responsible Metal Detecting in England and Wales
Endorsed by:
    Council for British Archaeology
    Country Land & Business Association
    English Heritage
    Federation of Independent Detectorists
    Museums, Libraries and Archives Council
    National Council for Metal Detecting
    National Farmers Union
    National Museum Wales
    Portable Antiquities Scheme
    Royal Commission for the Ancient and Historical Monuments of Wales
    Society of Museum Archaeologists
    The British Museum

Being responsible means:

Before you go metal detecting

1. Not trespassing; before you start detecting obtain permission to search from the landowner/occupier, regardless of the status, or perceived status, of the land. Remember that all land has an owner. To avoid subsequent disputes it is always advisable to get permission and agreement in writing first regarding the ownership of any finds subsequently discovered (see www.cla.org.uk/www.nfuonline.com).

2. Adhering to the laws concerning protected sites (eg those defined as Scheduled Monuments or Sites of Special Scientific Interest: you can obtain details of these from the landowner/occupier, Finds Liaison Officer, Historic Environment Record or at www.magic.gov.uk). Take extra care when detecting near protected sites: for example, it is not always clear where the boundaries lie on the ground.

3. You are strongly recommended to join a metal detecting club or association that encourages cooperation and responsive exchanges with other responsible heritage groups. Details of metal detecting organisations can be found at www.ncmd.co.uk or www.fid. newbury.net.

4. Familiarising yourself with and following current conservation advice on the handling, care and storage of archaeological objects (see www.finds.org.uk).

While you are metal detecting

5. Wherever possible working on ground that has already been disturbed (such as ploughed land or that which has formerly been ploughed), and only within the depth of ploughing.

If detecting takes place on undisturbed pasture, be careful to ensure that no damage is done to the archaeological value of the land, including earthworks.

6. Minimising any ground disturbance through the use of suitable tools and by reinstating any excavated material as neatly as possible. Endeavour not to damage stratified archaeological deposits.

7. Recording findspots as accurately as possible for all finds (ie to at least a one hundred metre square, using an Ordnance Survey map or hand-held Global Positioning Systems (GPS) device) whilst in the field. Bag finds individually and record the National Grid Reference (NGR) on the bag. Findspot information should not be passed on to other parties without the agreement of the landowner/occupier (see also clause 9).

8. Respecting the Country Code (leave gates and property as you find them and do not damage crops, frighten animals, or disturb ground nesting birds, and dispose properly of litter: see www.countrysideaccess.gov.uk).

After you have been metal detecting

9. Reporting any finds to the relevant landowner/occupier; and (with the agreement of the landowner/occupier) to the Portable Antiquities Scheme, so the information can pass into the local Historic Environment Record. Both the Country Land and Business Association (www.cla.org.uk) and the National Farmers Union (www.nfuonline.com) support the reporting of finds. Details of your local Finds Liaison Officer can be found at www.finds.org.uk, e-mail info@finds.org.uk or phone 020 7323 8611.

10. Abiding by the provisions of the *Treasure Act* and *Treasure Act* Code of Practice (www.finds.org.uk), wreck law (www.mcga.gov.uk) and export licensing (www.mla.gov.uk). If you need advice your local Finds Liaison Officer will be able to help you.

11. Seeking expert help if you discover something large below the plough soil, or a concentration of finds or unusual material, or wreck remains, and ensuring that the landowner/occupier's permission is obtained to do so. Your local Finds Liaison Officer may be able to help or will be able to advise of an appropriate person. Reporting the find does not change your rights of discovery, but will result in far more archaeological evidence being discovered.

12. Calling the Police, and notifying the landowner/occupier, if you find any traces of human remains.

13. Calling the Police or HM Coastguard, and notifying the landowner/occupier, if you find anything that may be a live explosive: do not use a metal detector or mobile phone nearby as this might trigger an explosion. Do not attempt to move or interfere with any such explosives.

BIBLIOGRAPHY

Abdy, R, 2006 After Patching: imported and recycled coinage in fifth- and sixth-century Britain, in *Coinage and History in the North Sea World, c.500–1250: essays in honour of Marion Archibald*, B Cook and G Williams (eds), Leiden, 75–98

Barford, P, 2006a Artefact hunting and the archaeological resource, *Rescue News* 98, 1–2

— 2006b Artefact hunting: the sequel, *Rescue News* 100, 4

Bland, R, 1996 Treasure trove and the case for reform, *Art, Antiquity and Law* 11, 11–26

— 1998 The Treasure Act and the proposal for the voluntary recording of all archaeological finds, Conference Proceedings, St Albans 1996, *Museums in the Landscape: bridging the gap*, Society of Museum Archaeologists, *The Museum Archaeologist* 23, 3–19

— 2005 Rescuing our neglected heritage: the evolution of the Government's policy on portable antiquities and Treasure, *Cultural Trends* 14 (4), No 56, 257–96

— 2006a Metal detecting and the archaeological resource: a response from the Portable Antiquities Scheme, *Rescue News* 99, 4–5

— 2006b Last words, *Rescue News* 100, 5

BM, 2006 *Portable Antiquities Scheme, Annual Report 2005/6*, The British Museum, London, available online at www.finds.org.uk (6 February 2008)

Chitty, G, 2001 *Review of Portable Antiquities Pilot Scheme*, Hawkshead Archaeology and Conservation, Lancaster

Chitty, G and Edwards, R, 2004 *Review of Portable Antiquities Scheme, 2004*, Hawkshead Archaeology and Conservation, Lancaster, available online at www.finds.org.uk (6 February 2008)

DCMS (Department for Culture, Media and Sport), 1999 *Portable Antiquities, Annual Report 1997–98*, Department for Culture, Media and Sport, London

— 2000a *Report on the Operation of the Treasure Act 24 September 1997–23 September 1998*, Department for Culture, Media and Sport, London, available online at www.culture.gov.uk (6 February 2008)

— 2000b *Portable Antiquities, Annual Report 1998–99*, Department for Culture, Media and Sport, London, available online at www.finds.org.uk (6 February 2008)

— 2001a *Report on the Operation of The Treasure Act 1996: Review and Recommendations*, Department for Culture, Media and Sport, London

— 2001b *Report on the Operation of the Treasure Act 24 September 1998–31 December 1999*, Department for Culture, Media and Sport, London, available online at www.culture.gov.uk (6 February 2008)

— 2001c *Portable Antiquities, Annual Report 1999–2000*, Department for Culture, Media and Sport, London, available online at www.finds.org.uk (6 February 2008)

— 2002a *The Treasure Act 1996, Code of Practice (Revised) England and Wales*, Department for Culture, Media and Sport, London, available online at www.culture.gov.uk (6 February 2008)

— 2002b *Report on the Operation of the Treasure Act 1 January–31 December 2000*, Department for Culture, Media and Sport, London

— 2002c *Portable Antiquities, Annual Report 2000–2001*, Department for Culture, Media and Sport, London, available online at www.finds.org.uk (6 February 2008)

— 2003 *Report on the Operation of the Treasure Act 1 January–31 December 2001*, Department for Culture, Media and Sport, London, available online at www.culture.gov.uk (6 February 2008)

— 2004a Report on the Operation of the Treasure Act 1 January–31 December 2002, Department for Culture, Media and Sport, London, available online at *www.finds.org.uk* (6 February 2008)

— 2004b *Dealing in Tainted Cultural Objects – Guidance on the Dealing in Cultural Objects (Offences) Act 2003*, Department for Culture, Media and Sport, London, available online at www.culture.gov.uk (6 February 2008)

— 2004c *The 1970 UNESCO Convention – Guidance for Dealers and Auctioneers in Cultural Property*, Department for Culture, Media and Sport, London, available online at www.culture.gov.uk (6 February 2008)

DNH, 1996 *Portable Antiquities: A discussion document*, Department of National Heritage, London

— 1997 *The Treasure Act 1996, Code of Practice (England and Wales)*, Department of National Heritage, London

— 1998 *Treasure Trove Reviewing Committee, Annual Report 1996–97*, Department of National Heritage, London

Dobinson, C and Denison, S, 1995 *Metal Detecting and Archaeology in England*, English Heritage/Council for British Archaeology, York, available online at www.britarch.ac.uk (6 February 2008)

Edwards, R, 2006 *Portable Antiquities Scheme User Survey 2006*, Arboretum, available online at http://www.finds.org.uk/news/ac.php

Gaimster, D, Hayward, M, Mitchell, D, and Parker, K, 2002 Tudor silver-gilt dress-hooks: a new class of Treasure find in England, *Antiquaries Journal* 82, 157–96

Hill, G F, 1936 *Treasure Trove in Law and Practice*, Clarendon Press, Oxford

Hobbs, R, 2003 *Treasure: finding our past*, British Museum Press, London

Jackson, R, and Burleigh, G, 2005 From Senua to Senuna, *British Museum Magazine* 52, 32–5

MLA, 2004 *Portable Antiquities Scheme, Annual Report 2003/04*, Museums, Libraries and Archives Council, London, available online at www.finds.org.uk (6 February 2008)

— 2005a *Portable Antiquities Scheme, Annual Report 2004/05*, Museums, Libraries and Archives Council, London, available online at www.finds.org.uk (6 February 2008)

— 2005b *Conservation Advice Notes*, Museums, Libraries and Archives Council and York Archaeological Trust, available online at www.finds.org.uk (6 February 2008)

Needham, S, Parfitt, K, and Varndell, G, 2006 *The Ringlemere Cup. Precious cups and the beginnings of the Channel Bronze Age*, British Museum Research Publication 163, London

Normand, A C, 2003 *Review of Treasure Trove Arrangements in Scotland*, Scottish Executive, Edinburgh, available online at www.scotland.gov.uk (6 February 2008)

O'Connell, M G, and Bird, J, with Cheesman, C, 1994 The Roman temple at Wanborough, excavation 1985–86, *Surrey Archaeological Collections* 82, 1–168

Palmer, N E, 1993 Treasure Trove and title to discovered antiquities, *International Journal of Cultural Property* 2 (2), 275–318

Resource, 2003 *Portable Antiquities Scheme, Annual Report 2001/2–2002/3*, Resource, London, available online at www.finds.org.uk (6 February 2008)

Saville, A, 2000 Portable antiquities and excavated finds in Scotland, in *Institute of Field Archaeologists Yearbook and Directory of Members 2000*, 31–2

NOTES

1. But not in Scotland, which has a completely separate legal framework governing finds: there is, in effect, a legal requirement to report all finds (Saville 2000; Norman 2003).

7

Treasure Trove and Metal Detecting in Scotland

ALAN SAVILLE

INTRODUCTION

The Scottish Treasure Trove system is aligned almost entirely differently from legislation and practice concerning archaeological finds in other parts of the UK. Its differences and legal underpinnings have been explained on numerous previous occasions (eg Carey Miller 2002; Saville 2002; 2006), and it is not proposed to rehearse them in detail here. Suffice it to say for present purposes that Scottish Treasure Trove embraces portable antiquities of any age and type (and of any raw material, not just metal) and that landowners do not possess rights of ownership over antiquities from their land. Recent administrative changes have included the renaming and expansion of the former 'Treasure Trove Advisory Panel' as the 'Scottish Archaeological Finds Allocation Panel', the rebadging of the panel's secretariat as the 'Treasure Trove Unit', and the publication of an annual report (Crown Office 2007a; 2007b).

Under the current implementation of the Scots common law of Treasure Trove/*bona vacantia*, all portable antiquities of archaeological, historical or cultural significance are subject to claim by the Crown and must be reported. This puts an obligation on finders, naturally including all metal detector users, to report any finds which they have reason to believe are, or suspect might be considered as, of significance.[1] Finds which have not been reported have no legal status, except as 'unreported Treasure Trove/*bona vacantia*', and cannot be owned or disposed of by their finders. Unreported finds are, in the terminology of the *Dealing in Cultural Objects (Offences) Act* 2003, 'tainted', even though this actual statute does not itself yet apply within Scotland (DCMS 2005, 15).

Once reported, finds are assessed against the criterion of their potential to contribute to the cultural record of Scotland. If this potential is present the find is claimed, if not it is unclaimed and returned to the finder. The statistics for claiming/unclaiming show a fluctuating yearly picture (Fig 7.1), but the recent trend has clearly been for more cases to be unclaimed than claimed.[2] It should be noted, however, that this does not mean that unclaimed finds are necessarily without any archaeological, historical or cultural merit. The latter is clearly seen in the case of individual coin finds, which are rarely claimed but

FIG 7.1: BAR CHART SHOWING THE NUMBER OF CASES OF CLAIMED TREASURE TROVE AND
UNCLAIMED PORTABLE ANTIQUITIES IN SCOTLAND FROM 1995 TO 2006.
(SOURCE: TREASURE TROVE UNIT DATA)

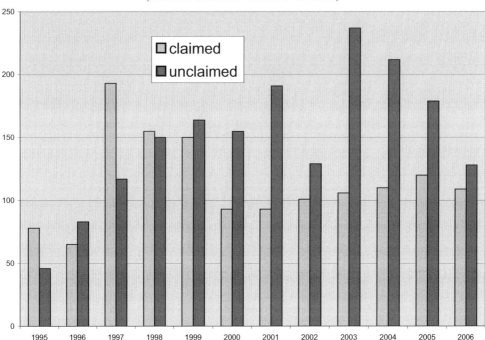

which are recorded in detail for their historical value before being returned (Bateson and
Holmes 2003, 246; Holmes 2004, 241–2).

Returned finds are accompanied by a certification sheet to confirm that they have
been reported and not claimed, which allows the finder to then treat a find as personal
property. Finders may in this situation decide to keep their find or to dispose of it in a
responsible fashion by exchange, sale, donation or otherwise (it would be irresponsible
casually to discard such a find). The certification sheet is important, since without it such
disposal would be illegal – no museum would be able to accept a found item as a donation
without this record of reporting,[3] nor would an auction house (including *eBay*) be able to
offer a non-certificated item for sale.

If an item is claimed as Treasure Trove on behalf of the Crown then the system has
a specific procedure (Fig 7.2), involving the independent Scottish Archaeological Finds
Allocation Panel, which operates to establish the museum to which a find should be
allocated, and the amount, if applicable, of any *ex gratia* payment which should go to a
finder as a 'reward' for a particular find (Crown Office 2007a; 2007b).

Following the recent review of Treasure Trove and the responses from the Scottish
Executive (Normand 2003; Scottish Executive 2004), there have been considerable

Fig 7.2: Flowchart summarising the process involved for any chance
or metal detected find under the Treasure Trove system.

Portable antiquity discovered
↓
If recovered, reported for Treasure Trove
(if left *in situ,* reported to local museum,
Council archaeologist, Historic Scotland,
or National Museums of Scotland)
↓
Find received and assessed at the TTU <——————> Find received and assessed at the TTU
↓   ↓
Claim   Unclaim
↓   ↓
TTU checks findspot details etc   Unclaimed certificate isssued
↓   by TTU and sent to finder
TTU advises QLTR of recommended claim   ↓
↓   **Portable antiquity returned to**
QLTR claims, allocates TT case number, and   **finder**
sends letter to finder
↓
TTU advertises case to Scottish museums
↓
TTU researches guideline valuation
↓
Application(s) for allocation sent by museum(s) to TTU
↓
SAFAP meets and considers ex gratia payment and allocation
↓
TTU advises museum(s) of SAFAP's recommendations
(in the event of multiple requests for a single case, there is a process
of consultation with the museums involved, which can lead to the case
being reconsidered at the Panel's next meeting)
↓
TTU advises QLTR of SAFAP's
    recommendations
↓
QLTR decides to accept SAFAP's
    recommendations
(if QLTR decides to reject a SAFAP recommendation
the case is returned to SAFAP for reconsideration at its next meeting)
↓
Recipient museum requested by QLTR to
 forward the ex gratia payment
↓
Recipient museum applies to NFA for grant aid then
    sends cheque to QLTR
↓
QLTR sends ex gratia reward payment and certificate to the finder
↓
Recipient museum collects the portable antiquity from the TTU and registers it as part
of its collection

Abbreviations
TTU: Treasure Trove Unit   QLTR: Queen's & Lord Treasurer's Remembrancer
SAFAP: Scottish Archaeological Finds Allocation Panel   NFA: National Fund for Acquisitions

changes in the operation of the Treasure Trove system and these are still in train, so that any detailed description of the operation of the system at the moment is likely to be slightly out of date by the time it appears in print. The latest overview of the system is that provided by the first *Annual Report on Treasure Trove* (Crown Office 2007a), but updated information is regularly provided on the TT website (www.treasuretrovescotland.co.uk), which has a copy of the current Annual Report in downloadable form. The situation will be clarified further once the authoritative Code of Practice, currently in final preparation, becomes available towards the end of 2008.

How do finders fulfil their obligation to report, and what happens next?

Finders who have any familiarity with the Treasure Trove system will normally have accessed the Treasure Trove website and downloaded the standard reporting form which requests basic information about the find location and the date and circumstances of finding, and which requires finders to sign off the form by declaring that they are indeed the finder. The find itself will normally need to be taken or sent to the Treasure Trove Unit in Edinburgh for assessment and, if claimed, for examination by the Scottish Archaeological Finds Allocation Panel.

Finders less familiar with the system are most likely to take their finds to their local museum and the system relies heavily on the cooperation of museum staff to facilitate the reporting process thereafter. Geographical and other constraints being what they are in Scotland mean there can occasionally be delays in the process of getting finds to Edinburgh for assessment, but finders have generally shown understanding of this difficulty when it occurs.

If a find is claimed the Treasure Trove Unit will normally send an identification report, a digital photograph and any other relevant available information to the finder. Finders will also be informed of the date of the meeting of the Scottish Archaeological Finds Allocation Panel at which their finds will be considered. After the meeting the recommendations of the panel as to museum allocation and level of *ex gratia* payment (if appropriate) will be passed to the Queen's and the Lord Treasurer's Remembrancer (QLTR) at the Crown Office and further correspondence with the finder comes from the QLTR Unit. This may include the issuing of a finder's certificate and the *ex gratia* payment. There can be further delays because the QLTR Unit requires payment of any sum involved from the museum to which a find has been allocated before it will pass that payment on to the finder, but normally the whole process from initial reporting to the finder receiving payment is completed within 12 months.

Museums will normally register the finds acquired in this way as having been purchased through the Treasure Trove system. Full documentation concerning all finds is retained by the Treasure Trove Unit and is available to museums, and claimed items are reported each year in *Discovery and Excavation in Scotland* (an annual publication by the Council for Scottish Archaeology). The Crown Office has recently consulted on whether the names of finders, the detailed grid references for findspots and the amounts of any *ex gratia* payments should be publicised (Crown Office 2007a, 43). The outcome so far is that the names of finders are now being published, but without actually indicating who found what in terms of the items claimed by the Crown (Crown Office 2007b, 31).

Metal detecting in Scotland

Anecdotal and other limited evidence would suggest that there are, *pro rata*, relatively far fewer active metal detector users in Scotland than in England (Dobinson and Denison 1995, 6). There are obvious reasons for why this might be the case, such as: the relative dearth of Roman sites north of the border and their primarily military rather than domestic nature; the acidic nature of many of Scotland's soils, which are therefore hostile to good preservation of metal artefacts; the limited extent of open arable land and the extensive afforestation and deep peat cover in many parts; and the distance of much of the landmass from centres of population. Some would also argue that the Treasure Trove system itself provides a discouragement, because all finds have to be reported.[4] In truth there is currently no facility for assessing the extent and productivity of metal detecting in Scotland other than from that which gets reported through the Treasure Trove system.

Taking as a sample 210 of the cases of Treasure Trove claimed in Scotland during 2005–6, the breakdown by method of discovery is as follows: metal detecting produced 101 cases (48 per cent); chance/casual finds produced 41 (20 per cent); and excavation produced 68 (32 per cent). These figures will, of course, be subject to fluctuation for various reasons: for example, the number of excavation assemblages has risen since the Scottish Archaeological Finds Allocation Panel took over the work of Historic Scotland's former Finds Disposal Panel (Crown Office 2007a, 5). However, the importance of metal detecting for providing Treasure Trove cases is clear.[5]

These 101 metal detected cases comprise approximately 915 individual items, plus a hoard of 314 coins. The finds were made by 63 individual detector users (61 male, 2 female). Some individuals were responsible for multiple cases: one for 10 separate cases; another for 8 cases; another for 6 cases; and another for 5 cases. Five individuals were responsible for 3 cases each, and six for 2 cases each.

Available information would suggest that these detector users are primarily individuals pursuing their hobby alone, within or adjacent to the areas of Scotland where they happen to live, though a few range more widely and may also detect in England. Even though it is known that a few of the people in this sample belong to detector users' clubs, it would appear that none of the above discoveries was made during club events, and only a few were made when two or more individuals were detecting together. The detector users involved are usually in regular contact with the Treasure Trove Unit and a two-way exchange of information tends to take place. The detector users are often well aware of the historical significance of their finds and sometimes undertake their own detailed research, and it should not be forgotten that detector users may often be extremely well-informed about the finds they are making (Saville 1999, 198).

Other finds get reported when serendipity intervenes and detector users not normally in contact with the system strike lucky with what are obviously important finds of precious metal or other distinctive objects easily recognisable from examples in museum displays or illustrated in books and magazines. Information about such discoveries tends to become known and sooner or later the finds are reported. To take a charitable view there may be instances when novice, foreign or occasional detector users are entirely ignorant of their obligations under Scottish Treasure Trove, but there can be few Scotland-based detector users who take up the hobby with any seriousness who could, hand on heart, admit to not being aware of the duty to report their finds.[6]

This makes it all the more surprising that there are some regions of Scotland from which metal detected finds are rarely, if ever, reported, yet in which it is extremely unlikely that no detector users are operating. The location by local authority area of all the cases in the above sample of 101 cases is shown in Table 1. There are interesting patterns here. The high number of cases from Highland is explained not by the huge area that this represents, but largely by the activity of one successful detector user on the east coast. Perth and Kinross probably features heavily because of a very active archaeological museum service in that council area, and there are other underlying special factors which could be suggested to explain the other higher numbers. It will, however, be apparent that the claimed cases do not correlate well with the main centres of population in Scotland and this snapshot does reflect a general tendency for low levels of reporting from the west, which perhaps, given that all official components of the Treasure Trove administration are Edinburgh-based, reflects the east–west divide prevalent in many other aspects of Scotland's culture.

More surprising still is that there are known metal detecting clubs in some parts of Scotland from which finds rarely get reported for Treasure Trove assessment, yet it is hard to imagine that the members of these clubs are entirely unsuccessful in their detecting forays. Generally speaking it is difficult to avoid the suspicion that throughout Scotland there is a considerable degree of under-reporting of metal detected discoveries. At the moment, however, there are no means whereby to monitor or document this.

At least two metal detecting rallies have been held in Scotland. The one attended by a member of the Treasure Trove Unit staff did not result in any items being found which were considered sufficiently significant to claim for the Crown.

The very recent establishment of a Scottish section of the National Council for Metal Detecting is already leading to improved dialogue with the club element of the detecting community, and the auguries are good for increased cooperation. Cooperation between clubs, individual detector users and field archaeologists is already increasingly taking place in Scotland. The classic instance of this is where detector users collaborate with excavation teams by searching spoil-heaps for any missed metal artefacts, especially small coins, or search zones within a development area where land is to be lost but which are not otherwise being investigated by the archaeologists. When detector users work collaboratively in this way they are taking part in organised fieldwork, and therefore all their finds will automatically be claimed as Treasure Trove along with the excavated part of the artefact assemblage.[7]

Another kind of cooperation which has been fruitful occurs after the initial reporting of finds. There have now been numerous occasions when museum archaeologists and

Table 1: Geographical distribution by local authority area of the most recent 101 cases of metal-detected finds claimed as Treasure Trove in Scotland. (Source: Treasure Trove Unit data)

Area	Number
Aberdeen City	-
Aberdeenshire	6
Angus	3
Argyll & Bute	4
Clackmannanshire	1
Dumfries & Galloway	7
Dundee City	1
East Ayrshire	-
East Dunbartonshire	-
East Lothian	7
East Renfrewshire	-
Edinburgh	1
Falkirk	3
Fife	13
Glasgow	-
Highland	18
Inverclyde	-
Midlothian	-
Moray	3
North Ayrshire	1
North Lanarkshire	1
Orkney	-
Perth & Kinross	14
Renfrewshire	1
Scottish Borders	10
Shetland	-
South Ayrshire	-
South Lanarkshire	1
Stirling	3
West Dunbartonshire	-
West Lothian	2
Western Isles	1
Total number	*101*

local authority archaeologists have returned to findspots with the original detector user finders to explore whether further artefacts, and in some cases other parts of the same fragmented artefact, remain in the ground, or whether the find has actually been part of an archaeological context (Figs 7.3 and 7.4). Specific instances of considerable success can be given here, such as the finding of the final missing central fragment of a late Bronze Age sword from a findspot in Perth and Kinross (Plate 7).

It is a feature of relationships in Scotland between metal detector users on the one hand and archaeologists, curators, and the various heritage administrators on the other

FIG 7.3: CURATOR AND DETECTOR USER IN DISCUSSION DURING AN INSPECTION
OF THE FINDSPOT OF PREVIOUSLY CLAIMED TREASURE TROVE ITEMS.

© STUART CAMPBELL; CROWN COPYRIGHT

FIG 7.4: CURATOR AND DETECTOR USERS UNDERTAKING EXPLORATORY
TEST-PITTING TO CHECK THE STRATIGRAPHY AT A LOCATION WHERE
ARTEFACTS HAVE BEEN DISCOVERED BY METAL DETECTION.

© STUART CAMPBELL; CROWN COPYRIGHT

that the same degrees of antagonisms as have bedevilled such relationships elsewhere in the UK seem never to have been so prevalent.[8] Although there would understandably be outrage if any nighthawking-type activities led to the despoliation of archaeological sites, this has not become a significant problem, perhaps because there are not the 'honey pot' types of sites in Scotland, such as Roman temples and villas, producing the sort of finds to attract the nighthawks. It is also perhaps because there does tend to be a greater respect for the nation's 'heritage', which would militate against any such gross vandalism by local detector users.

There have, of course, been incidents when conflicts between detector users and the authorities have arisen over detecting on Scheduled Ancient Monuments, which is banned under the Ancient Monuments and Archaeological Areas Act 1979.[9] The incidents of this type with which I have been involved have almost all occurred when detector users have genuinely been acting in ignorance of the fact that they were on scheduled land. These incidents have normally been resolved by warnings and undertakings, and by the finds being claimed for the Crown without any reward being paid.[10]

That relationships have not been so antagonistic is probably also influenced by the legal situation itself, whereby all parties know (or should know) from the outset that the finds made are liable to be claimed as Treasure Trove by the Crown.

Looking forward

The last 10 years or so have seen a steady improvement in the consistent and transparent application of the Treasure Trove system in Scotland, changing from a situation where just a few 'star' discoveries were dealt with on an *ad hoc* basis each year in the 1980s to the current norm of around 100 cases per year (Fig 7.1). Following on from the recent review (Normand 2003), there is now a clearly expressed government statement on Treasure Trove policy:

> The Treasure Trove system forms an important part of the Scottish Executive's approach to the preservation of the nation's cultural heritage. The Treasure Trove system will be used to safeguard Scotland's heritage of portable antiquities and archaeological objects by preserving significant claimed objects in the public domain. In accordance with the Executive's policy of increasing access to, and understanding of, our cultural heritage, claimed objects will be held by suitable institutions (usually the National Museums of Scotland or a local museum) for the benefit of the Scottish public. The presumption will be that display worthy objects will be placed on exhibition and, where appropriate, will be made available on loan to other museums. (Scottish Executive 2004, 8)

Increasingly there is also a recognition that all parties involved in the discovery and recording of portable antiquities are part of a common enterprise to foster knowledge of Scotland's past and to secure the preservation of all significant finds in the nation's museums.

My perception is that there is a measure of agreement from all sides that the way forward, in terms of increasing the level of reporting towards the 100 per cent level at which legally it should be, extracting the educational potential which finds of portable antiquities possess for informing the general public about past material culture, working more proactively with the metal detecting community and maximising the archaeological and museological benefits of the system, will only come from having a regional network for finds reporting. The Portable Antiquities Scheme network of Finds Liaison Officers in England and Wales provides an important analogue in this respect. Having a Liaison Officer on the ground locally to provide a contact point for reporting discoveries and to undertake outreach and education has been recognised as not only dramatically increasing the level of finds reporting (DCMS 2007, 5) but as having significant social benefit (PAS 2006, 2–19).

In Scotland much has been made recently of the concept of the 'cultural entitlement' which all citizens should expect to be delivered by central and local government (Scottish Executive 2006), and this has been given a specifically heritage gloss:

> Scottish Ministers have recognised that Scotland's people have cultural entitlements. One is that the people of Scotland are entitled to expect the historic environment to be protected, cared for and used sustainably so that it can be passed on to benefit future generations. (Historic Scotland 2007, 13)

The argument could be made that at present in Scotland the public in general, and metal detector users in particular, are significantly culturally underprivileged in comparison with their counterparts in England and Wales when it comes to locally available resources to assist them in identifying and reporting their finds.[11] It would undoubtedly be in the interests of all concerned if the present structure could be expanded to allow a regional Treasure Trove network to develop throughout Scotland, which would in turn allow the many advantages of having a robust national Treasure Trove system to be translated more generally into public benefit.

Acknowledgements

I am heavily indebted to my colleagues in the Treasure Trove Unit, Jenny Shiels and Stuart Campbell, for information and discussion, to Stuart Campbell for images, and to my curatorial colleague, Trevor Cowie, for perceptive comments, but the responsibility for this chapter rests entirely with me and does not necessarily reflect the views of any other officials or individuals connected in any way with the Treasure Trove system.

BIBLIOGRAPHY

Addyman, P, 2001 Antiquities without archaeology in the United Kingdom, in *Trade in Illicit Antiquities: the Destruction of the World's Archaeological Heritage*, N Brodie, J Doole and C Renfrew (eds), McDonald Institute Monograph, Cambridge, 141–4

Bateson, J D, and Holmes, N M McQ, 2003 Roman and medieval coins found in Scotland, 1996–2000, *Proceedings of the Society of Antiquaries of Scotland* 133, 245–76

Carey Miller, D L, 2002 Treasure Trove in Scots law, in *Summa Eloquentia: essays in honour of Margaret Hewett*, R van den Bergh (ed), University of South Africa Press, Pretoria, 75–89

Crown Office, 2007a *Treasure Trove in Scotland 04/06: Annual Report by the Queen's and the Lord Treasurer's Remembrancer*, Crown Office, Edinburgh

— 2007b *Treasure Trove in Scotland 06/07: Annual Report by the Queen's and the Lord Treasurer's Remembrancer*, Crown Office, Edinburgh

DCMS (Department for Culture, Media and Sport), 2005 *Combating Illicit Trade: due diligence guidelines for museums, libraries and archives on collecting and borrowing cultural material*, Department for Culture, Media and Sport, London

— 2007 *Treasure Annual Report 2004*, Department for Culture, Media and Sport, London

Dobinson, C, and Denison, S, 1995 *Metal Detecting and Archaeology in England*, English Heritage and the Council for British Archaeology, London and York

Historic Scotland, 2007 *Scotland's Historic Environment (Scottish Historic Environment Policy 1)*, Historic Scotland, Edinburgh

Holmes, N M McQ, 2004 The evidence of finds for the circulation and use of coins in medieval Scotland, *Proceedings of the Society of Antiquaries of Scotland* 134, 241–80

Kampmann, U, 2006 Who owns objects? A view from the coin trade, in *Who Owns Objects? The Ethics and Politics of Collecting Cultural Artefacts*, E Robson, L Treadwell and C Gosden (eds), Oxbow Books, Oxford, 61–76

Normand, A, 2003 *Review of Treasure Trove Arrangements in Scotland*, Scottish Executive, Edinburgh

PAS (Portable Antiquities Scheme), 2006 *Annual Report 2005/6*, Portable Antiquities Scheme, London

Renfrew, C, 2000 *Loot, Legitimacy and Ownership*, Duckworth, London

Robson, E, Treadwell, L, and Gosden, C (eds), 2006 *Who Owns Objects? The Ethics and Politics of Collecting Cultural Artefacts*, Oxbow Books, Oxford

Saville, A, 1999 Thinking *things* over: aspects of contemporary attitudes towards archaeology, museums and material culture, in *Making Early Histories in Museums*, N Merriman (ed), Leicester University Press, London, 190–209

— 2002 Treasure Trove in Scotland, *Antiquity* 76, 796–802

— 2006 Portable antiquities, in *Archaeological Resource Management in the UK: an Introduction*, 2nd edition, J Hunter and I Ralston (eds), Sutton Publishing, Thrupp, 69–84

Scottish Executive, 2004 *The Reform of Treasure Trove Arrangements in Scotland*, Scottish Executive, Edinburgh

— 2006 Draft Culture (Scotland) Bill: Guidance Document, Scottish Executive, Edinburgh

NOTES

1. There is by now sufficient case history about the types of artefact currently being claimed as Treasure Trove in Scotland for ignorance in this regard to be a poor defence for failure to report. Apart from the lists of claimed finds which have been published each year since 1996 in *Discovery and Excavation in Scotland*, and will henceforward be included in the annual Treasure Trove reports (Crown Office 2007a and 2007b), illustrated lists of recent claims are available on the website (www.treasuretrove.scotland.co.uk).

2. The number of objects involved in a 'case' will vary considerably. Chance finds normally comprise a single item, excavation assemblages often several hundred or even thousands of objects. Similarly, cases of metal detected finds can range from a single coin to a large hoard of coins, or from a single ring to hundreds of buckles, fitments, etc, from a medieval 'market' site. Over the past year or so it is calculated that, excluding excavated finds, approximately one-third of all actual objects reported are claimed, while the other two-thirds are unclaimed and are returned.

3. Since a cut-off date of the end of 1999, museums cannot legally acquire Scottish portable antiquities unless they have either been allocated through the Treasure Trove system or are certificated as unclaimed (or in certain rare cases when objects have been disclaimed by the Crown subsequent to having been claimed initially).

4. This raises the interesting issue of the degree to which metal detector users might be motivated by the desire to collect *per se* or to own antiquities. Much has been written about this, mainly in terms of non-British antiquities (Renfrew 2000; Robson *et al.* 2006) but there has been praise for the Portable Antiquities Scheme in England and Wales precisely because it does not deprive finders of their discoveries and for the *Treasure Act* because it does not extend to 'mass ware', thus allowing detector users freedom to collect and collectors and dealers freedom to buy and sell (Kampmann 2006, 64–7). On the other hand it has been suggested that the existence of the Portable Antiquities Scheme is itself a stimulus to the growth of metal detecting (Addyman 2001, 144), something which would be hard to gainsay when a culture minister calls detector users the 'unsung heroes of heritage' (*The Guardian*, 18 January 2007). The Scottish experience would suggest that detector users are motivated by the desire to discover more than to collect (with the possible exception of some coin enthusiasts), and that their interests in archaeology and history, and other factors such as pursuing an outdoor hobby and being interested in electronics, are of more significance. Nor should the feel-good factor of knowing that one's finds have made a contribution to the national archives of material culture and will be preserved for posterity in a museum be underestimated. For those with more financially inclined motivations the Treasure Trove system could actually be seen as an incentive, since, all things being equal, an *ex gratia* reward linked to 'full market value' will undoubtedly provide a better return for the finder than the black market ever would.

5. Only cases involving at least one metal object have been listed here as metal detected, though these will occasionally also include non-metal items from the same findspots, such as potsherds. However, it is known that at least two of the chance-find cases involving non-metal items were made by detector users, presumably while they were out detecting.

6. There is, admittedly, considerable confusion generated on this topic by the media, even within Scotland, which consistently carry reports about archaeological finds and treasure implying that the same regulations and practices apply in Scotland as in the rest of the UK. As often as this is pointed out, the mistake is repeated; seemingly an inevitable consequence of England's dominance within the UK.

7. In Scotland all finds recovered from archaeological excavation and other types of organised fieldwork must be declared through the Treasure Trove system and almost without exception are claimed by the Crown. No 'rewards' are payable for finds made in this way.

8. This might be painting a slightly over-rosy picture. As the current Historic Scotland metal detecting guidance leaflet expresses it: 'some archaeologists are strongly against it, while others believe that responsible detecting has a place in archaeological research' (www.historic-scotland.gov.uk/revised_metal_detecting.pdf).

9. Use of metal detectors on known archaeological sites, irrespective of whether they are Scheduled Ancient Monuments or not, is also prohibited under the conditions of certain agri-environment schemes in Scotland (see www.scottisharchaeology. org.uk/advice/farmingruralguides). There are also situations where there is a requirement for a metal detecting permit, such as on the Crown Estate foreshore (see www.thecrownestate.co.uk).

10. Thus far the only Treasure Trove incident I have dealt with which has involved a procurator fiscal and the police arose when a finder, who was not a metal detector user, refused to release for assessment a Neolithic polished stone axehead. This incident resulted in the axehead being claimed and the finder receiving no reward.

11. The annual cost of operating the existing Treasure Trove system in Scotland is currently around £65,000 (Crown Office 2007b, 18). The costs of operating the Portable Antiquities Scheme in England and Wales and the *Treasure Act* in England, Wales and Northern Ireland run to well over £1 million each year. As a consequence of this imbalance, people's lives in Scotland are arguably not being improved by the 'building knowledge, supporting learning, inspiring creativity and celebrating identity' which it is claimed is happening in England and Wales through the Portable Antiquities Scheme (PAS 2006, 5).

8

Metal Detecting in Northern Ireland

Declan Hurl

Northern Ireland, as many would appreciate, has had an individual set of circumstances from which to view opportunities and problems, and which extend into the field of archaeology in general and to the use of metal detectors in particular.

The 1971 *Historic Monuments Act (Northern Ireland)*, which replaced the *Ancient Monuments Acts* of 1926 and 1937, continued to outlaw digging for archaeological objects without a licence issued by the relevant government department. This situation, for a searcher for archaeological artefacts, was in contrast to the position of a chance finder of such an object, who was under an obligation to report the discovery and, if requested, to surrender it to the Ulster Museum for a period of study.

The Acts, and the subsequent Order in 1995 (see below), were attempts to prevent people 'digging for treasure'. What was unanticipated at the time was that the technology to allow people to target only metal objects would soon become publicly accessible, allowing treasure hunters to avoid digging trenches around ancient upstanding remains, which would be a labour-intensive and time-consuming activity as well as one which was relatively easy to spot.

World War II saw the development of the metal detector in its role of identifying mines, and for some time its use was restricted to such military purposes. While the 1970s saw the introduction and rise of its civilian popularity in the search for lost objects, interesting paraphernalia and, inevitably, treasure in other parts of the British Isles, the contrasting, more volatile, situation in Northern Ireland ensured that such equipment stayed more or less exclusively in military hands. That is not to say that there were no reports of such equipment being used to sweep known ancient sites for questionable purposes, but it did mean that the number of such cases was relatively small, and the likelihood of identification and successful prosecution was exceedingly remote.

It was a decade later that Northern Ireland saw metal detecting as a hobby really begin to take off. Unfortunately, but perhaps inevitably, with it grew the less savoury practice of illicit treasure hunting on identifiably ancient sites, often referred to as 'nighthawking' owing to the preference of such practitioners to avail themselves of the anonymity of darkness.

It is regrettable but, again, inevitable that those criminal activities tainted the image of the detector user community as a whole, especially within the archaeological profession, which experienced and railed against raids on protected monuments and research excavations by that maverick element. Indeed, such was the suspicion aroused amongst archaeologists in the field that they usually denied themselves access to this useful device. Even when detectors were purchased for investigative purposes by archaeologists, the general lack of experience among those wielding them practically guaranteed a poor result.

In 1990 efforts were made by members of both camps to build bridges, with government and museum staff attending meetings with detector users. Continuing suspicions and further treasure hunting incidents on protected sites, however, were more efficient in maintaining the breach, despite the fact that museum curators contracted detector users to search the dredgings along the River Blackwater (forming the border between Counties Armagh and Tyrone) in a search for Early Christian and medieval artefacts. This led to the discovery of many interesting objects, including the Early Christian reliquary known as the Clonmel Shrine. Overall, however, neither side displayed much interest in patching up old wounds.

One of the concerns among archaeologists was that, even when people were identified using detectors on known sites and were apprehended in possession of them, the law at the time only restricted the search for archaeological objects. Of course, none of those questioned were doing any such thing – they were trying to locate Victoriana, World War I memorabilia, lost hammers and penknives… on an Anglo-Norman motte! Others became belligerent when approached by archaeologists who were in the process of excavating the site on which they wanted to use their detectors. Even the police, when they became involved, were often unsure of the legal position, and the interest shown in pursuing the matter varied considerably. Add to this the equal uncertainty of the prosecution services as to the chances of winning a case under the existing legislation, and there is little wonder that no cases were ever successfully prosecuted.

For their part, some detector users considered that their activities were being restricted by archaeologists purely for selfish reasons – that is, the latter wanted to retain all the kudos and, frankly, excitement of finding ancient and beautiful objects for themselves; worse, since they apparently had every opportunity to find the masses of really valuable items which were undoubtedly out there, their apparent failure to

FIG 8.1: THE DRUMMOND PENDANT IS THE FRONT PLATE OF A 16TH CENTURY SILVER LOCKET DECORATED WITH THE ETCHING OF AN ANIMAL. FOUND BY A METAL DETECTORIST IN DRUMMOND TOWNLAND, IT WAS REPORTED TO THE ULSTER MUSEUM AND DECLARED TREASURE AT CORONER'S INQUEST.

do so led to suspicions that not everything was being reported from these professional investigations!

One of the main bones of contention was the contrast between legislation in England and Wales, Scotland and Northern Ireland, with the latter having the severest restrictions but, simultaneously, the most tenuous definitions. For example, how does one *prove* that someone is really digging for archaeological objects, the touchstone for criminal activity? And what is an archaeological object in the first place? This led to frustrations in both camps – detector users suspected that this imprecision was a deliberate ploy to assist archaeologists to regularly move the goalposts, while archaeologists felt that they had to constantly defend their interpretations of items and activities.

This was further underlined by the passing of the *Historic Monuments and Archaeological Objects (Northern Ireland) Order 1995*, in which it became illegal even to be in possession of a metal detector on a protected site (ie one that is scheduled or in State Care) without the permission of the Department of the Environment, which has been the body responsible for protecting the historic (and prehistoric) environment since 1981. This provided a measure of legal protection for such sites, though there was evidence that many were still persistently targeted by illicit detector users – but to prosecute such a crime, one has to catch the perpetrators in the act. The definition of archaeological objects, however, remains less detailed than many in both camps would like it to be.

FIG 8.2: THE MONEYGRAN FINDS CONSIST OF A SMALL INGOT OF SILVER MARKED WITH AN X AND THE TERMINAL OF A PENANNULAR BROOCH. FOUND TOGETHER BY A METAL DETECTORIST, THE TERMINAL HELPED TO DATE THE FINDS TO THE EARLY MEDIEVAL PERIOD AND, BY ASSOCIATION, WAS DECLARED TREASURE WITH THE INGOT, WHICH IS PROBABLY OF VIKING ORIGIN.

DECLAN HURL / CROWN COPYRIGHT

In 2000, a change began to occur. The Banbridge and District Metal Detecting Club (BDMDC), the largest (and at that time possibly the only) such association in Northern Ireland, sent an invitation to museum curators to attend one of its monthly meetings to talk to its members. This offer was taken up by me as, at the time, I was a government archaeologist. The talk basically described who archaeologists were, what they did, why they did it and why they had concerns about some of the detector users' practices. There followed a free and frank, though always civil, discussion of the hopes and concerns of the practitioners in both camps, during which a few amendments to the club's own voluntary Code of Conduct were suggested. Those changes, if adopted, would ensure that the detector users' field pursuits did not inadvertently stray over into activities or practices which were in contravention of the law.

There appears to have been a passionate exchange of views regarding the proposed changes at a subsequent meeting, with the majority appreciating the reasoning behind the suggestions and voting to adopt them. A minority, however, chose to leave the group and to form their own association, the North Down Metal Detecting Club.

There have been further informal meetings attended by government inspectors, museum curators and members of the BDMDC at which any remaining suspicions seem to have been allayed and offers were made to involve members of the club in joint projects. This resulted in the BDMDC members being called upon to carry out preliminary surveys of excavation sites and to check spoil-heaps for overlooked artefacts. They have also been prompt in reporting to both the Ulster Museum and the Department artefacts which they suspected were archaeological in nature. Indeed, not surprisingly, detector users have been responsible for around three-quarters of all Treasure reports since the introduction of the *Treasure Act* 1996. These items vary from small collections of medieval coins to a hoard of 3000-year-old bronze objects comprising bowls from Central Europe accompanied by a locally made sword.

Further, a research project along the Yellow Ford, the scene of an Elizabethan military encounter, involved the use of the club's detector users to survey the area under the direction of Paul Logue and James O'Neill, archaeologists specialising in such campaigns. Their work helped to ascertain the areas where volleys of shots both were fired and had landed. Excavation – under licence – of the signal spots indicating the location of lead shot also resulted in the identification of the size and condition of shot, the type of ordnance used, as well as the nature of its deposition (globular if dropped, flattened if fired) and, therefore, the side carrying out the shooting. This has helped to confirm and add considerable detail to the contemporary reports of the encounter. Several articles on the findings and the way that they have informed our understanding of the engagement have been submitted to *Post-Medieval Archaeology* and *Duiche Neill*.

Meanwhile, however, the reported incursions of the less conscientious practitioners on protected sites continue, but at least there is now 'clear blue sky' between the interested and concerned hobbyists and the 'nighthawks'.

Leaflets have been designed by the Department and distributed among club members and individual detector users explaining the 'do's' and 'don'ts' of practicing their hobby, and what to do if they find archaeological objects, especially Treasure items. Archaeologists and detector users occasionally meet up for a meal and a chat, just to maintain contact, to seek advice and to voice queries and concerns.

It is possible – maybe even inevitable – that field archaeologists themselves will eventually become owners of, and skilled in the use of, metal detectors. At least then the archaeologists themselves would have become detector users and the schism between the camps will have surely been sealed.

EXCERPTS FROM HISTORIC MONUMENTS AND ARCHAEOLOGICAL OBJECTS (NORTHERN IRELAND) ORDER 1995

Restrictions on possession and use of detecting devices

29.—(1) If a person has a detecting device in his possession in a protected place without the written consent of the Department he shall be guilty of an offence and liable on summary conviction to a fine not exceeding level 4 on the standard scale.

(2) In this Article—

'detecting device' means any device designed or adapted for detecting or locating any metal or mineral on or in the ground; and

'protected place' means any place which is the site of a scheduled monument or of any monument under the ownership or guardianship of the Department.

(3) If a person without the written consent of the Department removes any archaeological object which he has discovered by the use of a detecting device in a protected place he shall be guilty of an offence and liable on summary conviction to a fine not exceeding the statutory maximum or on conviction on indictment to a fine.

(4) A consent granted by the Department for the purposes of this Article may be granted either unconditionally or subject to conditions.

(5) If any person—

(a) in using a detecting device in a protected place in accordance with any consent granted by the Department for the purposes of this Article; or

(b) in removing or otherwise dealing with any object which he has discovered by the use of a detecting device in a protected place in accordance with any such consent, fails to comply with any condition attached to the consent, he shall be guilty of an offence and liable, in a case falling within sub-paragraph (a), to the penalty provided by paragraph (1), and in a case falling within sub-paragraph (b), to the penalty provided by paragraph (3).

(6) In any proceedings for an offence under paragraph (1) or (3), it shall be a defence for the accused to prove that he had taken all reasonable precautions to find out whether the place where he had the detecting device in his possession or (as the case may be) used it was a protected place and did not believe that it was.

Restriction on searching for archaeological objects, etc.

41.—(1) Any person who, except under and in accordance with any conditions attached to a licence issued by the Department under this Article, excavates in or under any land (whether or not such excavation involves the removal of the surface of the land) for the purpose of searching generally for archaeological objects or of searching for, exposing or examining any particular structure or thing of archaeological interest shall be guilty of an offence and liable on summary conviction to a fine not exceeding level 3 on the standard scale.

(2) A licence granted by the Department for the purposes of this Article—

(a) shall specify the land in relation to which and the archaeological purpose for which the licence has effect;

(b) may be granted subject to such conditions as the Department thinks fit; and

(c) shall not render lawful the doing of anything which would be unlawful apart from this Article.

(3) A person shall not, under the authority of a licence issued under this Article, enter on the land to which the licence relates except—

(a) with the consent of the occupier of the land and the owner (if the owner is known); or

(b) in exercise of a power of entry under Part II.

Reporting of archaeological objects found

42.—(1) Any person who finds an archaeological object (in this Article referred to as 'the finder') shall, within 14 days of finding the object—

(a) report to a relevant authority—

(i) the circumstances of the finding;

(ii) the nature of the object found; and

(iii) the name (if known) of the owner or occupier of the land on which the object was found; and

(b) subject to paragraph (2), deposit the object found with the relevant authority.

(2) Where the archaeological object found is not readily portable, the finder shall so specify in his report under paragraph (1), and shall state where any person authorised in that behalf by the Director or the Department may inspect the object.

(3) A police officer to whom a report is made under paragraph (1) shall forthwith—

(a) send details of that report to the Director; and

(b) where any archaeological object was deposited with the report, send that object to the Director unless for any reason he considers that the object is not suitable to be sent to the Director.

(4) An archaeological object which is deposited with the Director or the Department under paragraph (1) or sent to the Director under paragraph (3)(b) may be retained by the Director or the Department for the statutory period for the purpose of examining and recording it and carrying out

any test or treatment which appears to the Director or the Department to be desirable for the purpose of archaeological investigation or analysis or with a view to restoring or preserving the object.

(5) An archaeological object which is deposited with a police officer under paragraph (1) and not sent by him to the Director under paragraph (3)(b) may be retained by him for the statutory period to facilitate inspection of the object by the Director or a person authorised in that behalf by the Director.

(6) Except with the consent of the Director or the Department, the finder shall not, before the expiration of the statutory period, deliver the archaeological object to a person other than a relevant authority or otherwise part with the possession of the object.

(7) A finder who, without reasonable cause, acts in contravention of any provision of this Article, and any other person (other than a relevant authority) who, knowingly and without the consent of a relevant authority, obtains possession of any archaeological object before the expiration of the statutory period, shall be guilty of an offence and liable on summary conviction to a fine not exceeding level 3 on the standard scale.

(8) The Department may give financial assistance towards the purchase of any archaeological object, the finding of which has been reported under this Article.

(9) Financial assistance under paragraph (8) may be given subject to such conditions (including conditions as to the public exhibition of the purchased object) as the Department thinks fit.

(10) The Director shall make a report to the Department on every object deposited with or sent to him under this Article.

(11) Nothing in this Article—

(a) affects any right of the Crown in relation to treasure trove; or

(b) affects the right of any person to the ownership of an archaeological object.

(12) In this Article—

'the Director' means the Director of the Ulster Museum;

'relevant authority' means the Director, the Department or the officer in charge of a police station;

'the statutory period' in relation to an archaeological object means the period of 3 months beginning with the date on which a report of the finding of that object is made under paragraph (1).

9

Metal Detecting and Archaeology in Wales

MARK LODWICK

THE ESTABLISHMENT OF THE PORTABLE ANTIQUITIES SCHEME IN WALES

The Portable Antiquities Scheme was initiated in Wales in March 1999 in the second phase of the development of the pilot scheme (see Bland, chapter 6). The organisation of the scheme in Wales had to take account of the large geographic area to be covered and was accordingly structured differently from its English counterparts. After considerable consultation between interested parties, Richard Brewer (Keeper of Archaeology & Numismatics, Amgueddfa Cymru-National Museum Wales) and Jane Henderson (formerly of the Council of Museums in Wales) devised a pilot scheme that would be inclusive of many of the existing archaeological bodies and institutions in Wales. It was decided that the portable antiquities post should be based within the Department of Archaeology & Numismatics, National Museum Cardiff, where the post holder would coordinate the scheme throughout Wales. After consultation with the four Welsh Archaeological Trusts (Cambria (Dyfed Archaeological Trust); Clwyd Powys Archaeological Trust; Glamorgan Gwent Archaeological Trust; and Gwynedd Archaeological Trust), who are responsible for maintaining the Heritage Environment Records for their respective regions, it was decided that each of the trusts would be offered a service agreement in order to maintain and promote the scheme within its area. The coordinator and a representative from each of the trusts would then be able to support a nationwide network of reporting centres comprising regional and local museums.

The work of the coordinator is supported by the Royal Commission on Ancient and Historic Monuments of Wales and Cadw, and was initially administered through the Council of Museums in Wales, through funding by the Heritage Lottery Fund and the Welsh Assembly Government. In 1999 Dr Philip Macdonald was appointed to the post of Portable Antiquities Scheme Finds Coordinator: Wales, and he worked for three years establishing, building and developing the scheme in Wales, before the author took up the post in 2002. In 2003, a Welsh Assembly Government reorganisation resulted in the dissolution of the Council of Museums in Wales, and management of the scheme was passed to the National Museum of Wales.

The initial work of establishing the scheme in Wales was made considerably easier by the previous work of staff in the National Museum, who had offered a finds identification and recording service for a number of years. Among the most notable of the early outreach programmes of curators at the National Museum was a significant lithic recording programme undertaken by Elizabeth Walker (Curator of Palaeolithic & Mesolithic Archaeology, Department of Archaeology & Numismatics). Outreach to lithic fieldwalkers has continued within the Portable Antiquities Scheme and is demonstrated by a consistently high proportion of non-metallic finds recorded in Wales. In addition, Edward Besly (Numismatist, Department of Archaeology & Numismatics, Amgueddfa Cymru-National Museum Wales) had developed a numismatic identification and recording programme of which the PAS coordinator is still able to take advantage. The establishment of the scheme, however, provided a mechanism and structure for proactive outreach, reporting and recording, which was not previously available.

National Museum staff were able to respond to significant metal detecting discoveries, upon which the work of the PAS was able to build. In the early 1990s, before the PAS existed, a group of highly unusual early medieval metal detector finds was recovered from the Isle of Anglesey and reported by Mr Archie Gillespie and Mr Peter Corbett to Dr Mark Redknap (Medievalist, Department of Archaeology & Numismatics, Amgueddfa Cymru-National Museum Wales). Subsequent investigation of the findspot at Llanbedrgoch using geophysics and excavation revealed a Viking-age enclosure containing significant internal settlement evidence and human burial deposits within the enclosure ditches. The fieldwork project undertaken by the National Museum continued for a decade and was supported by the landowners, Roger and Debbie Tebutt, and finders, who were all included as essential members of the excavation team and provided an invaluable contribution to the project. The metal detector users provided archaeologists with markers to indicate the position of metallic finds within their archaeological context prior to excavation, as well as searching spoil for finds. In turn the metal detector users gained an insight into archaeological fieldwork methodology and an appreciation for the rigours of the archaeological process.

The inclusion of the finders in a fieldwork team is an ideal mechanism for demonstrating the complexities of the archaeological process and the importance of stratigraphy in site interpretation. The excavations provided Archie Gillespie with a platform and the experience to pursue his developing interest in field archaeology; subsequently he was involved in a number of museum, commercial and university archaeological fieldwork projects.

The number of finds recorded and input onto the PAS database by the Portable Antiquities Scheme in Wales tends to be variable year on year. This is, to some degree, dependent on additional administrative support available from the National Museum. During the years in which Wales has a comparatively high number of recorded finds, it is often because large lithic collections have been recorded and input onto the finds database.

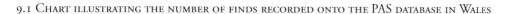

9.1 CHART ILLUSTRATING THE NUMBER OF FINDS RECORDED ONTO THE PAS DATABASE IN WALES

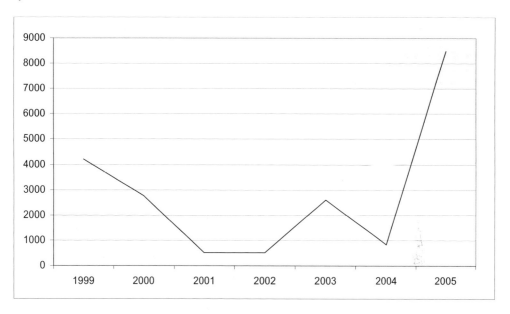

TREASURE IN WALES

The 1996 *Treasure Act*, introduced in 1997, was passed because of inadequacies in the common law of Treasure Trove. Recent problems in administering Treasure Trove and the protection afforded to precious metal artefacts have been outlined elsewhere in this volume (see Bland, chapter 6).

In return for administering Treasure Trove, the British Museum had the right of pre-emption of material from cases in both England and Wales. The National Museum of Wales, founded in 1907, acquired the right of pre-emption of Treasure Trove from Wales in 1943; however, this right was not exercised until 1955, when a hoard of three Bronze Age gold torcs was discovered at Heyope in Beguildy, Powys (NMW Accession number 55.543/1–3). From the 1960s curators at the National Museum advised coroners and appeared as expert witnesses in cases of Treasure Trove in Wales.

In the years before the introduction of the 1996 *Treasure Act*, the operation of Treasure Trove had been rendered increasingly problematical by modern legislative changes, by votive interpretations of precious metal deposits, by a requirement to guess the intentions of the original depositor and even by the definition of gold and silver in terms of precious metal purity. With the introduction of the 1996 *Treasure Act*, the question of deliberate deposition with the intention of recovery was no longer a factor. The Wales-wide role of the National Museum in dealing with Treasure Trove evolved into a similar arrangement under the 1996 *Treasure Act*. This was formalised in the official code of practice, and the National Museum of Wales was recognised as being the only body with the necessary

9.2 Chart illustrating the number of recorded Treasure
Cases in Wales since the 1996 Treasure Act

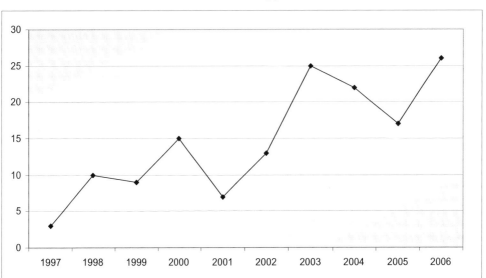

expertise to provide advice to coroners under the 1996 *Treasure Act* for all cases reported in Wales.

Treasure Trove cases in Wales were very rare, perhaps one to two cases every year at most. Often these were relatively small hoards of coins, but there were some spectacular Bronze Age gold finds, such as the Milford Haven gold torcs, and coin hoards, such as the Tregwynt Civil War coin hoard. In the first ten years of the 1996 *Treasure Act* in Wales, in contrast, there have been some 140 cases of potential Treasure reported, an average of 14 cases per year. Of the 100 reported Treasure cases since the introduction of the PAS in Wales, the Finds Coordinator or Welsh Archaeological Trust representative has been involved with approximately 90 per cent of cases. The PAS has an ever-increasing role in Treasure in Wales through outreach to finders, as a surprisingly high proportion of Treasure discoveries are not recognised as being Treasure by the finders before a PAS identification is able to initiate the Treasure process.

The extension of the 1996 *Treasure Act* to cover associated prehistoric base-metal artefacts in 2003 has not so far had a significant effect on the overall number of reported cases of Treasure in Wales. There have been five reported cases in the past three years which would not have been considered under the previous arrangement. Additionally, there have been five cases of prehistoric Treasure which have contained precious metal objects, three of which occurred since the extension of the 1996 *Treasure Act* in 2003. The 1996 *Treasure Act* can be shown to afford greater protection to significant prehistoric assemblages. Prior to 1997, only 15 or so of the 140 cases (10 per cent) would have been considered as Treasure Trove in Wales and the 1996 *Treasure Act* can again be shown to better protect ancient precious metal artefacts from Wales.

A high proportion of Treasure finds in Wales have been acquired by either the National Museum or regional museums. These Treasure discoveries can be seen as helping to develop public collections at both a national and regional level. The National Museum tends to acquire slightly over half the number of non-excavation Treasure cases, with regional museums acquiring the remainder, except for a small number of disclaimed cases (5 per cent).

PORTABLE ANTIQUITIES DRIVING RESEARCH AND LEARNING: CASE STUDIES

A key strength of the Portable Antiquities Scheme in Wales has proved to be the support of the National Museum in addition to the central PAS support. The finds coordinator is able to draw upon an extensive range of expertise, including curatorial, conservation, analytical, educational and illustration. Furthermore, facilities at the National Museum Cardiff make the job considerably easier, providing access to a comprehensive archaeological library, professional photographers, fieldwork equipment and cross-disciplinary expertise, helping with geological identifications and so on. The curatorial expertise within the Department of Archaeology & Numismatics has enabled joint PAS and museum projects to be rapidly initiated; thus important discoveries can receive a fitting level of research and, when appropriate, contextual information can be recovered.

Late Bronze Age metalwork in south-east Wales

Some of the most important recent discoveries reported through PAS have been in the late Bronze Age of south-east Wales. During 2001–2 a number of late Bronze Age metalwork hoards were recovered from south-east Wales. Seven hoards were reported in less than two years, comprising nearly 150 pieces of metalwork. All finds were made independently and by separate finders with the use of metal detectors. The discoveries were made prior to the extension of the 1996 *Treasure Act* to cover base-metal assemblages of prehistoric date and were all voluntarily reported to the PAS. Together, the hoard discoveries represent a highly significant local clustering of metalwork and have the potential to contribute greatly to our understanding of the late Bronze Age in south-east Wales.

The hoards were recovered from two areas within the region: the Vale of Glamorgan and central Monmouthshire. All metalwork is of the 'Ewart Park' metalworking tradition, dated to the period *c* 950–750 BC. The regional character of this metalwork has long been recognised and has been referred to as the 'Llantwit–Stogursey tradition' after the eponymous Llantwit Major and Stogursey hoards, now held at National Museum Wales and Somerset County Museum, Taunton, respectively. The 'Llantwit province' can be shown to extend across the low-lying ground from the River Neath in the west to the River Usk in the east and between the Bristol Channel and the Brecon Beacons. The overall focus of recovery, and presumably deposition, is in the Cardiff area, the Vale of Glamorgan and central Monmouthshire. These hoards are generally made up of tools and differ from hoards of the same age recovered from the Midlands, which generally contain a higher proportion of weapons, especially spearheads.

A substantial new body of material evidence has provided National Museum staff

9.3 SOME OF THE LATE BRONZE AGE METALWORK HOARDS REPORTED IN 2002

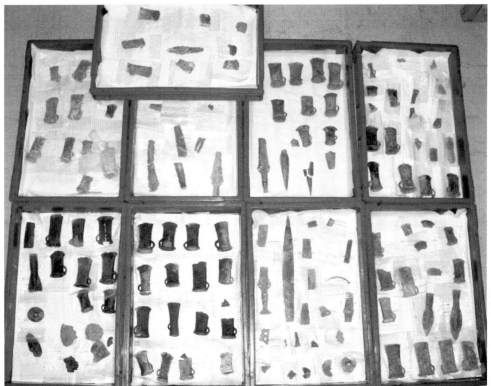

© MARK LODWICK / PAS.

(Adam Gwilt, Curator of Bronze & Iron Age Collections and Mary Davis, Archaeological Conservator) in conjunction with PAS an opportunity to reassess the regional character of this metalwork. The hoard discoveries have provided an insight into depositional practices and a number of the discoveries were followed up with small scale excavation.

It has become apparent that the hoards are generally deposited on hill slopes with little other contemporary archaeology in the immediate vicinity. Two hoards have a slightly different depositional character and were discovered in close proximity to one another. Follow-up fieldwork was able to propose that both assemblages had been placed at the edge of, or within, a lake or bog. Assessment of the position of these and other older discoveries within the landscape has shown that water deposition may play an important factor in their location. While only a few of the assemblages are believed to have been placed directly in water, most are deposited in the vicinity of rivers and water courses, with certain rivers attracting more depositional activity than others. We have been able to suggest that water-related depositional activity may occur around a water source, without the need for the metalwork to be placed within the water.

Further insights have been gleaned from observations of the treatment of the metalwork prior to deposition. A substantial proportion of the assemblages have been damaged, often with the removal of the blade and the violent splitting or closure of axe sockets, suggesting a consistent ritualised damage to the metalwork.

Detailed analytical study of the axe surfaces by Mary Davis has shown that the axes may have been deliberately coated with a tenorite deposit, resulting in a black surface colouring to the body of the axe. This would result in the axes having a visually dramatic appearance with the black axe body contrasting with the golden bronze colour of the sharpened blade and raised ribs of the axe. This hints at the importance of colour in prehistory, currently a poorly understood aspect.

Most of these metalwork hoards have been returned to the finders, but the recorded information is being studied in the Department of Archaeology & Numismatics at the National Museum Cardiff. The finds are being researched in conjunction with other recent late Bronze Age hoards from south Wales and The Marches to produce a regional synthesis of this material culture. This study will help to elucidate a poorly understood period of our history and has been able to demonstrate how PAS can initiate material culture research in collaboration with existing research institutions.

An early Iron Age feasting site

A further opportunity to research a different aspect of the late Bronze Age to early Iron Age in south Wales occurred when two metal detector users, Mr Steve McGrory and Mr Anton Jones, reported the discovery of an extraordinary assemblage from Llanmaes in the Vale of Glamorgan. The finds were recognised as cauldron and axe fragments dating to the Bronze and Iron Age transition, corresponding to the Llyn Fawr metalworking phase, dated to *c* 800–600 BC. The discovery of metalwork of this period is comparatively rare and its importance occasioned a site visit by Adam Gwilt, the finders and the author. The assemblage was recovered after the extension of the 1996 *Treasure Act* in 2003 to include prehistoric base-metal associated artefacts and therefore the discovery was initially pursued as a potential Treasure case. The site visit revealed that each of the finds had been recovered from a discrete location within an area of approximately 40 square metres, but any original association of artefacts was not clear. A need to understand the context for the metalwork as potential Treasure in order for the National Museum to fulfil its obligation to provide expert opinion to the local coroner, led to a geophysical survey, conducted by Dr Tim Young of Geoarch, and a week-long excavation over the concentration of metal detector pits and geophysical anomalies. The fieldwork revealed that the assemblage was unlikely to have been originally directly associated from the same find (eg a hoard or grave assemblage) and consequently the assemblage was unlikely to constitute Treasure. The excavated deposits yielded further cauldron and axe fragments together with a highly significant pottery assemblage, recovered from a period of sparse pottery production in Wales.

The importance of the archaeology and associated finds has since resulted in the instigation of a major research excavation, funded by the National Museum and supported by PAS. There have been four seasons of excavation and it is hoped the fieldwork will continue for a further three seasons. The excavations have revealed an extensive late Bronze

9.4 THE EXCAVATED ROUND HOUSE AT LLANMAES WITH THE TEAM POSITIONED
IN THE POST HOLES AND IN THE PIT CONTAINING THE CREMATION BURIAL

© MARK LODWICK / PAS.

Age and early Iron Age midden or rubbish deposit. This deposit contains a massive faunal assemblage, largely composed of pig bones and is likely to be the result of feasting activity on the site. Contemporary with the midden is a small scale and seemingly unenclosed settlement comprising at least three round houses, including one large example with a porch.

Study of aerial photographs has revealed a univallate enclosure of possible later prehistoric date in a neighbouring field with surrounding burial monuments of probable early Bronze Age date. The discovery of a middle Bronze Age cremation burial beneath the large round house hints at the continued importance of this landscape for burial around the earlier barrow monuments. Further geophysical survey has confirmed the presence of the enclosure and highlighted extensive internal features.

The rich potential for the preservation of environmental evidence and information on the formation, structure and later disturbance of the midden deposits has resulted in an excavation methodology of extensive sampling with on-site sieving and flotation. In 2006 this was funded by the award of a research grant from the Royal Archaeological Institute. Charred plant remains surviving within a range of feature fills were identified and quantified by Astrid Caseldine of University of Wales Lampeter. These revealed barley, wheat and oat grains and hazelnut fragments. Samples from the middle Bronze Age cremation pit yielded significant quantities of wheat, barley and oats. Very little is known of late Bronze and Iron Age crop husbandry in Wales, so this well preserved evidence will provide a significant addition to wider understanding.

Dr Richard Macphail, of University College London, has generated a series of thin sections from soil monoliths or columns which preserve the stratigraphy and were retrieved from the excavation. A brief assessment of their content has characterised the range of soils from the site, while informing our understanding of how the midden was formed, and then later modified. A range of crop processing and burning events are witnessed, with the presence of human and dog coprolites. These, and the high phosphate levels recorded, are typical of midden signatures. It is apparent that the deposit was also later mixed through animal trampling and truncated by later activity and ploughing.

Finds of axes of Armorican type, made in Brittany and Normandy, along with cauldrons with Irish attributes suggest widespread contact and influence on the site. The abundant finds of pig bones and cauldron fragments has enabled creative links to be forged with Welsh mythology and stories of the Mabinogion. Connecting archaeology with myth and legend has created opportunities in engaging with diverse audiences throughout Wales and has resulted in visits to the site by a number of poets and artists seeking inspiration for their work.

The community support for the excavations has encouraged the excavators with support from the National Museum to develop an educational programme offering innovative methods for learning and engagement with the past. This project has been coordinated by Kenneth Brassil, the Museum's Archaeology & History Education Officer. The practical process of discovery, through sustained seasons of survey and excavation, has provided a rich resource for learning and engagement. The excavation site can be considered a productive learning setting accessed by schools and the community.

A Schools Archaeology Project was initiated in 2005, following very positive local support for the excavations within the community of Llanmaes. Early presentations, excavation open days and behind-the-scenes museum tours ensured that the local community had an engagement and sense of ownership in the unfolding process of discovery of their prehistoric past. Kenneth Brassil established contact with the head teachers and teachers at the three local primary schools (Ysgol Llanilltyd Fawr, St Illtyd Primary School, and Eagleswell Primary School) in Llanmaes and Llantwit Major. During initial stages he visited the schools with handling collections and encouraged pupils to consider deep history through timelines and discussed excavation methodology. Engagement has been facilitated with the help of a number of creative individuals. A poet and crown bard, Iwan Llwyd, has worked with schools helping to compose poetic responses to the archaeology. Sean Harris, artist, has worked with a film company and primary school groups to create a piece of installation art and animation inspired by the Branwen story from the Mabinogion and utilising the archaeological discoveries made at Llanmaes. An Academi-sponsored storyteller, Michael Harvey, used an iron cauldron from the 'Celtic Village' at St Fagans: National History Museum as a focus for developing storylines.

One school group was ascribed the task of visiting the excavations as journalists and interviewed members of the excavation team, including volunteers, students, and professional archaeologists. Prior to the site visits, questions were prepared and digital cameras were made available. When the class arrived on site, they were given a tour of the excavation, finds processing and flotation activity. The children then worked in small teams, supporting each other's questioning and recording of responses. Back at the school, the notes were edited and a selection of stories and articles presented as a newspaper and circulated in the school. At National Museum Cardiff, their journalism was featured in a temporary exhibition as part of National Archaeology Days.

Another school was challenged with the task of filming and creating film narratives drawing upon personal artefacts in conjunction with the experience of visiting the Llanmaes excavations. Two half-days were spent with filmmakers Clwyd Jones and Gareth Bonello who involved the children in experimenting with video cameras and digital photography. The group gained confidence with the equipment by recording film and dialogue in the school. The experience of discussing material culture and the personal significance of artefacts inspired the children to explore their feelings towards personal possessions. Pupils brought their favourite object from home and worked together in the process of recording and filming. Their interpretations were personal and in some cases profound. This archive film of creating meaning and of identifying with a contemporary artefact became the core of the film. The resulting films have been shown at National Museum Cardiff to complement the display of artefacts.

A further group was given the role of landscape detectives. They focused on the context of exploring the location of the site by interrogating maps of different scales. Using gradually more detailed scales, they 'homed' in on the field in question on the edge of the village of Llanmaes before beginning the guided tour. By now there was a confident engagement within the class and a freedom to question the archaeologists and students who were excavating, planning, recording, sorting finds and processing sediment. With a single visit and limited introduction, they had begun to develop their own identity with the excavation project.

It is proposed that this partnership with the three schools continues for the duration of the fieldwork and beyond, with an involvement in the post-excavation programme and site interpretation.

The Llanmaes project is also collaborating with Cardiff University, and provides training for archaeology students in aspects of excavation technique, sampling, recording, finds and sample processing and survey. Collaboration with staff and research students is helping to frame wider research applications and access further funding opportunities.

The Llanmaes fieldwork project provides an insight into how the value of discoveries made through PAS can help diverse audiences engage and maintain an involvement with archaeology on a number of levels. It is able to enhance our understanding of the past and feed into current archaeological and academic debate; it is able to inspire and provoke the artistic community into visual and literal responses; it can involve the local community in both the process and discovery of archaeology and it can instigate cross-curricular learning in school audiences. Furthermore, the excavations have provided an ideal scenario for 'best practice' in metal detecting reporting and can be used in talks and displays to illustrate what can be learnt and achieved through working together.

A late Iron Age burial discovery

The importance of outreach to metal detector users was demonstrated when two detector users, Brian Gibison and Adrian Pierce, made a find at Boverton, Vale of Glamorgan, which they recognised as being of considerable archaeological importance. The finders contacted the PAS Finds Coordinator who was able to respond quickly and visit the site shortly after the discovery. Preliminary recording and survey was carried out and the Finds Coordinator was able to confirm that the find was an important neck ornament and associated bracelet of the late Iron Age to Roman conquest period, probably dating to the third quarter of the 1st century AD. The find was subsequently logged as potential Treasure and a small scale excavation was arranged by PAS and the National Museum to recover further contextual information. The excavation uncovered a second bracelet similar to the first and revealed evidence for an inhumation burial, which had been heavily disturbed by a post-medieval agricultural ditch. The second bracelet contained fragments of arm bones indicating that the bracelets had been worn when deposited.

Burials of this period and type are exceptional finds in Wales and the discovery again demonstrates the importance of effective outreach and good practice in metal detecting for recovering crucial archaeological data. Secondly, it illustrates the importance of rapid archaeological follow-up excavations in identifying the burial contexts of significant finds. The find was subsequently declared Treasure and is being acquired by the National Museum of Wales.

Lithics field-walking survey in Monmouthshire

A further research and community project has been initiated by PAS and the National Museum at St Arvans and Mathern, Monmouthshire. A local field-walker of lithic tools, Peter Bond, reported a large assemblage of lithic artefacts from the Chepstow area of Monmouthshire. Study of the assemblage by Elizabeth Walker recognised a number of implements that can be attributed to the late Upper Palaeolithic age (12 900–11 800 BP) on the basis of their typological characteristics. These flints all date to a period after the Last Glacial Maximum during which time people were not present in Britain. The climate had been so inhospitable at this time that people had moved to countries further south to escape the cold. As the climate improved, the vegetation began to re-establish itself and animals such as horse and reindeer returned, followed by late Upper Palaeolithic hunters. The climate remained stable enough for these people to survive in Britain until 10 800 BP when a short but very cold period (the Younger Dryas) forced them south and out of Britain again. These finds are sufficient for us to claim a rare discovery of a new open-air Upper Palaeolithic site.

An ongoing field-walking project has begun over the farm where the initial finds were recovered. Members of the local community and local historical and archaeological societies are participating in the field-walking. The lithic finds and their positions are beginning to suggest an emerging pattern of the utilisation of the landscape from the Upper Palaeolithic to the Bronze Age. Further Upper Palaeolithic finds have been recovered on organised field walks and independently by Peter Bond which have been located up to a kilometre away from the initial finds. It is hoped that continued systematic field-walking will inform and provide finer resolution on the location of these prehistoric sites.

The future for Portable Antiquities in Wales

At the time of writing, PAS has been operating in Wales for more than seven years. This period has seen the growth and development of the Scheme into an established and successful initiative supported by archaeological institutions and members of the public. Throughout this period the operation of the Scheme has remained largely unchanged with only a modest increase in budget, and may be seen as offering a high standard of service and value for money. There are, however, problems in maintaining a consistent standard of coverage throughout Wales. The PAS regional museum liaison relies on a basic level of archaeological expertise or interest within a museum. The recent loss of several such curators from Welsh regional museums may result in the non-reporting of archaeological finds shown to the museums. Increasing pressures on funding to unitary authority museums have the potential to threaten the effective operation of the PAS museum network.

A significant existing problem with PAS in Wales is the inconsistent coverage caused by the scale and geography of Wales. A significant number of metal detector users based in north-east Wales are not routinely visited by a PAS representative at their meetings. The challenge over the next few years for the PAS is to ensure that the level and the quality of service are equal and consistent throughout Wales.

10

Building Bridges between Metal Detectorists and Archaeologists[1]

Trevor Austin

When I was first asked to speak to the conference about building bridges, my first thought was that detector users have been trying to build bridges for the past 25 years, with varying degrees of success.

I began metal detecting in the late 1970s, a time when most metal detector users were quite happy to pursue their hobby in their own individual way, going out at the weekend and discovering finds which they recorded in their own personal log or notebook. PCs or laptops worthy of the name had yet to surface, the only database being the card index, filing system or crosses on a map, all discreetly and jealously guarded. The Portable Antiquities Scheme was still a good 20 years away.

But even in those early days many detector users wanted to know more about their finds and to share that information with their local museum. Regrettably, many museums would turn finders away, but there were those who had already seen the light; such unorthodox collaborators as Kevin Leahey and Tony Gregory were working with detector users, recording their finds, and receiving much criticism from their contemporaries for doing so. But the seeds were sown. Slowly, through persistent group effort and mediation, detector users became genuinely welcome at some of the more enlightened museums.

Metal detecting is first and foremost a legitimate recreational hobby which can be pursued by all, young and old, rich or poor; that is one of its endearing qualities. It gives

FIG 10.1: CHILDREN CAN HAVE A REWARDING TIME. SHOWS MY GRANDDAUGHTER JODIE WITH A GOLD RING WHICH SHE FOUND WHILE METAL DETECTING AT CHAPEL ST LEONARDS. IT WAS HER FIRST RING. SHE WAS SEVEN AT THE TIME.

© TREVOR AUSTIN

Fig 10.2: The two pictures from the Robin Hood Rally of Sestertii are of two young people who had found their first hoard. They had not been detecting long.

© Trevor Austin

us all the opportunity to enrich our lives with a greater understanding of our past. But it is a hobby that has responsibilities, and most detector users recognise those responsibilities; once a find has been removed from the ground, the finder then becomes the custodian of that find; the custodian of our heritage, a heritage that belongs to us all.

Since its inception, the Portable Antiquities Scheme (PAS) has been instrumental in awakening the general public, and the media, to our hobby of metal detecting. The National Council for Metal Detecting (NCMD) has always shown great enthusiasm toward the PAS, which has given finders the opportunity to be constructive and meaningful and to be a part of a new experience. Detector users regularly record their finds, both on their personal database and with the PAS, many recording findspots on customised map-making programmes such as 'Mapmaker'.

Now that the PAS is a permanent part of heritage affairs in this country, detector users would like to see a broadening of horizons; they want involvement, discussion, information, debate, research and conservation, and more opportunities to work alongside archaeologists. By becoming cohesive we will all have a greater understanding about historical landscapes and the hidden secrets they contain. The PAS can provide all these channels.

FIG 10.3: LLANMAES, SOUTH WALES; TAKEN BY THE HIDDEN TREASURE FILM
CREW ON A SITE WHICH HAD PRODUCED QUITE A FEW BRONZE AGE AXE HEADS.
THE PICTURE SHOWS ARCHIE GILLESPIE, A WELL-KNOWN DETECTOR USER AND
AMATEUR ARCHAEOLOGIST, HELPING THE MUSEUM OF WALES ON THE DIG.

© TREVOR AUSTIN

The PAS has also woken up English Heritage, the Forestry Commission, English Nature, DEFRA, ALGAO, Tony Robinson and 'Uncle Tom Cobley and all', and, not to be trumped by the PAS, all these bodies are producing reams of documents, codes and guidelines. Despite promises to the contrary, some organisations – for example, The National Trust – have produced metal detecting policy without consultation with the NCMD. Some of these policies have been threatening, some pointless. Not only has the NCMD been deluged with mountains of paper, but this has been very counterproductive to the mission of the PAS and has at times served only as a threat to the success of the Scheme. Today I want to send a clear message to all these bureaucrats: 'get off our case', and leave the responsible hobby alone. Attempts to inflict archaeological controls prevent serious cooperation; matters that relate to the detecting hobby should be channelled through the PAS. The Scheme had already succeeded in gaining our confidence while other bodies were messing about formulating rulebooks! It has taken 200 years for archaeology to get its act together and create standards, and there are still many internal divisions within the discipline. It has only taken 25 years for metal detecting to reach a stage where results are being proudly achieved, revolutionising archaeological thinking in the process. The responsible hobby is ready to move forward in tandem with the now

Fig 10.4: Cei and Kevin being interviewed by the Hidden Treasure
Team for the final programme in the series at Charlcotte Park, an
Elizabethan manor house in which the programme was set.

permanent PAS, and show what can be achieved in future years, but we will not tolerate meddling in the hobby or the Scheme. The Finds Liaison Officers of the PAS not only understand the metal detecting hobby and discuss issues surrounding metal detecting frankly and honestly, they also understand the needs of archaeology and environmental issues. I believe the PAS needs to evolve as the coordinating body that combines the interests and concerns of us all.

Regardless of whether we use a detector or a trowel, providing the PAS continues to treat the detector users as 'customers' and does not become over-confident, then customers will remain loyal. And providing there is meaningful dialogue to and from the archaeological world, via the Scheme, we should all see the benefits. However, not everything is sweetness and light – far from it. Since I first began attending executive meetings of the NCMD in 1990, through *Treasure Trove*, the *Perth Bill* and finally the 1996 *Treasure Act*, it has been a hard and sometimes uphill struggle to achieve the kind of cooperation we have today.

There are detector users that have no interest in what we are achieving, and there are still archaeologists who for their own purposes would be rid of metal detection, or attempt to control the hobby with meaningless unworkable rules and regulations. As we in the NCMD have seen many times, the hobby has come under continued attack from various sources, usually from those who do not, or do not wish to, understand the hobby. And let us remember that some of these people are still out there, and still recruiting. There are still the nighthawks to be dealt a damaging blow, but enlightened detector users and archaeologists are now, I believe, the mainstream of today and the future of our past.

As the shining new PAS train gets ready to leave the station (without any baggage), it will be mainstream, forward-thinking detector users, archaeologists, historians and the like that are on board, leaving behind those that cannot see further than their noses or bury old prejudices. They will be the losers, while we are debating our passion, the finds, the landscapes, the meanings, and putting flesh on our past. The others, both detector user and archaeologist, will be left standing on the platform in a time warp, with outdated ideologies and misconceptions, shouting abuse at each other and probably us.

I believe the future is ours, and the more distant we are from the disbelievers, the more isolated and vulnerable they will become; eventually they will have to catch up, give up, or join the 'dark side'. I believe and expect the future of the PAS and the NCMD will be to empower everyone to share in the understanding of our past, set achievable, acceptable standards for all, and create a vehicle – my 'train' – that we all want to be on and be part of.

When Dionysius invited his courtiers to that luxurious banquet, Damocles enjoyed the delights of the table, until his attention was directed upward and he saw a sharp sword hanging above him by a single horsehair. 'That sword! That sword!' whispered Damocles. 'Don't you see it?' 'Of course I see it,' said Dionysius. 'I see it every day. It always hangs over my head, and there is always the chance someone or something may cut the slim thread.' Damocles realised the ever-present peril. I say to you all – let not one of us be the one to cut that slender thread.

NOTES

1. This chapter is the unaltered text of the opening address of the *Buried Treasure: Building Bridges* conference held at Newcastle University and the Hancock Museum on Saturday 18 June 2005.

11

The Construction of Histories: Numismatics and Metal Detecting

PETER D SPENCER

I have had an interest in coins for over 40 years. As a schoolboy I collected Victorian pennies but after leaving school I developed an interest in British hammered and early milled silver. On the positive side, coins were very cheap when I first started to collect, but on the negative I had very little spare cash to devote to my hobby. I therefore took up dealing on a part-time basis. This was in the mid-1960s, a time when there were few dealers – despite the fact that coins were in great demand. Prices rose year on year and I speedily built up a list of clients in the UK and overseas. Many fine and rare coins passed through my hands and quite a number entered my private collection. Pressure from my full-time employment forced me to stop dealing in the mid-1980s but through collecting and dealing I had broadened my knowledge of coins and coinages. Besides my own coins, I had viewed others in museums and in the collections owned by other numismatists, as well as a huge range of material on view in numerous salerooms. One can learn much through reading reference works, but I always tell budding numismatists that the best way to become familiar with any series of coins is to see and handle as many specimens as possible. For example, pennies of Edward I, II and III might all look alike to the novice but anyone who has handled or seen thousands will be speedily able to spot the subtle differences between the numerous classes. Having said this, I must not underestimate the knowledge I gained through reading numerous numismatic reference works. Starting with general works, such as Seaby's *Standard Catalogue of British Coins*.[1] I quickly moved on to more specialised publications on specific series. This reading gave me a firm grounding in the subject, one that has developed and expanded ever since.

Therefore, my knowledge of numismatics was gained through practical experience – collecting, dealing in and viewing countless coins – and through countless hours spent reading reference works written by experts on several different series of coins. Added to this, over the last 12 years I have been deeply involved in the identification and cataloguing of metal detecting finds.

THE DEVELOPMENT OF METAL DETECTING

Metal detecting is a hobby that first took off during the 1960s (see, for example, Palmer 1997; Addyman, chapter 5). As specially designed detecting machines became widely available the popularity of the hobby grew, as did find rates – but the latter not, initially at least, to any great degree. Many enthusiasts gave up the hobby when after only a few search sessions they failed to find anything significant. At first most detectorists targeted parks, beaches, woods and footpaths when searching for finds. These places tended to produce little other than coins and artefacts from the Victorian period onwards. When the main focus shifted to farmland the situation changed, for it was soon discovered that areas which produced crops of one kind or another regularly produced finds that dated back hundreds or thousands of years. The focus on farmland, together with further improvements in the efficiency of detecting machines and the increasing skill of metal detecting enthusiasts, led to an improvement in find rates. I date the start of this improvement to roughly 1975.

My own introduction to metal detecting and its enthusiasts dates from 1996, when I was asked to talk about coins to a local club. As my talk had been announced at a previous meeting, members had brought in several of their finds to show me. I remember being quite amazed at the range and quality of the coins I saw and being very impressed by the enthusiasm of the detectorists themselves. By way of thanks for my short talk I was made an honorary member of the club and was invited to attend an outing. I said that I would love to go out with the club but that I did not drive, so could not get to a site, and in any case I did not own a detecting machine. To my surprise I was offered a lift and the loan of a machine and the following Sunday I had my first practical experience of metal detecting. This is a hobby that most certainly would not suit everyone but I was immediately hooked. That an electronic gadget could tell me if there was a metallic object hidden just below the surface of the soil seemed quite fantastic. My first outing produced a number of pieces of scrap metal and little else, except a very worn Victorian halfpenny. However, many other club members found several coins each, which seemed to indicate that I could look forward to a higher degree of success when I gained more experience. On my third or fourth outing with the club I saw a member unearth a Roman fibula in quite astonishing condition and over the months that followed I saw many, many more finds of equal quality. Of course, intermixed with these were thousands upon thousands of pieces of scrap metal removed from various sites.

Metal detecting had often received a bad press over the years, so when I became involved in the hobby I set out to attempt to improve its image. Choosing the popular rather than the academic press, as I wished to spread the word to a wide audience rather than a very narrow one, I wrote articles for a number of publications, always stressing the positive aspects of the hobby (see, for example, Spencer 1998a; 1998b; 1999a; 1999b; 2000b). Around the same time I started to write for *The Searcher*, the leading monthly publication focusing on metal detecting, and have continued to do so ever since.

As a result of doing identifications for detectorists, giving talks to numerous detecting clubs and societies and being present during many search sessions, I have seen far more rare coins through my involvement in metal detecting than I did during the much longer period when I was purely a numismatist.

THE IMPACT OF METAL DETECTING FINDS ON MY UNDERSTANDING OF COINAGE PRODUCTION, USE AND CIRCULATION

Before being introduced to metal detecting I had a broad knowledge of numismatics from the Celtic period up to the demise of the pre-decimal system. As already stated, this knowledge had been built up through seeing and handling coins and from in-depth reading about coins and coinages. I was therefore pretty confident as to what detectorists would find. I knew about the peaks and troughs of cash economies and believed that coin finds would be in line with these peaks and troughs. In some series the coins produced from the soil confirmed my expectations. For example, I saw significant numbers of small Roman base-metal coins being unearthed and heard of many more. If confirmation were needed that in Roman Britain a cash economy stretched far and wide, the material evidence has been provided by metal detecting finds (Fig 11.1). In most areas there was then a long gap in time before coins, once again, became widely used during the reign of Henry II. I have calculated that for the period from then to the start of the reign of Charles II, not far short of 20,000 individual hammered coins are found every year (Spencer 2000a). Numismatists know that few silver coins of George I, II and III (pre-

FIG 11.1: GROUP OF SMALL BASE-METAL ROMAN COINS. HUNDREDS OF THOUSANDS OF SIMILAR COINS HAVE BEEN UNEARTHED AS SINGLETON FINDS ON MANY, MANY SITES IN DIFFERENT PARTS OF BRITAIN.

© PETER SPENCER

1800) actually circulated; should proof have been needed then it is provided by the rarity of these coins as detecting finds.

However, in part owing to the sheer numbers being found, coins belonging to some other series did not match my expectations. Anglo-Saxon silver sceattas, for example, used to be quite rare. During the 20-year period in which I was dealing in coins not a single specimen passed through my hands, so I expected to see very few as detecting finds. In actual fact, over fairly recent years, *thousands* of sceattas have been unearthed by metal detectorists in many different parts of the country. I myself have recorded scores of examples, including a number of previously unrecorded varieties. Fewer Saxon pennies have been found but those that have turned up have not followed the pattern I would have expected. For example, in general early Saxon pennies are rarer than the later ones (from Aethelred II onwards), yet I have seen more early coins as detecting finds than later ones. And when it comes to the later pennies I expected the more common mints, moneyers and types to predominate; this has not been the case, as I have seen a disproportionate number of new mint/moneyer/type combinations. Few coins circulated during the Norman period, so I believed that few would be found. Sure enough, this is what has happened. However, rather than being of known mint/moneyer/type combinations, a high percentage of those I have seen have been unrecorded mints for type or moneyers for mint.

In some cases, therefore, my expectations – based upon my previous knowledge of numismatics – were questioned as I realised that the soil seemed to be producing things that it 'should not'. The most significant example relates to the early–middle Plantagenet period, where my understanding was questioned quite dramatically. Many coins were produced by the Norman kings but the soil tells us that few actually circulated. During the first coinage of Henry II (the cross and crosslets or 'Tealby' coinage, 1158–80) a greater quantity of coin was struck but certainly not enough to say there was a cash economy during this period. The situation changed very quickly indeed with the voided short cross coinage of Henry II, which commenced in 1180. The standard unit of currency (the silver penny) was struck in far greater numbers than ever before. Prior to my key date for the impact of metal detecting – 1975 – tens of thousands of voided short cross coins were on record; metal detectorists have dug up many thousands more since 1975. This could be expected, since if a coin is common out of the soil I would expect it to be common in the soil. During the Anglo-Saxon period, when the silver penny had become the standard unit of currency, when a halfpenny or farthing was needed a penny was cut in half or into quarters. This practice continued through the Norman period and into the Plantagenet, only ceasing when round halfpence and farthings were struck in quantity with the introduction in 1279 of the New Coinage of Edward I. Cut fractions dating from the Saxon and Norman period are very scarce, which is only to be expected of periods when few coins actually circulated. Back in 1975 cut coins of *any* period were scarce, including those dating from the early–middle Plantagenet period. I would estimate that in 1975 no more than 1000 examples of voided short and long cross cut coins were known to exist; this total includes all the examples in museum and private collections. In the 20-year period in which I was dealing in British hammered coins not a single cut coin

Fig 11.2: A group of cut halfpence and a cut farthing. Voided short cross type: Henry II, Richard I, John and Henry III (up to 1247), and voided long cross type: Henry III (post 1247).

© Peter Spencer

passed through my hands. On the basis of the knowledge I had built up about coins and coinages I would therefore expect the soil to produce many whole pennies but very few cut fractions. This, though, has certainly not been the case. In actual fact, for each whole penny of the early–middle Plantagenet period the soil produces roughly two cut fractions (Allen and Doolan 2003; Spencer 2006; see Fig 11.2 for examples of these cut coins). This is an astonishing revelation.

The implication of the finds being produced by metal detectorists could only have one explanation, but it was a very exciting one: in some cases the soil must contain a different range of material to that on record in 1975. Exciting this may be but how could it happen? How could the range of currency extant in 1975 be in some cases different to that found in the soil? Only when the material available in 1975 is examined in more depth does the answer become clear.

The sum total of these coins provided the main primary material evidence for the study of numismatics from the Iron Age onwards. There was, of course, other primary evidence – in documentary form, such as contemporary chronicles, written records of mint accounts, die production and other details of currency use and production – but the basic material, coins, changed little year on year. In the UK there would be a few additions over time – random finds of single coins and perhaps a hoard now and then;

among these there might even be a significant discovery, but these were certainly few and far between. Additionally, over the years scholarly research produced more background information about coins and coinages. From the sum total of this – the primary material, documentary evidence and scholarly research – knowledge was founded and books were written.

However, the accuracy of at least some of these pre-1975 books must now be questioned. Such questioning depends on the book's intent: Seaby's *Standard Catalogue* aimed to provide a list of all the known main varieties and dates of coins struck from the earliest time up to the present day, together with their retail prices. To this extent the *Standard Catalogue* was very accurate. However, more specialised works contained information based upon research done by the author or by others. Later research might question earlier work, or could lead to completely fresh conclusions being drawn, which might be accepted as definitive or be questioned in turn by other scholars. A tiny minority of scholars might have been careless in their approach to numismatics but the great majority tried to be as accurate as possible. However, in 1975 numismatic scholarship was based upon the material evidence then available. Research moved forward, as it had done for decades previously, but most of the research and study was on existing material, rather than on anything new. Reference works, therefore, were as accurate as they could be in the light of the material available to scholars in 1975.

To make sense of the finds made by metal detectorists since 1975 the collections, both private and institutional, in which pre-1975 coin finds were kept had to be reappraised. How had they survived? Where had they come from? All the coins known in 1975 would originally have fitted into one of the six different categories listed in Table 1. When we take into consideration how the coins came to be in these categories we begin to understand why in some cases a different picture (to that available in 1975) has begun to emerge over more recent years.

In the case of early coins the majority of those known in 1975 would originally have formed part of a hoard. A small proportion will have been random finds or have been used as votive offerings. In total, there would be a large number of coins from categories 4, 5, and 6, but most of these would probably date from the 15th century and later. A high proportion of the coins in categories 2 and 3 would not only be old, they would also be contemporary with the period they were donated or lost and would be likely to be of low face value.

There are two basic types of hoard: savings and currency. Savings hoards were put together over a period of time and therefore contain coins with a range (sometimes a wide range) of dates. Currency hoards are made up of coins in circulation at the time they were assembled; this type of hoard is likely to have been deposited during times of strife, when there was a need to speedily bury the cash owned by an individual, family or business. The contents of each type of hoard tended to be selected, but more so with the former than the latter. Forgeries would be rooted out, often only higher denomination coins chosen, and sometimes only full weight coins would be included. Coins in hoards might have been selected twice – first by the original owner and then for a second time

TABLE 1: SIX CATEGORIES OF PRE-1975 COLLECTIONS

Category	Type	Comment
1	Hoards	The Romans dug up Greek coins, various nationalities dug up Roman coins, later coins dug up by later generations. It seems certain that the vast majority of coins extant *c* 1975 would originate from hoards: witness the huge accumulations found over recent years and the many others on record from times past.
2	Votive offerings	At shrines (very many), special sites (many), the soil (offerings to farmland), etc. These coins, of various periods, were found during later periods. A large number, but the overall percentage low in comparison to hoards.
3	Random finds (single coins)	These represent random losses in the past on sites and in places where activity took place. For example: towns and villages; fair and market sites; areas where sporting events were held; farmland and other places where people worked. Coins in this category will have turned up throughout history, mostly as odd surface finds. For the numismatist random finds are most useful for determining where and when certain coins and coinages were in use.
4	Passed down	Through businesses and families. An indeterminate quantity (could be quite high) for this category.
5	Banks	Early 18th century onwards. Sacks of coins kept in vaults. Large amounts involved. Some sacks not opened until the 20th century.
6	Collectors/collections	From the later medieval period onwards. Some blurring with category 4. Large numbers involved, the total perhaps second only to hoards.

by a later finder, owner, collector or museum. For example, from the approximately 6000 coins found in a hoard of Henry II silver pennies at Tealby in Lincolnshire in 1807, over 5000 were melted down, with only the finest being selected and saved (Sturman 1989).

Most of the coins in categories 4, 5, and 6 would also be selected, with those in worn condition being melted or placed back in circulation. Therefore, coins in four of the six categories, including the major one, hoards, would be subjected to a selection process prior to them being buried, passed down, accumulated in bank vaults or added to collections. Furthermore, in the past most people were very poor and the majority would never even see a high denomination coin, let alone actually own one. Therefore, most of the coins falling into categories 1, 4, 5, and 6 would originally have been in the possession of wealthy individuals or families. Only in categories 2 and, in particular, 3 would ordinary folk be involved.

The fundamentally important point is that the vast majority of coins extant in 1975 would originally have been in the possession of the wealthy. Therefore, though it was unrealised at the time, the range of material available to numismatists in 1975 was not necessarily the same as the range of coins that was in everyday use in the past. In effect, in 1975 a significant part of the history of numismatics had over the centuries been constructed through selection. Rather than being a history that included every section of society that had at one time or another been involved in the receipt or payment of cash, it was to a great extent the history of a narrow section of society: the wealthy.

The realisation that the history of numismatics had been constructed through selection, and was therefore a history of the wealthy only, has come through metal detecting finds. Post-1975 coin finds do not alter the whole history of numismatics but in some cases they do have nothing less than a dramatic impact. Coins that used to be very rare out of the soil are not necessarily as rare in the soil. Hoards of Saxon sceattas and early pennies, for example, have rarely been found and this is still the case. However, many, many individual examples – including previously unknown types and varieties – regularly turn up as detecting finds.

The majority of later Saxon and Norman pennies have been found in hoards. However, a good proportion of those that turn up as individual detecting finds bear the names of new mints and/or moneyers for the type. Therefore, the range of coins *hoarded* during the later Saxon and Norman periods often appears to be different to the range of coins that actually *circulated*. It is in the sphere of what could be described as small change (halfpence and farthings) that the greatest change had occurred. The huge number of cut halfpennies and farthings of the early–middle Plantagenet period unearthed by metal detectorists alters the whole complexion of coinage use during this period (see Fig 11.2). In 1975 whole pennies of Henry II, Richard I, John and Henry III outnumbered cut coins by approximately 150 to 1; in 2006 metal detecting finds suggest that in most areas cut fractions in circulation outnumbered whole coins by two to one (Spencer 2006). This alteration is quite staggering and would not have come to light had not metal detecting produced the material evidence. Later records (from the reign of Edward I) show that round halfpence and farthings were struck in large quantities during most reigns, yet in 1975 the coins themselves were in many cases very rare or completely unknown. However, many thousands of examples, including numerous new types and varieties, have been found by metal detectorists, and continue to turn up quite regularly. A generation ago it was almost impossible for numismatists to build up a representative collection of round halfpence and farthings (Edward I onwards), but today that task can be accomplished with relative ease.

Three of the six categories (4, 5 and 6) making up the total number of coins extant in 1975 can be now discounted, as these categories will produce nothing new. Category 1 (hoards) will still produce more material over the years, as will category 2 (votive offerings). In 1975 category 3 (random finds) would have produced some of the coins then known, but nowhere near the number built up over the last 30 years by metal detecting finds. The total number of coins in this category today might be even higher than the total found in hoards; it has for some time been the main source of new material and will continue to grow at a very rapid pace in the future.

If it is accepted that the soil produces coins that actually circulated in particular places during specific periods then a more comprehensive picture of the currency that was used in everyday monetary transactions in the past can be built up. In some cases the patterns that have emerged indicate that the use of coins was restricted. In other cases, where significant numbers of coins of the same period have been found in many different areas, material evidence given up by the soil indicates that the use of currency was more widespread. In particular, when low denomination coins are found in significant numbers it seems safe to assume that the use of currency had spread down the social scale. Quite how far down the scale this went has yet to be assessed. However, through metal detecting finds we do know that at times a huge number of low denomination coins were in circulation, and that these coins were largely ignored by the wealthy members of society. The post-1975 picture which has developed introduces ordinary folk into the frame and thus can be said not only to be more inclusive, but also to provide a more rounded, realistic and accurate view of coinage production, circulation and use at various times in the past. Had metal detecting finds not significantly added to the range of basic material evidence available this sharper picture would never have emerged. I personally have gained a better understanding of coins and coinages, and numismatic scholarship in general has benefited and will continue to do so through the discoveries made by metal detecting enthusiasts.

Conclusion

Those who set out to write history books choose from a vast range of subject matter, write for a particular audience and select a suitable style. Academic works are perceived to be the most authoritative, but all history books have one thing in common: their authors select evidence in order to construct the history they present. This is not to say that the histories are necessarily distorted, biased or false – though at times they might be – but that any historical narrative is always constructed through a process of selection (see, for example, Carr 1987).

The history of metal detecting in the UK suggests that the material evidence available to us prior to 1975 regarding coinage had been constructed through a not dissimilar selection process during past ages. There are similar implications for many other categories of finds. Detectorists unearth a very wide range of other items – for example, tokens, jettons, buckles, pendants, harness mounts, jewellery, keys, weights, thimbles and seal matrices. While some of these will have been produced for high-status individuals and families, a high percentage will have been made for ordinary folk and are therefore far less likely to have been hoarded, collected or passed down and now be in private or museum collections. Coin finds can tell us what ordinary folk used in everyday cash transactions, and the other low-status items that are turning up as metal detecting finds can offer pointers as to what the lower ranks actually bought with their hard-earned cash.

With a staggering range of material being unearthed on a daily basis it might be assumed that archaeologists, museologists and numismatists would all be keen to develop good relationships with individual detectorists and detecting clubs. Apart from a few exceptions, this is not and never has been the case. Of course, the Portable Antiquities Scheme has now been running for a few years and Finds Liaison Officers (FLOs) regularly attend detecting club meetings.

However, not a few detecting clubs rarely, if ever, have guest speakers, even though most would welcome the offer of a talk from an expert on a topic relating to metal detecting finds. FLOs do record a wide range of finds on the PAS database and in the case of coins there is the *Celtic Coin Index* and the *Corpus of Early Medieval Coin Finds*, both of which record material from specific series. I myself, in the pages of *The Searcher*, have also set on record several important finds (see Figs 11.3–11.6). Having said this, the great majority of finds – be they coins or artefacts – are never recorded. A far more concerted effort is therefore required, otherwise important information will be lost forever. There is much expertise in the detecting world, expertise gained by individuals through years of in-depth research into their own finds and those unearthed by their colleagues. It is no exaggeration to say that archaeologists, museologists and numismatists need detectorists more than detectorists need them. This is not to say that detectorists shun the help, advice and expertise that can come from outside their hobby. The fact is that they welcome it, when it is offered and provided it is not presented in a condescending manner. However, in most cases they have no real need to seek it out. It is therefore up to archaeologists, museologists and numismatists to forge links with metal detecting clubs, societies and federations. In doing so they have much to gain and nothing to lose. And, importantly, through these links a far greater proportion of finds will be placed on record than is presently the case.

© PETER SPENCER

FIG 11.3: ECGBERHT, KING OF WESSEX 802–39, PENNY OF ROCHESTER. THE REVERSE AN UNRECORDED TYPE FOR THE MINT.

© PETER SPENCER

FIG 11.4: HAROLD II (1066) PENNY OF CHESTER. MONEYER DUNINC. THE MINT EXTREMELY RARE FOR THIS REIGN AND THE MONEYER PREVIOUSLY UNRECORDED FOR CHESTER UNDER HAROLD II.

© PETER SPENCER

FIG 11.5: HENRY I (1100–35) PENNY OF WORCESTER. TYPE 4. MONEYER AELFGAERD. THE MONEYER PREVIOUSLY UNRECORDED FOR TYPE 4 AT WORCESTER.

© PETER SPENCER

FIG 11.6: HENRY III (1216–72) ROUND HALFPENNY OF LONDON. VOIDED SHORT CROSS CLASS VII. MONEYER ILGER. THE DENOMINATION EXCESSIVELY RARE AND THE MONEYER UNIQUE ON A ROUND HALFPENNY. ROUND HALFPENNIES WERE STRUCK DURING THE ANGLO-SAXON PERIOD, THOUGH NOT IN GREAT QUANTITIES AND NONE AT ALL AFTER THE REIGN OF EADGAR (959–75). THEY WERE STRUCK FOR ONLY ONE OF THE NORMAN KINGS, HENRY I; ABOUT ONE DOZEN DATING FROM THIS REIGN ARE KNOWN, MOST OF WHICH ARE UNIQUE TYPE/MINT/MONEYER COMBINATIONS AND NEARLY ALL ARE METAL DETECTING FINDS. EVEN THOUGH THEY ARE MENTIONED IN CONTEMPORARY RECORDS, ROUND HALFPENNIES OF HENRY III WERE UNKNOWN UNTIL 1989, WHEN THE FIRST EXAMPLE WAS PUBLISHED BY PETER SEABY (SEABY'S *COIN AND MEDAL BULLETIN*, SEPTEMBER 1989). ANOTHER WAS DISCOVERED IN 1990 AND A FEW OTHERS HAVE TURNED UP SINCE THAT DATE. THE EXAMPLE ILLUSTRATED HERE WAS FOUND BY A METAL DETECTORIST AND IS NOW IN THE BRITISH MUSEUM. SEABY ENDED HIS DISCUSSION OF THE FIRST ROUND HALFPENNY BY SAYING: 'PERHAPS WE MAY LOOK FORWARD TO THE DISCOVERY OF OTHER SPECIMENS OF THIS DENOMINATION AND EVEN TO ROUND FARTHINGS OF THE SHORT CROSS PERIOD.' HIS WORDS PROVED TO BE PROPHETIC, FOR THE FIRST ROUND FARTHING OF HENRY III WAS DISCOVERED VERY SHORTLY AFTER SEABY HAD PUBLISHED THE HALFPENNY.

BIBLIOGRAPHY

Allen, M, and Doolan, P D, 2003 Finds From Dunwich, *British Numismatic Journal* 72: 85–94

Carr, E H, 1987 *What is History?* Editorial matter in the 1987 edition by R W Davies, Penguin, London

Corpus of Early Medieval Coin Finds, available at http://www.fitzmuseum.cam.ac.uk/coins/emc/ (24 July 2008)

Oxford Celtic Coin Index, The, available at http://www.finds.org.uk/CCI/ (24 July 2008)

Palmer, A, 1997 *The Metal Detector Book*, B T Batsford Ltd, London

Spencer, P, 1998a Not poachers, rather fellow gamekeepers, *Museums Journal* 98 (4): 20–1

— 1998b Buried treasure under your land, *Farmers Weekly* (July 31–August 6): 86–7

— 1999a Any old iron?, *Home & Country* (February): 22–4

— 1999b Starting a collection? Try digging one up! *Collect It!* (March): 60–2

— 2000a A Survey of Coin Finds, Part I and Part II, *The Searcher* (April): 41–3 (Part I), (May): 26–8 (Part II)

— 2000b Unearthing the past – literally! *Antique Collecting* (September): 44–7

— 2006 Cut Halves and Quarters: Statistics, *The Searcher* (July): 19–21, (December): 45–7

Sturman, C, 1989 Sir Joseph Banks and the Tealby hoard, *Lincolnshire History and Archaeology* 24: 51–2

Suggested reading

Van Arsdell, R D, 1989 *Celtic Coinage of Britain*, Spink & Son Ltd, London

Brooke, G C, 1976 *English Coins from the Seventh Century to the Present Day*, Spink & Son Ltd, London

Hobbs, R, 1996 *British Iron Age Coins in the British Museum*, British Museum Press, London

Mattingly, H, *et al*, 1923–94 *The Roman Imperial Coinage*, ten volumes, Spink & Son Ltd, London

North, J J, 1975–80 *English Hammered Coinage*, 2 vols (Vol 1: 1994, Vol 2: 1992), Spink & Son Ltd, London

Peck, C W, 1964 *English Copper, Tin and Bronze Coins in the British Museum 1558–1958*, British Museum, London

Robertson, A S, 2000 *An Inventory of Romano-British Coin Hoards*, R Hobbs and T V Buttrey (eds), Royal Numismatic Society Special Publication 20, London

NOTES

1. The first edition of the *Standard Catalogue of British Coins* was published by B A Seaby Ltd in 1929. In 1998 Spink and Son Ltd took over the publication and have continued to expand the *Standard Catalogue* ever since. It provides information and prices for coins from the earliest times up to the present day and is regarded by all numismatists as an essential reference.

12

Cumwhitton Norse Burial

Faye Simpson

Introduction

The summer of 2004 saw the discovery and excavation of the nationally important Cumwhitton Norse Burial Site, Cumbria. The site was identified as a result of a metal detector user's discovery of a pair of late 9th-century oval brooches, which was reported to the Portable Antiquities Scheme Finds Liaison Officer for Cumbria and Lancaster. The project enabled archaeologists and metal detector users to uncover a site which would have been otherwise destroyed in a matter of years through the farming practice of deep ploughing. This chapter discusses the process of uncovering a rare furnished early medieval cemetery following the reporting of a single pair of 'Viking' oval brooches, and the light that this has shed on the socio-dynamics in this undocumented and, it was previously assumed, sparse archaeological period in the North West. It highlights the benefits of archaeologists working with metal detector users and farmers to rescue this non-renewable resource and all the other data that are being lost through intensification of farming and lack of awareness about what lies beneath people's feet.

Background to the Portable Antiquities Scheme in the North West

It was not until December 2003 that Cumbria and Lancashire received Heritage Lottery Fund funding for its first area Finds Liaison Officer (FLO). Until this point the whole of the North West had been covered by Nick Herepath, based in Liverpool, which was no mean feat in terms of the scale of the area, the extent of metal detecting activity and the variety of finds. There had been some tension between archaeologists and metal detector users in the North West which was similar to the tensions reflected in the rest of the country, mainly relating to trust between the two groups.

In comparison to the rest of the country, the North West was assumed to be an archaeologically sparse area (Fox 1943) where people seldom chose to settle in ancient times, an idea perpetuated by the Romans' written accounts of Cumbria and Hadrian's Wall, which describe the area and weather as inhospitable. This perception has been sustained by patterns in the development of commercial archaeology and the principle of 'the developer pays'. The landscape of Cumbria is either farmland or National Trust land (Lake District) and, with a large proportion of archaeology since 1990 being initiated only when the land is commercially developed, limited archaeology took place in the region. In comparison to the south of England, the development or redevelopment of landscapes had not been rapid, and there was under-investment in the archaeology of this area. As a result, much of what was known about the archaeology relates to 19th-century antiquarians and early archaeological excavation of the area, especially as regards the early medieval period (Edwards 1998).

THE CUMWHITTON NORSE BURIAL SITE, CUMBRIA

At nine o'clock one Saturday morning I was awoken by a phone call from a local metal detector user from the Kendal Metal Detector Club, Peter Adams, saying he had found what one of his fellow metal detector users had suggested could be something interesting, even possibly a Viking oval brooch. I arranged to meet with Peter that morning to have a look at the object. This was my first sighting of a Viking oval brooch, other than detailed illustrations and photographs in archaeological reports. The rarity of these objects in the United Kingdom is well known. A further telephone call from Peter the following morning confirmed the discovery of a second oval brooch from the same site.

On Monday morning, armed with conservation materials, camera and books, as advised by Ben Edwards, the local Viking expert, I made my way to Barrow-in-Furness to meet with Peter. The brooches were stunning; as Peter pulled them from the safe and started to unwrap them I realised these were something really special. The brooches were identical in style; both were cast copper-alloy and double-plated, with openwork design (Portable Antiquities Scheme Annual Report 2005, 60), with gilding in both silver and gold colour and stylised zoomorphic design. I had read, and been informed, that these pairs of brooches had only ever been found in association with burials, and having studied the period at university I realised that it was not only important for Cumbria and the North West region but for the United Kingdom as a whole. I needed some help because if these were part of a Viking burial site, as many people started to suggest, then there were the potential problems of dealing with preservation and security – for example, from nighthawks – coupled with the possibility that even more contextual evidence might have been destroyed when the brooches were taken out of their graves. Many of the colleagues that I contacted for advice shared this opinion, especially James Graham-Campbell, an expert on the Viking period; Leslie Webster, Curator at the British Museum; Richard Hall, the Viking expert with the York Archaeological Trust (YAT); and Helen Geake, an early medieval expert with the Portable Antiquities Scheme.

It became necessary to work quickly as the brooches had been disturbed and were already suffering from some form of bronze disease (Hobbs *et al* 2002). There was also evidence of residual materials inside the hollow dome, including the remains of an iron pin and possible textile. Immediate stabilisation and conservation was required. There was a need for immediate intervention by specialists and it was with this in mind that I contacted Jim Spriggs and Eleanor Patterson at YAT's Conservation Department. A pair of brooches had recently been found in Yorkshire, and had been analysed and conserved by the Trust. At this stage no formal funding was in place to deal with the objects. I delivered the brooches personally to the laboratories in York, where I met with Penny Walton-Rogers, a material expert with the Anglo-Saxon Institute. Once the brooches had been stabilised by YAT she was able to identify them as Type P55 (Jansson 1985), a Scandinavian style of oval brooch dating from approximately the early 10th century AD. A direct comparison can be found with an antiquarian find from Bedale in Cumbria (Hall 1978).

What was particularly interesting in terms of potential archaeological investigation was the work that Eleanor Patterson did on the brooches, which confirmed that the remains on the back of the brooches were ionised textiles, indicating that the brooches were attached to clothing, possibly when the people were buried. Second, there was evidence of worm casts, which form only during the decomposition of flesh. This provided sufficient evidence to warrant further investigation of the site as a burial ground with at least one grave of 10th-century date.

A few days after the initial meeting with Peter, I met with him and George Robinson, Peter's metal detecting partner, at a service station just south of Carlisle so they could lead me to the site and introduce me to the farmer. This cautious approach was essential in protecting the location of the site. But I needed to find out more about the site and its location, and to talk to the farmer about the possibility of a trial excavation to understand the context of the burial ground and its characteristics.

Contextual evidence

The site is located in the Eden valley area of Cumbria. To the east is the River Eden, approximately six miles from the well-known discovery of the furnished Viking period burial in 1822 at Hesket (Edwards 1998, 7). The Hesket burial site was covered in large stones, and although skeletal remains had not survived, weapons found suggest a male interment (Edwards 1998, 11). Many of the Viking burial sites in the area are located in mounds; however, this site provided no evidence of mounds. Instead, the location was on a natural plateau near a stream, north of the village of Cumwhitton. The first grave was discovered in a prominent position on the top of the plateau. The antiquity of the village can be traced back to the 13th century but, following the end of Roman activity on and around the nearby Hadrian's Wall, we have no direct evidence of the area in the early Middle Ages.

Archaeological investigation

The next stage was to discuss how to carry out the evaluation and excavation in order to assess the financial implications of such a project. There was no budget available through the Portable Antiquities Scheme to evaluate findspots; much of the work on metal detector finds locations has been carried out by the local Finds Liaison Officer, with the metal detector users involved, and sometimes with the county archaeologist. However, with this site a different approach was adopted because of the possibility that the site could be of national importance. If the site did prove to be a Viking inhumation site, the excavation of human remains required both osteological expertise together with a knowledge and understanding of the layout of grave goods of this period. This may, at times, require expert knowledge of block-lifting finds. Of critical importance was precise 3D recording to ensure no vital evidence was lost in the process. I was aware of the potential for professional criticism if the correct approach was not adopted.

A number of organisations were approached for advice and for financial support for an evaluation, including Oxford Archaeology North (Rachel Newman, Director), Lancashire Country Museum Services (Edmond Southwark, Head of Museum Services), and Cumbria County Council (Richard Newman, County Archaeologist). Unfortunately, English Heritage was not able to provide the type of funding needed in this case because at this preliminary stage there was insufficient evidence of the site's national importance.

Oxford Archaeology North, who were the local archaeological unit, supervised the initial evaluation of the site, which was co-directed by English Heritage and myself; this revealed the inhumation that had been expected. What was not expected, because of the sandy composition of the soil, was the survival of skull fragments, together with a knife and a wooden chest. The chest was block-lifted using a freeze-drying technique recommended by English Heritage and York Archaeological Trust. Peter Adams carried out a metal detector survey of the plough soil in the area surrounding the initial grave, which was an integral part of the evaluation. These results were plotted in 3D using global positioning software. It transpired that this course of action proved invaluable for the continuation of the project.

Over 100 years ago there were excavations of Viking burials conducted in the area, at Claughton Hall, Heskett, Beacon Hill and Aspatric (Edwards 1998), but only scant written reports detailing evidence from these excavations exist today. These burials had been considered as individual high-status burials, and no consideration had been given to the surrounding landscape or the possibility of multiple graves. For the first time in the region, the distribution of artefacts revealed by the metal detector survey suggested other possible graves, as well as recovering fragments of an oval brooch of a different style and earlier date than the first pair, part of a key, fragments of brooch, iron rivets and the hilt of a sword. These were distributed within a radius of 4–8m around the original discovery.

The sword hilt provided one of the most conclusive pieces of evidence for the preserved multiple graves. This was not unequivocal evidence that there were further graves but the presence of swords *together with* oval brooches would be highly unusual if buried with a single person. Brooches are normally associated with females, and swords with males. Moreover, they were too far away from the original location to have been placed there by plough movement.

These finds provided the evidence required for English Heritage and the County Archaeologist to be consulted once more, to seek funding for continued excavation of the surrounding area. Arguing such a case is neither easy nor quick. What made the whole thing possible was the formation of a partnership with academics, professionals and the public from the outset. Evidence from the excavation of the first burial provided proof of the extensive plough damage, and statements from the farmer suggested that his plans to plant potatoes during the coming September would lead to further, if not total, destruction of the site.

The funding came with the proviso that any ownership issues had to be resolved and that the farmer and the finder had to sign over all finds (excluding Treasure) found during the archaeological excavation to the local museum, Tullie House. After a period of consultation, both agreed to this proviso, as they understood that the required conservation work needed to preserve such artefacts is a specialised, extensive and expensive enterprise. They were also given the assurance that the artefacts would be displayed in their local museum rather than ending up in one of the big, national museums, like many of the other Viking finds, including the Pikehead and Curedale hoards (Graham-Campbell 2001).

Funding was granted, permissions obtained, Home Office licences secured, and agreements signed between parties; the excavation of Cumwhitton Norse Burial site commenced in July. Funding for eight weeks of fieldwork had been secured, five full-time staff employed, and the excavation of an extensive area of 40m x 40m on top of the ridge commenced, largely by hand. There was a high risk factor attached to the project, and no doubt many sleepless nights for those involved in the decision-making process. But three weeks into the dig there was no evidence of grave cuts, despite the finds. There was the possibility that we were too late and the site had been completely ploughed out. The sandy soil did not help and when the grave cuts did appear the evidence was extremely subtle, made obvious only by dampness. When the excavation team eventually unearthed the grave cuts there were five in total, all tightly clustered together. A total of five further graves were found, all richly furnished (see Table 1). The lack of human remains made it impossible to determine whether they were female or male, although evidence from the grave goods, and comparison with graves of a similar date from Scottish excavations, provided support for gender ascription based on the objects recovered from sexed skeletons. Making sex assumptions on gendered objects is always problematic, because it relies on the supposition that individuals choose their own burial items. A further difficulty with this approach was highlighted by grave number 27, where an assortment of female- and male-associated items was found.

Consideration must always be given to the fact that some of the grave finds might well be from an earlier period, having been included as heirlooms, so some of the sword hilts dating from the 8th or 9th century might actually be discovered in a 9th- to 10th-century context.

The nature of the site meant that a cautious approach had to be adopted, and although there was the desire to share information there was also an awareness that much of the detail of the excavation needed to remain confidential, at least in the short term, to ensure security of the site. Questions posed by the public were answered as honestly as was possible. Once the excavation was completed, an open evening for the local community provided the opportunity for those with an interest to have a tour of the site, ask further questions and handle reconstructed objects. It was the generosity of the landowners, David and Jenny, which enabled the success of this project.

FIG. 12.1: COMPILED BY AUTHOR USING INFORMATION OBTAINED DURING EXCAVATION, FROM X-RAYS AT ENGLISH HERITAGE AND POST EXCAVATION ASSESSMENT OF FINDS BY CAROLINE PATTERSON.

Grave No	Contents	Sex
4	Oval Brooches Chest: containing, shears, jet arm ring, beads, needles, ring, lock component, riveted hinge, small hammer. Glass Bead Knife	Female
24	Sword (Petersen's Saertype 1/2) with highly decorated hilt. Ring Pin Pivot Knife Perforated Whetstone Knife Buckle Silver Rings Beads (Melon and Amber) Flint Iron nail Strap end	Male
25	Sword Spearhead Pair of Spurs and associated strap mounts Knife (sheath) Drinking horn terminal 3x Ring Pins Buckle Strap End Drinking horn mount Linked chain Beads x 2 – incl. Amber, Mosaic	Male (delimited by a form of ring ditch)
27	Buckle (Hiberno-Norse Type) Arm-ring (Jet/ Lignite) Finger ring (Jet/lignite) Shears Spindle Whorl Grass Beads (x7) Mount Copper alloy pendants (x2) Comb (bone/ antler) Possible drinking horn mount Pair of Shears	Male/ Female

Grave No	Contents	Sex
Grave 32	Spearhead (decorated) Knife Buckle (hiberno norse type) (Possible associated sword fragments in plough soil)	Male
Grave 36	Sword (Petersen type L) hilt without pommel Axehead (Petersen Type E) Spearhead (Petersen Type K) Shield Boss Ring Pin Buckle Strap end	Male
Plough Soil	Key Sword Hilt, Berdal type oval brooch (early 9th century) Ring pin (with textile) Spearhead Knife Arrowhead Beads Comb fragments Borre style buckle Hammer head	

The whole team involved in this project learnt the value of a strategic metal detector survey, and not to dismiss what may at first appear to be 'a scrap of metal'. Everything that was found was catalogued, plotted, bagged and taken away to be X-rayed. It proved to be a mammoth task because of the vast number of items recovered – well over 1000. X-ray evidence revealed belt buckles, fittings, brooches, rivets or small fragments of horse equipment, all of incredible value. An example of this was the 20 pin brooches that were found in the plough soil; they are highly unusual, not just in terms of the number but because of the amount of textile still attached, suggesting the distinct possibility of ploughed-out graves, perhaps indicating that the cemetery was originally much larger than the group that was uncovered.

This astonishing discovery led to intense media interest. The site swiftly became one of 2004's most scrutinised sites, with extensive global media interest ranging from the *New York Times* and *Der Spiegel* to the Channel 4 *Richard and Judy* show. The ensuing media frenzy focused predominantly on stereotypical views of the Vikings and almost overshadowed the importance of the archaeological discoveries in shedding new light on the early medieval period.

The discovery of the site in Cumwhitton has raised many questions, one of these being the location of the contemporary settlement. Identifying settlements in the early medieval period is difficult because of the lack of archaeological finds and building remains – many of which, of course, were built of timber. Therefore, the search for settlements of this period becomes a matter of interpreting minor soil changes rather than more substantial material remains. The geophysical investigation by Oxford Archaeology North of the surrounding landscape, undertaken during the excavation, indicated a small anomaly to the south, at the base of the ridge. This might indicate a small farmstead, although to date the investigations have yet to be completed. The preferred theory is that the early medieval settlement is located underneath the modern-day village, although there is no architectural or archaeological evidence of this. Further analysis of the area to the east of the cemetery – encompassing the adjacent field – is needed, as this could give evidence of the extent of the cemetery. This area was under crop at the time of the original excavation. What appears certain is that the original cemetery is unlikely to have existed in isolation to the rest of the early medieval landscape. The assumption has always been that artefact-rich inhumations signify isolated high-status burials. However, the Cumwhitton project raises the possibility that this may not always be the case.

The origins of the Cumwhitton Hiberno-Norse (Scandinavian) settlers are still not entirely clear. It is suggested by other evidence in the area that these people were of Norse origin; the finds, burial, place-name evidence and date of this site all tally with this idea. Their route to this area of England is less clear; did they come via Scotland? Or were they from Ireland via the Isle of Man? Both possibilities are plausible: the place-name evidence suggests some Scottish connection and the burial customs seem similar to some of the examples from Scotland (Graham-Campbell and Batey 2002), while the finds in the graves, including the strap ends, suggest an Irish influence; the idea of Irish connections is backed up by sculptural evidence in the area. The Irish connections, however, are made more tenuous by the possible earlier date of this cemetery in relation to the other evidence of Vikings in the North West (Graham-Campbell 1997, 75). The other factor that needs to be considered is that these graves could be those of local people taking on similar cultural traditions passed on through contact with Hiberno-Norse people.

Conclusions

There are many lessons regarding liaison with metal detector users to be learnt from a project such as this. Projects which entail partnerships require patience and perseverance from all parties involved in working together because of the range of views and the agenda that each brings to the project. One overriding factor that kept the whole team going was the belief that the Cumwhitton project was spectacular, and therefore a common goal was to preserve, record and rescue as much of the Viking past as possible. Without metal detecting in the area the site might never have come to light and it is likely that deeper and further ploughing would have caused a great deal more damage in the forthcoming years. Many sites are probably lost in this way. This loss of archaeological sites can be related to changing farming practices and the lack of awareness by the farmers of the archaeological potential in the rural landscape of the North West, a lack of awareness which means that there is the potential that when archaeological sites are disturbed by plough damage and finds come to the surface, the farmers are unaware of what they have uncovered and the finds may go unnoticed. The project changed the view held by both the archaeologists and metal detector users involved. Those who worked on this project realised that the two pursuits are inextricably linked. It has also changed policy in the area and metal detector users' surveys are now written into many of the planning policy consent policies which involve the need for archaeological work in Cumbria.

In numerical terms the discoveries on this site have added exponentially to the number of graves of this period in England, and it is one of the few sites with multiple graves. Furnished graves – that is, those containing artefacts – are rare in 10th-century England, and appear to belong to a brief period, perhaps only a generation or so in length (Newman *pers comm* 2005), before the Norse population adopted orthodox Christian burial practices. The site has therefore increased our understanding of Norse burial rites in England. What has made this site particularly interesting is the possibility of a mixing of burial rites, with an east–west alignment of graves more commonly associated with Christian burials (prior to and following the Vikings) combined with ornate and elaborate grave goods, including hilts of swords and brooches decorated zoomorphically with animals, which tend to be associated with pagan burial customs.

The location of the Cumwhitton burial ground and the mixture of female and male burials would indicate a form of social integration within an area, with more common associations possibly signifying a family plot. This would indicate the settling, or at least direct influence, of Scandinavian people in Cumbria, with an intermixing of beliefs and possible marriages. Evidence from this site indicates some form of assimilation of Norse or Hiberno-Norse culture into the local population. The fact that the bodies are buried with all their riches would suggest that, rather than being 'pillaging pirates', these people brought riches to the area. The findings and conclusions drawn from this site are helping to dispel some of the common notions of Vikings as invaders and pillagers of England and establish the idea that they were, rather, traders, settlers and integrators, supporting the idea that the historical accounts of marauding Vikings were largely politically and religiously motivated, rather than fact; these were written by monks a few centuries after the Viking period, and represented a few cases in which Scandinavian people did loot churches and monasteries. The Cumwhitton excavation suggests looting during the late 9th to early 10th century might have been an exception to the rule. One further aspect which was surprising was that the similarities between the riches of the grave goods found in both male and female burials suggests a similar status was accorded to both sexes, at least in death but perhaps also in life.

The Cumwhitton Project proved beneficial to all parties involved: curators, individuals and organisations such as English Heritage, the Portable Antiquities Scheme, Oxford Archaeology North and Tullie House Museum and Art Gallery. These individuals and organisations brought expertise in both conservation techniques and the early medieval period. Collaboration established a new level of understanding between different stakeholders.

BIBLIOGRAPHY

Edwards, B J N, 1998 *Vikings in North West England*, University of Lancaster Press, Lancaster

Fox, C, 1943 *The Personality of Britain. Its influence on inhabitant and invader in prehistoric and early historic time*, National Museum of Wales, Cardiff

Jansson, I, 1985 *Ovala Spännbucklor: en studie av vikingatida standardsmycken med utgångspunkt från Björkö-fynden*, (*Oval brooches: a study of Viking Period standard jewellery based on the finds from Björkö (Birka) Sweden*), Aun 7, Uppsala Universitet, Uppsala

Graham-Campbell, J, and Batey, C E, 2002 *Vikings in Scotland: an archaeological survey*, Edinburgh University Press, Edinburgh

Graham-Campbell, J, 2001 *The Viking World*, Frances Lincoln Limited, London

Hall, R A, 1978 *Viking Age York and the North*, Council for British Archaeology, London

Hobbs, R, Honeycombe, C, and Watkins, S, 2002 *Guide to Conservation for Metal Detecting*, Tempus Publishing Ltd, London

Pitts, M, Adams, P, Lupton, A, and Simpson, F, 2004 Cumwhitton Norse Burial, *British Archaeology* 79: 28–31

13

The Portable Antiquities Scheme in the North

Philippa Walton and Dot Boughton

Introduction

Every year many thousands of archaeological objects are discovered through the Portable Antiquities Scheme (PAS), which was established in 1997 to promote the recording of these finds and broaden public awareness of the importance of objects for understanding our past (see Bland, chapter 6). At the heart of the Scheme is its network of Finds Liaison Officers (FLOs), who promote the Scheme, record finds, give advice on conservation and the 1996 *Treasure Act*, and encourage liaison between members of the public, metal detector users, archaeologists and museums.

The North

Prior to 2003, there were no Finds Liaison Officers north of Liverpool and York. Occasional finds were reported to local museums such as the Museum of Antiquities in Newcastle, Tullie House Museum and Art Gallery in Carlisle and the Museum of Lancashire in Preston, but there was no framework in place to ensure the dissemination of this valuable information to Historic Environment Records and researchers. The situation improved with the expansion of the Portable Antiquities Scheme nationwide in 2003. Two FLOs have been appointed in the North, one covering Lancashire and Cumbria and the other the counties of Northumberland, Tyne and Wear, Durham and Teesside. However, the PAS is still very much in its infancy in this region and faces several challenges.

Challenges

In common with most other areas of England and Wales, the largest group of finders of archaeological objects are metal detector users, most of whom belong to metal detecting clubs. At present there are 14 clubs in the North East and five clubs in the North West, with a total membership of approximately 300. However, both the numbers of clubs and members fluctuate quite substantially from year to year, making regular contact difficult at times. Unfortunately, the relationship between the archaeological profession and the metal detecting hobby is less developed in the North than in other parts of England, such as East Anglia. This situation has been exacerbated in recent years by high-profile cases of unauthorised detecting, known as 'nighthawking', on the nationally protected sites at Corbridge, Binchester, Yeavering and Wigton, drawing the focus away from responsible metal detecting. This background has meant that establishing contact and maintaining regular liaison with metal detector users has been a difficult process.

For information to be useful in research or the development control process, findspot accuracy for material recorded is crucial. However, eliciting grid references and even parish information from finders has proved very difficult. Indeed, some metal detecting clubs have elected to withhold all useful findspot information and, in 2004, 38 per cent of finds recorded by the PAS in the North East and 18 per cent of finds from Lancashire and Cumbria had no national grid reference (NGR) at all. In 2005, 8.5 per cent of finds in the North East and 15.5 per cent from Lancashire and Cumbria lacked an NGR. It is anticipated that these figures will improve as relationships of trust are cemented. The reasons for the reluctance to report findspot locations are diverse, complex and controversial. Many finders are convinced that as a result of recording such details the area would immediately be protected as a Scheduled Monument (even though there are no examples of this happening), future detecting would be prevented or the site would be overrun by other eager detector users. Unfortunately, this reluctance has always made it difficult to transform individual finds into meaningful clusters or to attribute finds to known archaeological sites.

DISCOVERIES

Despite these difficulties, more than 3400 objects were recorded in the period 2004–5 and figures continue to rise. They range in date and type from Neolithic flint tools to post-medieval hammered coinage, and their distribution spreads from Northumberland to Cambridgeshire. Among these finds are more than 30 Treasure cases, some of which have been acquired by local museums. These include a large number of early medieval stycas from Bamburgh, Northumberland, and a hoard of Bronze Age metalwork from near Haggerston, Northumberland. Interestingly, a large percentage of finds which were recovered outside the North East and North West continue to be reported. The counties of North and East Yorkshire account for a substantial number of finds reported, as do Norfolk and Gloucestershire, indicating that detector users from the North travel considerable distances in pursuit of land to investigate.

As the number of finds recorded continues to rise, it is obvious that the PAS in the North is beginning to fulfil its aim of advancing knowledge of archaeology and history. In the North West the FLO, Dot Boughton, has worked with the local community to record finds from a Roman cremation cemetery in Beckfoot, Cumbria, a site which has been severely affected by coastal erosion. Over the course of many years, members of the public have reported objects that they have recovered from the beach at Beckfoot to Senhouse Roman Museum in Maryport. These have included cremation urns, iron nails, copper alloy brooches and coins. It has always been suspected that they represented only the tip of the iceberg, and that more unrecorded artefacts are in private hands. By

13.1: EARLY ROMAN DENARIUS OF NERO
FROM WALTON-LE-DALE, LANCASHIRE
(LANCUM-3599F1, FINDER: JOHN FORDE)

13.2: POST-MEDIEVAL GROAT OF ELIZABETH
I FROM PRESTON, LANCASHIRE (LANCUM-
3572A0, FINDER: JOHN FORDE)

13.3: MIDDLE BRONZE AGE FLANGED AXE FROM THE RIBBLE VALLEY,
LANCASHIRE (LANCUM-D84888, FINDER: NEIL BARRY)

13.4: ROMAN FLAGON FROM BECKFOOT, CUMBRIA (LANCUM-BA9242, RECORDED AT FINDS DAY IN MAWBRAY, CUMBRIA)

13.5: ROMAN BEAKER FROM BECKFOOT, CUMBRIA (LANCUM-BAEE35, RECORDED AT FINDS DAY IN MAWBRAY, CUMBRIA)

holding a series of 'Finds Days', Dot was able to catalogue a range of objects including four intact Roman vessels – a flagon, a black burnished ware urn and two smaller cups. None of these items had been recorded previously and they therefore represent exciting new information about the Roman cemetery.

In the North East, a further important discovery was the large assemblage of Roman finds recovered from the River Tees at Piercebridge by divers Bob Middlemass and Rolfe Mitchinson in the late 1980s and 1990s. The assemblage comprises more than 3000 objects, including coins, brooches and pottery vessels which the FLO, Philippa Walton, and her assistant Frances MacIntosh packaged, photographed and catalogued. Preliminary analysis suggests that the finds are a combination of refuse from the fort and a series of votive deposits, possibly associated with the conjectural location of a bridge across the river. They represent an important assemblage, complementing material recovered from excavations within the fort during the 1970s. They have the potential to provide tremendous insight into army and religious life in the Roman North in the 2nd and 3rd centuries AD.

On a smaller scale, some individual detector users are building up detailed pictures of the archaeological landscape in the areas in which they undertake their hobby. Although most have not embraced GPS technology, several finders make a considerable effort to ensure the accurate plotting of their finds with Ordnance Survey mapping. For example, Wayne Clynes has identified significant Bronze Age and medieval finds scatters near Warkworth, Northumberland, as a consequence of his meticulous plotting of all finds. Similarly, Peter Hayes has contributed to the understanding of the archaeology of the Preston area by following a similar process and recording the findspot of every object he has ever found.

Conclusion

We hope to have shown in this short paper that the Portable Antiquities Scheme is making a real contribution to our understanding of the archaeology of the North. From unusual Bronze Age hoards in Northumberland to a Viking cemetery in Cumbria, objects recorded by the FLOs have proved to have both local and national significance. The challenge for the future is to build on these initial successes and continue to cultivate a culture of cooperation with the metal detecting community.

14

Wanborough Revisited: The Rights and Wrongs of Treasure Trove Law in England and Wales

SUZIE THOMAS

INTRODUCTION

Wanborough is a small, pleasant village near Guildford in Surrey, famed for its 14th-century Great Barn (Guildford Borough Council 2007) and recommended as a 'delightful situation' for prospective homebuyers (*The Good Move Guide* 2004). Yet in the past few decades its name has become synonymous in British archaeology and metal detecting with an infamous looting incident, when the Romano-British temple site was raided, and the almost equally infamous subsequent series of trials of metal detector users. While Wanborough is not unique in its status as a looted site in England – other documented cases include Corbridge in Northumberland (Dobinson and Denison 1995; Addyman and Brodie 2002, 181) and Donhead St Mary in Wiltshire (McKie 1996) – it is this chapter's argument that the significance of Wanborough was not so much in its importance as an archaeological site, but in the opportunities taken to politicise the looting of this site, and also the subsequent trials, ultimately contributing to a major change in the law concerning the treatment of finds of archaeological importance in England and Wales.

The initial incident of looting at Wanborough, in 1983, is analysed in view of its significance for the attempts by archaeologists to curtail and control treasure hunting in England and Wales, especially their growing concern in the late 1970s and 1980s with the rise in popularity of metal detecting. It is also analysed in terms of the incident's impact on laws relating to archaeology in England and Wales. England and Wales are focused on in this chapter rather than the whole of the United Kingdom simply because of legislative differences in Scotland and Northern Ireland and in the UK Crown Dependencies. At the time of the Wanborough looting incident, the predominant law affecting portable antiquities in England and Wales was the Treasure Trove common law, which was replaced by the 1996 *Treasure Act* (which came into force in 1997). This change came about, however, only after years of campaigning for a change in the law, a pursuit that was arguably assisted by the severity of the damage at Wanborough and the determination of those involved to use the unfortunate incident to their advantage as a way of illustrating the need for change.

It is self explanatory to all archaeologists that much of the information to be discovered from an artefact stems from its physical context within the landscape, whether this is underground or within a standing structure. Without this information, an object is 'orphaned' from its past and that of the people who produced it (University of Cambridge 2001). Yet it is this information that is often lost before there has been any opportunity for the object to contribute to the archaeological record.

Many authors have already discussed the international trade in antiquities and its implications for the study of archaeology. They argue that it is, and has been, a major contributor to the problem of archaeological material being illicitly removed from its site of origin (eg Skeates 2000; Renfrew 2000; Brodie 2002). Renfrew (1995, xvii) has stated that '… the looting of archaeological sites has become what is probably the world's most serious threat to our archaeological heritage', and specific examples of sites and artefacts known to have suffered from looting for commercial gain are numerous. Angkor Wat, Cambodia (Thosarat 2001, 8), Sipán, Peru (Alva 2001, 93), and the Lydian Hoard (Kaye and Main 1995) are only a few of the most prominent examples from thousands of instances. This chapter only touches on the consideration of the loss of irreplaceable information about a site and its place within the context of its assemblages and the wider landscape that looting causes, and how to tackle that threat. The primary focus, instead, is the political context of the looting, and its impact on metal detecting. While much of the more high-profile international trade deals with prices much higher than the market value of objects most commonly found in the UK, it is not unknown for items of huge financial value to be discovered in England or Wales, as coin hoards such as Wanborough have demonstrated. The issue of market value is, however, only one of the features that made Wanborough significant.

'THE BATTLE OF WANBOROUGH TEMPLE'

'The Battle of Wanborough Temple' (*sic*) (Gilchrist 2003) has been cited as a turning point in the relationships between archaeologists and amateur metal detector users, sometimes referred to as treasure hunters, in the UK. The relationships between archaeology and metal detecting in the UK was initially largely antagonistic, with alarmist reactions from professional archaeology to the growing hobby and the potential threat that it represented to the integrity of archaeological sites, which could now be easily combed for metal artefacts. There were also angry retaliations by metal detector users towards archaeologists, through treasure hunting magazines, for example. There were, of course, exceptions to this stance among archaeologists. The counties of Lancashire, Hampshire and Yorkshire saw working relationships established between archaeologists and local metal detecting groups as early as the 1970s (STOP Committee 1980). In East Anglia in the late 1970s a system had even been arranged to encourage metal detector users to record their finds (eg Green and Gregory 1978), on which model the current Portable Antiquities Scheme (PAS) is based (Bland 2005, 442).

When the looting of the site at Wanborough occurred, however, it demonstrated the need for cooperation between archaeologists and responsible metal detector users, who were concerned not only with the damage to the physical remains of the past but also the damage to the reputation of metal detecting. It has been credited with changing the 'ancient treasure trove law' (Gilchrist 2003), with Surrey Archaeological Society claiming that the 1996 *Treasure Act* 'came about as a direct result of the Society's experiences' with Wanborough (Graham 2004, 307). On the other hand, it has also been identified as a key example in the deterioration of relations between metal detector users and archaeologists (Hobbs 1999, 7). But is it possible that just one incident in the 1980s could have had such a far-reaching effect?

Apart from an initial discovery of Roman pottery and roof tile in 1969 and a small excavation in 1979 (Graham 2004, 7), not much attention had been given to the Romano-British temple site at Wanborough until the 1980s. In 1983 metal detector users discovered a number of coins at the site. Initially the discoverers acted responsibly by reporting their finds to a local museum. During a coroner's inquest – the procedure used for investigating possible Treasure Trove cases – the location of the site was given out publicly in open court (Hanworth 1995, 173). This release of information led to the large-scale looting of the site. Before an emergency dig by the Surrey Archaeological Society could take place, looting had occurred on such a scale that it was reported that, at times, up to 30 or 40 individuals were digging illegally on the site overnight (Sheldon 1995, 178). It is unknown how much material was removed in this period, but some estimate that around £2 million in coins was lost, possibly appearing on American and European antiquity markets (Hanworth 1995, 173), and the site's integrity was severely disturbed (Fig 14.1). 'Nighthawks' – 'illicit metal detectorists who go secretly and illegally by night onto private land in search of marketable antiquities' (Renfrew 2000, 86) – were responsible for this loss. Even during rescue work carried out by Surrey Archaeological Society in 1986, involving metal detecting surveys of the site using 'five known and trustworthy metal detector users', fresh holes were discovered between the two survey days, indicating that unauthorised detecting was continuing (Graham and Graham 1986). In 1986 too, astonishingly, some of the looted coins were sent to Surrey Archaeological Society, accompanied by an anonymous letter from a 'well-wisher' (Anon 1986). The anonymity of the sender indicates their anxiety not to be recognised, not only to avoid prosecution by association with the looting, but also to remain anonymous to the illegal detector users from whom they (the sender) had received the coins (Anon 1986).

Criminal trials of some of the treasure hunters deemed responsible for looting the site followed in June, July and August 1986 at Kingston Crown Court in Surrey (Wakeford 1986a; 1986b; 1986c; 1986d). Five of the six initial trials were noted by Joan Wakeford on behalf of the Surrey Archaeological Society. The first trial, involving three servicemen, ended when a *nolle prosequi*[1] was entered, with indications after the closure of the case that they had 'turned Queen's evidence' and assisted the police in tracing coin dealers who were 'trading in the W coins' (Wakeford 1986a, 1). According to the Wakeford notes, another trial collapsed and one defendant was found not guilty. Two more men were found guilty in subsequent trials.[2] Of those who were found guilty one was fined £1000, one £400, and one £250 along with the confiscation of his metal detector, with imprisonment threatened in all cases if they failed to pay their fines in the time required (Wakeford 1986a; 1986b; 1986c; 1986d).

FIG 14.1: JOHN GOWER, JOINT HONORARY SECRETARY OF THE SURREY ARCHAEOLOGICAL SOCIETY, EXAMINING DAMAGE BY TREASURE HUNTERS AT WANBOROUGH IN 1985.

(PHOTO: MARIAN GOWER 1985, REPRODUCED BY KIND PERMISSION OF MARIAN GOWER)

EFFECT ON TREASURE LAWS IN ENGLAND AND WALES

The Treasure Trove law was, until its cessation in 1997, the oldest law still in use in Britain (Gilchrist 2003). Its history traced back to the 12th century, and it remained largely unchanged since its description in the account of Henry de Bracton *c* 1250 (Graham 2004, 312). Its principal features were based on the notion that anyone finding gold or silver in the ground was obliged to report it to the coroner: this was effectively a medieval safeguard against tax evasion by hiding one's valuables rather than declaring them to the monarch. Hence, if it was demonstrated at the coroner's inquest that the objects were probably buried with the intention of recovery but that the owner could not be found then they were determined to be Treasure, and as such property of the Crown. If the inquest was satisfied that the objects had been lost accidentally or buried without the intention of recovery, then ownership passed to the landowner (Cleere 1984, 57).

Although it was widely accepted that the site at Wanborough was a temple, it was the interpretation of the context of the objects that was significant in court. The objects included sceptres and chain headdresses, some of which are now displayed in Guildford Museum, as well as substantial quantities of coins (Sheldon 1995, 178). The most obvious interpretation of the objects, given the nature of the site, was that they were votive offerings. This would mean that the people who deposited the objects had no intention of recovering them, and thus the objects could not be classified as Treasure Trove. However, if the prosecution could demonstrate convincingly that at least the gold and silver was not votive, but deliberately hidden and/or intended for recovery at a later date, the Crown would have been identified as the owner. The objects would have gone to the British Museum, or another museum, and prosecutions could take place on the grounds that the material had been stolen from the Crown (Collis *pers comm* 2004).

One archaeological interpretation offered by the prosecution was of a tower-like wooden temple, in which the Treasure may have been stored on an upper floor; the argument runs that when the temple fell down, or was destroyed or burnt, the coins would have been scattered (Collis *pers comm* 2004; Wakeford 1986c, 3). As it could not be demonstrated in the end whether it was deposited for recovery, lost or votive, no ownership could be demonstrated. The looted site covered land belonging both to Surrey County Council and to a private landowner. Interestingly, it was noted by Wakeford (1986a) in her records of the trials that the prosecution had decided not to bring in the issue of landowners' rights to artefacts found on their land, instead focusing on Treasure Trove – in other words, theft from the Crown. This was apparently to avoid 'straying into the realms of Chancery' (Wakeford 1986a, 2). Yet without ownership through Treasure Trove, no theft from the Crown could be demonstrated. Another reason for following the avenue of Treasure Trove rather than theft from a private individual could have been that, if the prosecutions had been successful, the British Museum would automatically have claimed ownership of the artefacts on the Crown's behalf. If the items in question had been treated as private property, although the *Theft Act* as well as trespassing laws could have been applied, ownership would have stayed with the landowners, leaving no guarantee that the owners would wish for the artefacts to go to an institution such as the British Museum.

Interestingly, the defence for one of the metal detector users on trial even called a university archaeologist, John Collis, as an expert witness to testify to the likely votive nature of the objects found (Wakeford 1986d, 9–12). This move caused concern among some professionals, and naïveté was suggested in the handling of the matter (eg Cleere 1986). Yet, in light of the attempts to demonstrate Treasure Trove in the trial, it also raises the question of how ethical it was of the prosecution and its supporters to try to interpret objects in a certain way, when evidence suggested otherwise, in order to obtain the desired verdict, of a finding of Treasure Trove, and hence Crown ownership, in a court case.

What was especially demonstrated through the Wanborough cases was the weakness of the laws intended for the protection of archaeological sites: that the undoubted importance of what was allegedly found on site could not be protected, not only through Treasure Trove restrictions, but also because the site in question was not scheduled, and thus not protected under the other most relevant law, the 1979 *Ancient Monuments and Archaeological Areas Act*. This Act includes Section 42, which came into force in 1980 (Munro 1980), making it an offence to use a metal detector without permission on protected (ie scheduled) sites (HMSO 1996, 31).

Ultimately it was the system of Treasure Trove that was criticised for its inability to support the case satisfactorily in the criminal trial (Hanworth 1995, 174). There had been previous attempts to pass Treasure Trove amendments, which would have strengthened the law's protection of archaeological material. The *Abinger Bill* had been presented to the House of Lords in 1982, just before the incidents at Wanborough, and had sought to broaden the categories classed as Treasure Trove, and to remove *animus revertendi* – the 'guessing game, in which one seeks to decide the intention of the person who deposited something in antiquity' (Hanworth 1995, 174). Even one of the successful Wanborough prosecutions brought for theft was overturned in 1990 by the Court of Appeal, based on the argument that the Crown Court Judge had 'misdirected the jury' about whether they had to be sure that the coins in the case were Treasure Trove, rather than simply sure about the possibility of them being Treasure Trove (as happened in the 1986 trials), before a conviction could be made (Ayres 1992, 404). As it is virtually impossible to prove beyond doubt the conditions under which archaeological material was originally deposited (as was required for the concept of *animus revertendi*), the success of the appeal further demonstrated the weakness in the Treasure Trove law when trying to secure a criminal conviction (ie theft from the Crown).

The *Abinger Bill* was successful in the House of Lords, but then failed in the House of Commons. Explanations for this have differed: for example, Cleere (1984, 57) suggests a certain amount of cynicism and deliberate action on the part of the Commons. Cleere's stance is supported by McKie's newspaper article in 1996, in which he claimed that the 1982 Bill was '… killed by infanticide when the Tory MP who had volunteered to steer it through the Commons deliberately throttled it, revealing that he'd secretly been opposed to it all along' (McKie 1996, np). However, other parliamentary debate suggests that the *Abinger Bill* failed 'not because of opposition in either House but because of a lack of parliamentary time' (Hansard 1996, col 570). Whichever version is closer to the truth, it took another ten years after the Wanborough trials for the Treasure Trove common law finally to be discarded and replaced by the 1996 *Treasure Act*, which came into force in 1997.

'STOP TAKING OUR PAST!'

The looting at Wanborough occurred within a broader political context of the aftermath of an arguably controversial campaign entitled STOP (Stop Taking Our Past), which was launched in 1980 by several key organisations representing the archaeological profession (see Addyman, chapter 5). Even before STOP was planned and launched, treasure hunting (ie metal detecting) had already been identified as a threat to archaeology by groups such as Rescue, the British Archaeological Trust (eg Fowler 1972, 15). STOP tried to persuade public opinion against the growing metal detecting hobby, particularly the irresponsible side of it, but, in reality, 'probably did more harm than good' (Addyman and Brodie 2002, 179). The campaign has been criticised for creating a polarity between metal detector users and archaeologists (Gregory 1986, 26). Public opinion was an important issue: 'A professional approach is vaguely deplored – or savagely attacked as a means of getting public money for a private hobby, according to recent polemics by the metal detecting treasure hunters', according to Cleere (1984, 61).

STOP seems far removed from the current initiative of the Portable Antiquities Scheme (PAS), which was launched in 1997 to coincide with the 1996 *Treasure Act*. One aim of the nationwide PAS is: 'to increase opportunities for active public involvement in archaeology and strengthen links between metal detector users and archaeologists' (Resource 2003, 7). There had, however, been a number of cases emerging of nighthawking around the time of STOP, adding to the concern felt by the heritage sector at that time. Wanborough was by no means the only case of looting that had occurred in England in the 1980s. However, in contrast to the later 1990s (when PAS started), metal detecting was still seen as a relatively new hobby, even though the technology had been around since World War II (see Addyman, chapter 5).

The STOP campaign itself took the form largely of posters and leaflets (Fig 14.2), as well as an educational strategy for use in schools, but a significant war of words began between some prominent archaeologists (through STOP) and metal detector users and manufacturers, primarily through the Detector Information Group (DIG), an organisation formed by a number of metal detector users with the support of metal detector manufacturers around the same time that STOP was being formed. One notable article in a prominent metal detecting magazine declared as its title 'STOP SCUM (that's you)', claiming the letters to be that of the archaeologists' campaign (Payne 1979, 4). It

FIG 14.2: SECTION FROM A STOP CAMPAIGN LEAFLET, 1980. (REPRODUCED COURTESY OF CBA)

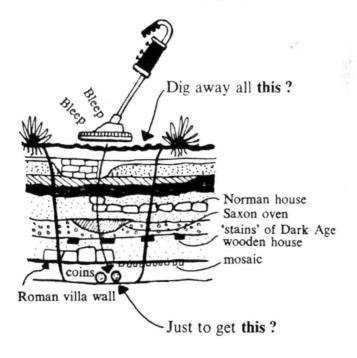

would seem that the 'SCUM' part of the headline had been taken from the acronym for Standing Conference of Unit Managers, and was not at all related to the language of the STOP campaign (Cleere 1979). Whether this was a deliberate misinterpretation of STOP or not, the intention of the article to expand further the existing animosity of metal detector users towards archaeologists is clear.

Conclusions

Wanborough still formed a bone of contention in the continuing tensions between archaeologists and metal detector users almost a decade later. In 1990, in light of the draft Bill to change Treasure Trove (nicknamed the '*Surrey Bill*'), speculations of a conspiracy were even put forward in *Treasure Hunting*, one of the leading metal detecting magazines, when John Castle asked of archaeologists' actions towards the still unscheduled Wanborough site: 'Did they deliberately allow the site to get looted to: (1) exert pressure on the landowners to allow them access to the site which he had previously refused to do? (2) provide an excuse for another attempt to change the law?' (Castle 1990, 50).

While it is not alleged in this chapter that such a conspiracy occurred, the tone of Castle's article indicates wider feelings of scepticism and suspicion on the part of many metal detector users towards archaeologists, no doubt at the time reciprocated. Herein lies an important, and sometimes under-emphasised, issue in the relationships between archaeologists and metal detector users. There are, of course, metal detector users who would never have been comfortable with, or prepared to work alongside, archaeologists, particularly if they are metal detector users who indulge in nighthawking. And equally, even the most responsible metal detecting causes concern to some archaeologists, even today, owing to the fact that even the most diligent of finds recording by metal detector users cannot provide the same level of detail as professional archaeological excavation, taking into account as it does stratigraphy, related non-metal finds, organic material and so forth. However, campaigns such as STOP had their own part to play in closing doors to possible communication. Some have even claimed that many responsible metal detector users, who were keeping detailed records of their finds, site information and so on, were so discouraged by the messages of STOP that they promptly destroyed their records rather than have them be seen by museums and archaeologists (Critchley *pers comm* 2007). Thus, what records there had been of much of the metal detecting hobby in the STOP period were deliberately removed as a reaction to the campaign.

As with all cases of looting and undocumented removal of archaeological material, it is the loss of information from the context of the site and its relationship to the surrounding area which is irretrievable. That the initial looting of Wanborough took place within a period marked by the STOP campaign and the promotion of the doomed *Abinger Bill* probably accounts greatly for its notoriety. Hobbs asserts that when the looting happened it even led to calls for metal detecting to be banned (2003, 18). Certainly, authors on the subject have referred to high-profile cases of looting from England and Wales: the Salisbury Hoard (Stead, cited in Renfrew 2000, 85–9), for which investigations began in 1988 (Stead 1998), although the site is believed to have been looted in 1985 (Addyman and Brodie 2002, 180); incidents at Corbridge between 1989 and 1993 have been cited as an example of a site vulnerable to metal detecting (Addyman and Brodie 2002, 181); and the 2002 incident of looting at Yeavering Bell, which has been cited at conferences and seminars (eg Allan 2004) and made national news when it was discovered (Kennedy 2002); all these occurred, or at least were addressed, later than the Wanborough case. Wanborough remains the 'best documented' of looted sites in terms of the damage caused, and seems to have achieved 'almost mythic status with illicit treasure seekers' (Addyman 2001, 142).

Another important aspect to the fame of Wanborough are the reports of how much money might have been made from the illicit findings in the 1980s, with dealers even buying the coins at the site as they were being uncovered in some instances (Graham 2004, 307). The power of money, both as incentive to loot and as a way of emphasising the severity of an instance of looting, must not be underestimated.

Perhaps one of the most important factors for the significance of Wanborough, however, was the determination of the individuals involved in its exploitation to make changes to the law. Although it was another decade before legislation was passed, Surrey Archaeological Society, along with staff from the British Museum and the Department for Culture, Media and Sport (DCMS) were persistent in pursuing the legislation. In the words of Lady Hanworth, the then President of the Surrey Archaeological Society, the *Surrey Bill*, which eventually became the 1996 *Treasure Act*, was successful '… because of our persistence – we persisted in this for ten years before we achieved our goal.' (Hanworth *pers comm* 2006).

The timing of the incident, and even the unsatisfactory result of the trials for the archaeologists involved in the prosecution, seem to have been crucial for the site's 'value' as a key example for the argument to amend legislation in England and Wales. To take a recent legislative example, the Private Members Bill which led to the *Dealing in Cultural Objects (Offences) Act* 2003 arguably benefited from the media publicity regarding cultural property under threat, and the attention given to this issue by the Government, which resulted from the conflict in Iraq and its ramifications for Iraqi heritage and museums (Allan *pers comm* 2004; Stone 2005, 940–1). The 2002 looting by nighthawks of Yeavering Bell Iron Age hillfort in Northumberland also found a role as an example in the arguments for the Act to be passed (Allan 2004).

Since 1985, Wanborough has been looted on other occasions, as in 1997 (*British Archaeology* 1997, 4) and even in 2005 (Graham *pers comm* 2005; Fig 14.3). However, on these occasions there was no STOP campaign, and with relations far improved since the 1980s, local metal detecting clubs even joined archaeologists in condemning some of the raids (*British Archaeology* 1997, 4). Even since the arrival of the 1996 *Treasure Act*, other instances of looting have occurred. This raises the question of whether changing legislation makes any difference to the rate of nighthawking. In the case of the 2003 *Dealing in Cultural Objects (Offences) Act* it is still early days, but it will be interesting to see how many convictions are made as a result of it. With a national survey of nighthawking commenced in 2007, further data should shed light on this issue and whether illicit metal

Fig 14.3: Recently disturbed soil at the Romano-British temple site at Wanborough, the foreground is on privately owned land, while behind the trees is Green Lane, owned by Surrey County Council.

© Suzie Thomas 2005

detecting still occurs at such a rate as previously believed. Whether it does or not, one has to wonder whether another incident infamous (or famous?) on the scale of Wanborough will ever emerge.

BIBLIOGRAPHY

Addyman, P V, 2001 Antiquities without archaeology in the United Kingdom, in *Trade in Illicit Antiquities: the destruction of the world's archaeological heritage*, N Brodie, J Doole and C Renfrew (eds), 141–4, McDonald Institute for Archaeological Research, Cambridge

— and Brodie, N, 2002 Metal detecting in Britain: catastrophe or compromise?, in *Illicit Antiquities: the theft of culture and the extinction of archaeology*, N Brodie and K W Tubb (eds), 179–84, Routledge, London

Allan, R, 2004 *The Dealing in Cultural Objects (Offences) Bill 2003*, unpublished lecture delivered at DCMS Open Seminar 'Recent measures to restrict the illicit trade in cultural objects', 15 January 2004, at British Museum, London

Alva, W, 2001 The destruction, looting and traffic of the archaeological heritage of Peru, in *Trade in Illicit Antiquities: the destruction of the world's archaeological heritage*, N Brodie, J Doole and C Renfrew (eds), 89–96, McDonald Institute for Archaeological Research, Cambridge

Anon, 1986 Unpublished letter to D Bird, accompanying a parcel of artefacts, 15 October

Ayres, A, 1992 Comment, on Treasure Trove: dumb enchantment or new law? (by N Cookson), *Antiquity* 66: 403

Bland, R, 2005 A pragmatic approach to the problem of portable antiquities: the experience of England and Wales, *Antiquity* 79: 440–7

British Archaeology, 1997 In Brief, *British Archaeology* 24: 4

Brodie, N, 2002 Introduction, in *Illicit Antiquities: the theft of culture and the extinction of archaeology*, N Brodie and K W Tubb (eds), Routledge, London, 1–22

Castle, J, 1990 Back to Wanborough, in *Treasure Hunting*, December: 50–1

Cleere, H, 1979 Series of unpublished letters to R Smith, various dates

— 1984 Great Britain, in *Approaches to the Archaeological Heritage*, H Cleere (ed), University Press, Cambridge, 54–62

— 1986 Unpublished letter to Viscountess R Hanworth, 8 October

Dobinson, C, and Denison, S, 1995 *Metal detecting and archaeology in England*, available at http://www.britarch.ac.uk/detecting/cont.html (18 July 2004)

Fowler, P, 1972 Archaeology and the treasure hunters, *Rescue News* 2: 15

Gilchrist, A, 2003 There's gold in them there hills, *The Guardian*, 17 November, available at http://www.guardian.co.uk/arts/features/story/0,11710,1086627,00.html (4 February 2005)

Graham, D, 2004 To change the law: the story behind the Treasure Act 1996, *Surrey Archaeological Collections* 91: 307–14

Graham, D, and Graham, A, 1986 Unpublished report on metal detector survey at Green Lane, Wanborough, dated 22 July, Surrey Archaeological society

Green, B, and Gregory, T, 1978 An initiative on the use of metal-detectors in Norfolk, *Museums Journal* 4: 161–2

Gregory, T, 1986 Whose fault is treasure-hunting? in *Archaeology Politics and the Public*, C Dobinson and R Gilchrist (eds), York University Archaeological Publications, York, 25–7

Guildford Borough Council, 2007 The Great Barn – Wanborough, available at http://www.guildford.gov.uk/GuildfordWeb/Tourism/Groups/The+Great+Barn+-+Wanborough.htm 926 March 2007)

Hansard, 1996 House of Commons debate on 8 March 1996, column 571, available at http://www.parliament.the-stationery-office.co.uk/pa/cm199596/cmhansrd/vo960308/debtext/60308–05.htm (18 February 2005)

Hanworth, R, 1995 Treasure Trove: new approaches to antiquities legislation, in *Antiquities Trade or Betrayed*, K W Tubb (ed), Archetype, London, 173–5

HMSO, 1996 *Ancient Monuments and Archaeological Areas Act 1979*, available at http://www.culture.gov.uk/NR/rdonlyres/02D66156-A8A6–4889–888A-497C95FE6F55/0/AncientMonumentsAct1979forCase3276.pdf (20 June 2007)

Hobbs, R, 1999 Showing our metal, *British Archaeology* 46 (July): 7

— 2003 *Treasure: Finding our past*, British Museum Press, London

Kaye, L, and Main, C, 1995 The saga of the Lydian Hoard antiquities: from Uşak to New York and back some related observations on the law of cultural repatriation, in *Antiquities Trade or Betrayed*, K W Tubb (ed), Archetype, London, 150–61

Kennedy, M, 2002 Thieves pillage Iron Age fort, *The Guardian*, 21 October, available at http://www.guardian.co.uk/uk_news/story/0,3604,815938,00.html (29 October 2002)

McKie, D, 1996 Peasants revolt in the fields of England, *The Guardian*, 3 January, np

Munro, H, 1980 Unpublished letter to Tam Dalyell MP (Labour), 14 April

Payne, G, 1979 STOP SCUM (that's you!), *Treasure Hunting*, November: 4–5

Renfrew, C, 1995 Introduction, in *Antiquities Trade or Betrayed*, K W Tubb (ed), Archetype, London, xvii–xxi

— 2000 *Loot, Legitimacy and Ownership*, Duckworth, London

Resource, 2003 *Portable Antiquities Scheme Annual Report 2001/02–2002/03*, Resource, London

Sheldon, H, 1995 The lure of loot: an example or two, in *Antiquities Trade or Betrayed*, K W Tubb (ed), Archetype, London, 176–80

Skeates, R, 2000 *Debating the Archaeological Heritage*, Duckworth, London

Stead, I, 1998 Catching the Salisbury Hoard looters, *British Archaeology* 38 (October): 10–11

University of Cambridge, 2001 *Stealing History*, touring exhibition text, available at http://www.mcdonald.cam.ac.uk/IARC/Display/Interactive.htm (8 February 2005)

Stone, P, 2005 The identification and protection of cultural heritage during the Iraq conflict: a peculiarly English tale, *Antiquity* 79: 933–43

STOP Committee, 1980 Unpublished minutes of STOP Committee Meeting, 10 June

The Good Move Guide, 2004, available at http://www.thegoodmoveguide.com/Locations/Surrey/Boroughs/Guildford/Guides/villages/wanborough.htm (26 March 2007)

Thosarat, R, 2001 The destruction of the cultural heritage of Thailand and Cambodia, in *Trade in Illicit Antiquities: the destruction of the world's archaeological heritage*, N Brodie, J Doole and C Renfrew (eds), McDonald Institute for Archaeological Research, Cambridge, 7–17

Wakeford, J, 1986a *Wanborough coins cases*, unpublished notes of the trials at Kingston Crown Court (9 June 1986) of treasure hunters connected with Wanborough, Surrey

— 1986b *Wanborough coins cases*, unpublished notes of the trials at Kingston Crown Court (9, 10, 11 June 1986) of treasure hunters connected with Wanborough, Surrey

— 1986c *Wanborough coins cases*, unpublished notes of the trials at Kingston Crown Court (16, 17, 18 June 1986) of treasure hunters connected with Wanborough, Surrey

— 1986d *Wanborough coins cases*, unpublished notes of the trials at Kingston Crown Court (18, 19, 20 June 1986) of treasure hunters connected with Wanborough, Surrey

NOTES

1. 'nolle prosequi definition: in a lawsuit, a nolle prosequi is an entry made on the record, by which the prosecutor or plaintiff declares that he will proceed no further.' (www.legal-definitions.com, accessed 27 March 2007)
2. One of these three was found guilty of the charge of 'going equipped for theft (with a metal detector etc)' but the jury were directed to find him not guilty of the charge of 'handling stolen goods, viz a Celtic gold coin' (Wakeford 1986c, 1)

15

The Real Value of Buried Treasure. VASLE: The Viking and Anglo-Saxon Landscape and Economy Project

Julian D Richards and John Naylor

Introduction

In a review of the first edition of *Viking Age England* (1991) in the *Treasure Hunting* magazine, one of us (JDR) was castigated for failing to acknowledge that many of the finds discussed had been recovered by metal detector users, not archaeologists (Fletcher 1994). The project described in this chapter attempts to redress that error.

It is certainly the case that many metal detector users are much better informed about the location of some categories of site than are most archaeologists. This is especially true for those times and places when large numbers of non-ferrous artefacts were lost or otherwise deposited, such as in early medieval England. Indeed, the recovery of large numbers of copper alloy artefacts and coins from particular Anglo-Saxon sites has led to them being classified by a new name, as 'productive sites' (Richards 1999a). Travelling across the landscape with an experienced detector user can be a salutary experience. Driving through the Yorkshire Wolds one day, it seemed that there was a site at every turn: an Anglo-Saxon cemetery in that field; a Roman villa in that one; a settlement which produced gold and silver Anglo-Saxon coins on that hillside. None of these sites was recorded in the local Historic Environment Record (HER), and each was unknown to archaeologists. The density of human occupation revealed was comparable to that discovered in some regions in the dry summer of 1976, one of the first times when aerial photography revealed that England had been much more densely settled in the past than had previously been thought. Yet none of these new metal detected sites were visible from the air, and even to the trained archaeological eye, nothing was visible on the ground.

These sites are under threat from a combination of modern agriculture and detector users working on sites illegally (nighthawks). It is no secret that many detector users commute daily to East Yorkshire from North East England, where unemployment levels are high and detecting is less productive than in the richer lands to the south. In the ploughing season one can drive down quiet Yorkshire lanes, spotting the nighthawks cruising during the day, earmarking freshly ploughed fields to return to, like vultures circling around fresh carrion. It is clear that they are well organised, using spotters to follow the tractors, and email and the Internet as well as mobiles to keep in touch. It is alleged that some are tipped off by locals, willing to take a cut of the proceeds, in return for turning a blind eye to the rape of the past. At night the hawks arrive in teams, parking their minibuses down hidden tracks and disgorging across the fields. They come armed with miner's lamps and shovels and local farmers and gamekeepers are reluctant to tackle them. Even where the police can be encouraged to show much interest the task is hopeless. How can they possibly guard every ploughed field all night? To protect such sites one has to be quicker than the nighthawks, to detect the sites as soon as conditions are right, leaving nothing of value for them to find. But even a night's delay can be too late, and a visit the following morning reveals the tell-tale footprints and the holes where a promising signal has turned out to be a rusty horseshoe thrown back in disgust, or where something far more precious has been removed.

There are rich pickings for those willing to break the law. Sensational finds make the news, and many may well be reported as Treasure, but it is the insidious trickle of coins and objects, often sold over the Internet, that represents the major damage. It is possible for experienced nighthawks to make a good living from selling their finds, often out of the country. One contact alleged that he could always spot when a particular Anglo-Saxon site in Yorkshire was ploughed as it was swiftly followed by a rash of particular types of silver sceattas appearing for sale on *eBay*.

Landowners and farmers may resent that another individual is making a living by robbing their property, but can do little about the problem. Banning metal detecting

15.1: One of the co-authors (JDR) working with Mr David Haldenby

© University of York

and refusing to give permission does little to help, and usually exacerbates the situation, preventing legitimate detector users who would report their finds and share the proceeds from working the fields, and driving all detecting underground.

The only solution is to work with the vast majority of detector users – those who have a genuine interest in the past and are happy to report their finds, and even sometimes to donate them to a museum. Here the Portable Antiquities Scheme (see Bland, chapter 6) has had a major impact in providing a national framework for finds reporting and taking forward the liaison and public relations work pioneered by archaeologists such as Tony Gregory in Norfolk and Kevin Leahey in Lincolnshire and by metal detector users such as Jim Halliday in York. To thwart the nighthawks one has to gain the confidence of landowners, and actively encourage them to give permission to responsible detector users to work their land. At least one group of responsible metal detector users actually target nighthawked fields with the express intent of retrieving objects before the nighthawks return. With the explicit permission of landowners they search the affected fields in daylight as soon as the field has been ploughed and in many cases even follow the plough. Their very presence has a positive effect in reducing night-time looting. But one has to be as cunning as the nighthawks to beat them. One of us (JDR) was surprised to learn that he had introduced himself to a farmer and asked for permission for a group of detector users to work on a field, when at the time he was 30 miles away in his office in the University of York.

However, the potential knowledge gain from working with detector users, facilitating their access and helping them record and publish their finds is worth all the trouble. The rest of this chapter gives some examples of the potential of portable antiquities in helping to write archaeology. Whilst drawn exclusively from the early medieval period, it is equally valid for every era since the Bronze Age.

VASLE: The Viking and Anglo-Saxon Landscape and Economy Project

The Viking and Anglo-Saxon Landscape and Economy (VASLE) Project was established in October 2004 with a three-year research grant from the Arts and Humanities Research Council (AHRC). The aims of the project were to utilise coin and artefact data for the period AD 700–1050, primarily recovered by metal detecting, to (1) plot national distributions of artefact types in order to chart social and economic development and change; (2) study settlement hierarchies by defining characteristic assemblage 'fingerprints'; and (3) study the development and settlement morphology of specific sites through limited fieldwork. It is intended that these will then also contribute to the broader aim of improving our understanding of the development of settlement, landscape and economy in the early medieval period. There is not space to cover the full range of results here, but some examples are given of the value of site level work (Aim 3), as well as the importance of the Portable Antiquities Scheme data for looking at national distributions (Aim 1). The full results and an interactive database are to be published in the online journal *Internet Archaeology* at the end of the project (Richards *et al* in prep.)

WORKING ON SITE WITH METAL DETECTOR USERS

Archaeologists have had a troubled relationship with detector users and many have been wary of letting them on site. Yet a metal detector is just another type of remote sensing equipment, and one which in skilled hands is highly effective at identifying the position of artefacts with a high ferrous or non-ferrous content. More archaeologists are now prepared to let metal detector users on the spoil-heap, but this misses the point. If used properly, a metal detector can provide much higher levels of finds recovery than the most experienced excavator. Most detectors will not detect small artefacts at any great depth, but can be used to locate the position of metal objects in the next layer, alerting the excavator to their presence and avoiding damage. Obviously, they can occasionally miss objects, particularly items that are standing on their edge and hence give off little 'reflection', but they can identify traces of human activity that the human eye can fail to see. Excavating on a chalk site, tiny lumps of lead-working debris were indistinguishable from chalk grit to the naked eye; only the tell-tale beep gave away their presence.

Metal detector survey is another method to add to the range of remote sensing techniques. Handheld GPS units are now both cheap and accurate and where detector users can be persuaded to record the precise coordinates of finds, important horizontal stratigraphic information can be derived, even without excavation, to a higher level of resolution than is provided by traditional survey methods such as field-walking. We have worked with one group of detector users who conscientiously log all finds recovered and transfer them to a specialised database for recording purposes. All finds are recorded by national grid reference (NGR) coordinates and depth, and are meticulously cleaned, measured, weighed and photographed. They even go so far as to X-ray obscure artefacts to ensure identification is correct and, if the metallurgy of the object cannot be defined, a spectrometer is used to verify metallurgical composition. The standard of their reports would be a credit to any archaeological contracting unit.

The important point here is that the majority of detected finds are recovered from the plough soil. Within a few years they would be abraded to the point of destruction, but in the interim it appears that they generally do not travel far from their original position. Thus the horizontal distribution of artefact types may tell us a lot about the distribution of human activity and even the chronological development of the site (see Richards 1999b). On shallow stratified rural sites it is even possible to use metal detector survey in combination with more traditional geophysics survey to plot the features from which the artefacts had been disturbed, and excavation can subsequently be used even to reunite finds with their original archaeological context.

At Cottam B it was possible to use the map of artefacts recovered by Dave Haldenby and his colleagues, plotted by pacing out their position in relation to the modern field boundary, to study the horizontal distribution of artefacts. The distribution of datable artefacts indicated a chronological shift in settlement from the 9th to 10th centuries, but this dating then allowed the refinement of the dating of two broad classes of strap ends by showing that geometric forms were found only in the Anglian 9th-century settlement area (Richards 1999b, 8–15, illus 8; Richards 2001, Fig 30). Using Thomas'

15.2: Distribution of strap ends at the 'productive site' of Cottam B

● geometric strap-ends

○ zoomorphic strap-ends

■ Thomas Class B4

0 5 10 20 30 40 50
Metres

© VASLE Project

recent classification of strap ends allows us to draw out other patterns (Thomas 2003). Geometric types include Class A2 (convex-sided with geometric decoration), which are clearly concentrated around the area of the 8th-/9th-century Anglian enclosure, with few other geometric types associated with the Anglo-Scandinavian 10th-century settlement to the north (Fig 15.2). Thomas (2003, 2) describes Class A2 as a 9th-century type fossil, although he does suggest that they probably start in the 8th century. However, he also suggests that they extend well into the 10th century in the North. On the basis of the Cottam evidence this seems unlikely. By comparison, both examples of Class B4 (parallel-sided shaft, wedge-shaped split end, multiple headed) were found within the Anglo-Scandinavian site, and this probably represents an early Anglo-Scandinavian type. Thomas (2003, 5) states that the multiple heads are 'replicated … on a selection of metalwork of Scandinavian and Anglo-Scandinavian origin, including the strap mounts from Borre'. The 'other strap ends' category includes three examples of Class A5 (with niello inlay and silver wire decoration). An East Anglian concentration with a few outliers in Yorkshire was noted by Thomas (1996, 82–3), and there are now a few more examples known from Yorkshire, as well as some in Lincolnshire and Nottinghamshire. It is interesting to note that their distribution almost exactly matches that of Ipswich Ware (Blinkhorn 1999, Fig 2), and it seems reasonable to suggest that the Cottam and other Yorkshire examples came up the coast with other trade goods from Ipswich. At Cottam, therefore, the distribution of Classes A2 and B4 is mutually exclusive, indicating a small but significant change in dress between the Anglian and Anglo-Scandinavian phases.

THE NATIONAL PICTURE

The VASLE project has utilised Anglo-Saxon objects reported to the PAS to study settlement patterns and economic activity at a coarser national level. Like all distributions, such maps have to be treated with great care, and the reporting of detected finds is susceptible to a range of biases, but our work demonstrates that they have great archaeological value.

One of the most important initial objectives has been the determination of the nature of the constraints and bias in the data. A number of techniques have been developed to assess this, built around GIS-based analysis exploring the VASLE data against a range of control data (Figs 15.3–15.4) and a number of base maps including a 'constraints' base map (Fig 15.5). This was specifically designed to illustrate where finds recovery may be problematic, limited or unduly affected by modern features, including urban areas, forests, lakes and the limits of ploughzone farming. We have also used basic topographic mapping, comparing data to the height of land and river systems, and have produced plots of kernel density to determine areas of relatively higher concentrations of finds across the country.

In assessing the potential constraints on recovery it was decided that the best approach would utilise as many records as possible from all periods, rather than a period-specific dataset such as VASLE's. The data for this was compiled from all material with grid references held by the PAS dating from early prehistory to the modern period: a total of 122,379 records. This gives a broad overview of metal detected data across England and Wales with which period-specific datasets can be compared and conclusions drawn relating to settlement patterns for particular periods. The density of all PAS records in Fig 15.3 shows a greater concentration of finds in the South and East, especially in East Anglia, Kent, North Lincolnshire and parts of Yorkshire, with large numbers also visible in the central Midlands, especially Northamptonshire. In north-west England, Wales and the South West (Devon and Cornwall) noticeably fewer finds are known. It

15.3: Density plot for all PAS data, as at July 2006

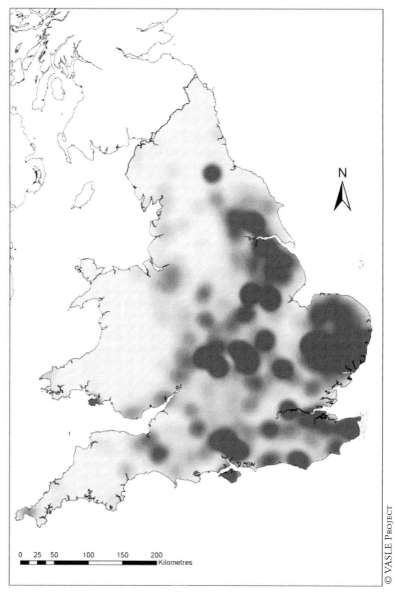

© VASLE Project

is clear that urbanism and the limits of ploughzone farming are the major constraints on data collection, but any area where access is restricted, including woodland and military 'danger' zones, also has a negative effect on recovery. Urbanism has a two-fold effect – there are virtually no finds made in built-up areas, with little detecting and few stray finds, but, conversely, clusters of finds are often made in the immediate vicinity of many larger towns and cities, as a result of detector users working on land relatively local to them. Across the country, most finds have been made below 100m OD, and the vast majority below 300m OD, although some can be seen at this height in the southern Pennines. Historical landscape elements have also affected recovery patterns produced, with the majority of finds made dating to the period before AD 1500. It is most obvious in areas such as the Weald and the finds around the Wash, where archaeological work has illustrated a low density of occupation for much of pre-modern times.

A critical question in attempting to utilise such distributions for research, however, must be the extent to which distribution patterns are a product of constraints on modern recovery of artefacts and how much they can be considered a real indicator of ancient settlement patterns. Obviously, it is clear that this is a difficult question to answer, and it must be recognised that there is much regional variation, producing the complex patterns summarised above. Some of the higher densities relate to those areas where finds reporting is well established (even though Norfolk finds have been recorded in local systems and are under-represented in the national database). However, in general, we can be quite confident that the dearth of finds on higher ground is an indication of ancient settlement patterns and not just the limits of arable agriculture, especially given that even on higher ground *within* the ploughzone the number of finds made is generally lower. In eastern England (excluding the North East and South East), constraints on data recovery are generally low, and so here it is likely that the distributions have a basis in ancient patterns of settlement. In the North East there are known problems of access to land and so the sparse distribution there is governed by constraints on modern recovery. South-east England faces very similar problems to the North West and much of the Midlands. Those associated with urban areas are most pertinent, and the density of finds immediately outside these areas would be expected across the country. Therefore, in the Midlands, North West and South East, outside of the highland areas, it should be expected that a more general spread of finds should be seen but urban areas distort this picture to produce a biased pattern.

The data derived from the PAS form the basis for the mapping of artefact distributions for the period AD 700–1050, and has been cleaned and amended where necessary (for further discussion of this process see Naylor and Richards 2005). Additional information about single coin finds was derived from the Corpus of Early Medieval Coin Finds (EMC) maintained at the Fitzwilliam Museum, Cambridge, but is not used here.

The PAS-derived VASLE database contains 3379 records, over 96 per cent of which have at least a four-figure national grid reference. As for the overall PAS data, Fig 15.4 shows a greater concentration of finds in the South and East, especially East Anglia, northern and eastern Kent, the Sussex coastline, North Lincolnshire, and the Vale of York and Yorkshire Wolds. However, it is the differences between the density distributions for AD 700–1050 and the total density that are most important, as these cannot result from differential recovery. Any differences must therefore relate to specific factors determining the loss of portable artefacts in the Anglo-Saxon and Viking Age.

The major variations relate to areas in the west. There are fewer VASLE finds and correspondingly lower densities in the North West, South Wales and the Midlands, and

15.4: Density plot for VASLE PAS records, as at end Oct 2005

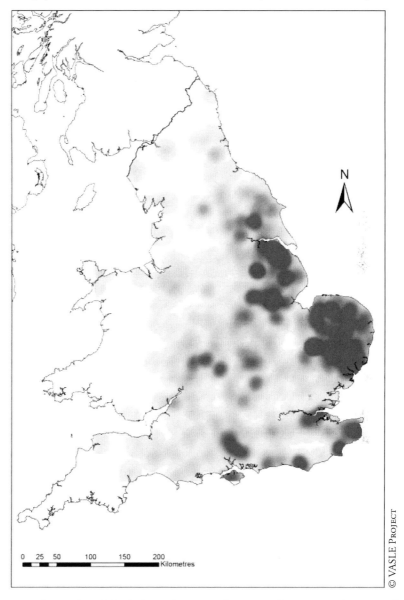

© VASLE Project

virtually no early medieval finds have been made in south-west England. As for most pre-Conquest periods, the Weald has produced few finds, and this corresponds well with most early medieval archaeology. Variations are also present in East Anglia, especially in north-east Suffolk, where the relative finds density is very low. These variations must be a reflection of settlement patterns in the period.

15.5: DISTRIBUTION OF VASLE PAS RECORDS, AGAINST POSSIBLE CONSTRAINTS ON DATA RECOVERY

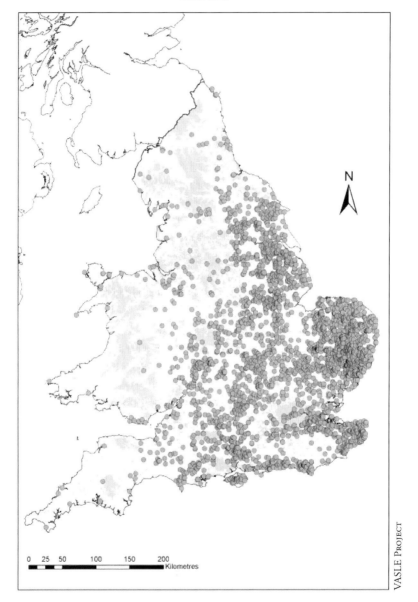

VASLE PROJECT

The distribution of all VASLE finds against the constraints background (Fig 15.5) makes clear the influence of external factors on data recovery and reporting and helps identify which blank spots are real gaps in the distribution of Anglo-Saxon settlement, and which are simply products of biases in the data.

15.6: Distribution of strap ends, against possible constraints on data recovery

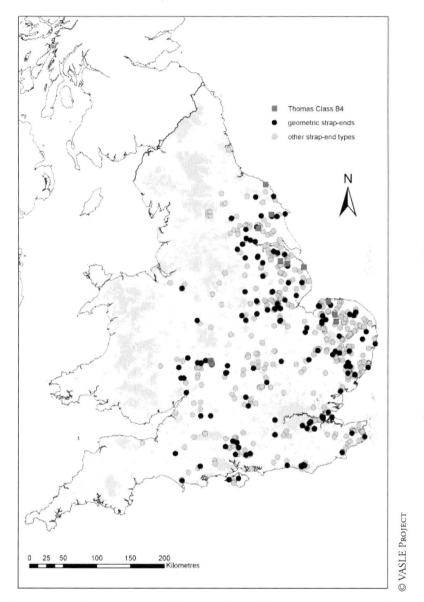

To a large extent the national distribution of one of the most common artefact classes – strap ends (Fig 15.6) – simply mirrors the general distribution of early medieval finds, with the main concentrations in Norfolk and Suffolk, Lincolnshire and Yorkshire, but with examples in Kent, the Midlands, Wiltshire and Hampshire as well. The obvious gaps south of the Wash and in the Weald are preserved. When the same categories which showed intra-site patterning at Cottam (Fig 15.2) are considered, it is clear that geometric types are found throughout this area, but are not as concentrated in Norfolk and Suffolk. As part of Anglo-Saxon dress it is unsurprising that they should be found throughout lowland England. The distribution of type B4, however, is much more constrained, with a strong northern emphasis; most examples are from Norfolk, Lincolnshire and Yorkshire, all prime areas of Anglo-Scandinavian settlement, with just two outliers in Warwickshire. Clearly such minor dress accessories were used as an active means of constructing and marking cultural identity in the 9th and 10th centuries. Even this single example demonstrates that the patterning reflected in the PAS database provides a valuable research tool in identifying zones of cultural influence on a national level, to match those patterns isolated on specific sites.

Conclusion

Archaeologists have often argued that unless artefacts have an archaeological context (and by implication have therefore been discovered during a professional excavation) then their knowledge value has been destroyed, and only their monetary value persists. This is not the case. The recording of portable antiquities and metal detected finds provides valuable information for scholarly research which, in turn, can contribute to the enrichment of public knowledge. Precise locational information about where objects have been recovered on a specific site can help interpret the development of the site. Indeed, properly conducted detecting provides a more accurate survey than most field-walking, whilst national distributions of finds reported to the PAS can illuminate settlement patterns and cultural zones. The VASLE project has successfully made use of portable coins and artefacts to investigate the Anglo-Saxon and Viking settlement of England. This is the real value of buried Treasure to society at large.

Acknowledgements

We are grateful to Roger Bland, Helen Geake and Simon Holmes and other colleagues from the Portable Antiquities Scheme for their help and encouragement in using their datasets. We are also grateful to the countless metal detector users who have made this research possible by logging their finds with the Portable Antiquities Scheme. Our cooperation with Dave Haldenby, Mark Ainsley, and Geoffrey Bambrook has been of particular assistance to this project. The background map detail used in the figures in this paper is based on copyright digital map data owned and supplied by HarperCollins Cartographic and is used with permission. Contours are derived from LANDMAP datasets and are used with permission. The project's website can be found at: http://www.york.ac.uk/depts/arch/vasle/. The project was funded by the AHRC under Research Grant APN18370.

BIBLIOGRAPHY

Blinkhorn, P, 1999 Of Cabbages and Kings: production, trade, and consumption in middle-Saxon England, in *Anglo-Saxon Trading Centres: Beyond the Emporia*, M Anderton (ed), Cruithne, Glasgow, 4–23

Fletcher, T, 1994 Review of *Viking Age England*, by J D Richards, *Treasure Hunting*, May: 58

Naylor, J, and Richards, J D, 2005 Third-party data for first class research, *Archeolgia e Calcolatori* 16: 83–91

Richards, J D, 1991 *Viking Age England*, B T Batsford/English Heritage, London

— 1999a What's so special about 'productive sites'?, in *The Making of Kingdoms: Anglo-Saxon Studies in Archaeology and History* 10, T Dickinson and D Griffiths (eds), Oxford, 71–80

— 1999b Cottam: An Anglian and Anglo-Scandinavian settlement on the Yorkshire Wolds, *Archaeological Journal* 156: 1–110

— 2001 Anglian and Anglo-Scandinavian Cottam: linking digital publication and archive, *Internet Archaeology* 10, available at http://intarch.ac.uk/journal/issue10/richards/index.html (7 February 2008)

Richards, J D, Naylor, J, and Holas-Clark, C, in prep Anglo-Saxon landscape and economy: using portable antiquities to study Anglo-Saxon and Viking Age England, *Internet Archaeology*

Thomas, G, 1996 Silver wire strap-ends from East Anglia, *Anglo-Saxon Studies in Archaeology and History* 9, Oxford: 81–100

— 2003 Late Anglo-Saxon and Viking-Age strap-ends 750–1100: part 1, Finds Research Group Datasheet 32

16

'The Rust of Time': Metal Detecting and Battlefield Archaeology

Tony Pollard

Introduction

The archaeological remains of battlefields are almost unique in that they exist largely as decontextualised artefacts in the plough soil and topsoil rather than as features in the less disturbed subsoil or as upstanding remains (this chapter will not discuss the concept of battlefields as landscapes or the issue of graves). As a result, battlefields have by and large escaped any form of legal protection as archaeological sites, which is unfortunate as they are at risk from a number of quarters, including both modern development and the activities of hobbyist metal detectorists. Somewhat ironically, however, the practice of battlefield archaeology, which in the UK is a relatively recent innovation, would be impossible without the use of metal detectors and indeed their non-archaeologist operators, a number of whom have made invaluable contributions to our understanding of these sites and the violent events they represent.

This chapter will explore both sides of this situation, providing background on current legislation as it impacts on the use of metal detectors on battlefields and using examples to suggest how both archaeologists and detectorists can work productively together. The discussion, which in part focuses on Scottish examples, will also consider the practicalities of metal detecting survey on battlefield sites and briefly assess the effectiveness of the various methodologies which have been adopted.

Battlefield archaeology – a historical introduction

In 1788 William Hutton published his treatise on the Battle of Bosworth, fought in 1485, and in his preface to the 1813 edition wrote:

> Whatever omissions I may be charged with, want of assiduity, and enquiry are not of the number. My pursuits as might be expected, were attended with difficulties. I could not even examine the wood in Bosworth Field, without being repeatedly set fast in the mire; though possessed of two feet, I could sometimes use neither, if in searching the rubbish of antiquity, I found an imaginary prize, it appeared so cankered with the rust of time, as to baffle judgement. I have more than once put a whole family into silent amazement, by the singularity of errand. (Hutton 1813 (1999 facsimile), 29)

These sentiments will be familiar to any modern battlefield archaeologist who has stumbled through muddy fields or tried to glean some clue as to the identity of the rusted lump of iron thrust into their hand by a metal detectorist. Hutton's search for battlefield relics at Bosworth bears some obvious similarity to modern battlefield archaeology, where the recovery and identification of battlefield artefacts represents a key component of the multi-faceted approaches which have over the past few years been applied to a number of sites.

The relationship between metal detectors and battlefields is a long one – the modern metal detector is, after all, a direct descendant of the mine detectors developed during World War II to clear minefields. It is a little-known fact, however, that the first use of a metal detector really dates back to the 19th century, on an occasion also related to conflict. In 1881 the President of the USA, James Garfield, was shot by an assassin, but he was to linger on for two and a half months before dying with the bullet lodged in his chest. Various attempts were made to extract the bullet but it could not be found. Alexander Graham Bell, famous as the inventor of the telephone, was at the time working on his device and along with Simon Newcom used a primitive metal detector, in part based on his telephone, to try to locate the bullet buried deep inside the President's chest; alas, the attempt failed. The reason for this failure was that the President was lying on one of the newly invented coil spring mattresses, which had the effect of masking the signal produced by the bullet (Scott 2006).

Although it would not be until the 1980s that the metal detector began to make a real impact on battlefield archaeology, there were pioneers in the UK some time before the subject hit the headlines, with the much referenced work of Doug Scott, Richard Fox and others on the American battle site of Little Bighorn (Scott *et al* 1989), which was investigated to such great effect in the wake of a brush fire in 1983. The work of Peter Newman at the English Civil War battlefield of Marston Moor (1644) is notable here. In the 1970s he recovered hundreds of musket balls from the site of the battle and plotted their location, but most of his early finds were simply picked from the surface of ploughed fields as he walked over them (Newman and Roberts 2003). In the UK, however, it was hobbyist metal detectorists rather than archaeologists who really demonstrated the worth of the technology.

As the hobby grew in the post-war era so battlefield sites, which represented an obvious source for finds, became favoured haunts of these relic hunters. Unfortunately, the vast majority of these finds went unrecorded, with detectorists by and large failing to realise the importance of recording the findspot if any attempt is to be made to interpret metal finds as part of the archaeological record. Without this information the object, especially if it has no intrinsic value, is by and large just a piece of scrap metal – and this applies to all types of metal artefact, not just those collected from battlefields. But while most detectorists simply dropped their musket balls or copper alloy buckles into jam jars a small number did plot their finds on maps or at least record which fields they were found in. Perhaps more surprising, though, was the failure of archaeologists to recognise the importance of battlefields. Although the English Heritage *Register of Historic Battlefields* was launched in 1994, and despite the efforts of earlier exponents such as Newman, battlefield archaeology began to be taken seriously in the UK only in the late 1990s.

Pioneers among the metal detecting community included Simon Richardson at Towton and Jon Pettet and Barry Seger at Sedgemoor, all of whom recorded the position of their finds on maps. Richardson's work came to the attention of archaeologists in the wake of the excavation of a mass grave in 1996 (Fiorato *et al* 2000), and since then he and Tim Sutherland, an archaeologist on that project, have worked together to recover and record a dramatic collection of finds from across the battlefield, including the only substantial collection of arrowheads to be recovered from a British medieval battle site (Sutherland 2005). The collection of finds from Sedgemoor by Pettet and Seger came to the attention of the author when a limited archaeological survey of the site was carried out as part of the *Two Men in a Trench* television series in 2002 and the former has since then continued to demonstrate the value of hobbyist detectorists working under the supervision of archaeologists (see below). Another noteworthy addition to this list is Captain Scott, an army officer who, in the late 1970s, was based at the ammunition depot at Kineton, which was built during World War II on the battlefield of Edgehill (1642). During his off-duty hours, Scott searched a number of fields around the base and plotted his finds, including musket balls and cannon shot, on maps before handing them over to the Warwickshire County Archaeologist to be integrated in the local Sites and Monuments Record (SMR). Scott's efforts provided an important base line for later investigations carried out first by the author and his team (Pollard and Oliver 2003) and then by Glenn Foard (Foard 2005).

Despite these few examples of what can be done right there are numerous cases of sites where detectorists have removed collections of important finds without any attempt to record or report them. The author has yet to visit a British battlefield which has not been affected by the attentions of metal detectorists, as evidenced by numerous conversations with detectorists. The aim of the Portable Antiquities Scheme (PAS) is to encourage detectorists to record and report their finds to Finds Liaison Officers on a voluntary basis. There can be little doubt, however, when the annual reports for the Scheme are consulted, that battlefield finds such as musket balls are not being brought forward, as they are largely absent from the record (eg PAS Annual Report 2005/6). Any suggestion that this absence is indicative of metal detectorists avoiding battlefields would appear to be at odds with the large amounts of battle-related material for sale on *eBay* (Ferguson *pers comm* 2007). No equivalent scheme exists in Scotland and in order to understand more fully the differences between legislation as it impacts on metal detecting in Scotland and in England, some background is provided below.

LEGISLATION AND METAL DETECTING

It would not be an exaggeration to say that archaeologists have tended toward a less than harmonious relationship with metal detectorists. Metal detecting on battlefields is an especially thorny issue as, unlike most other types of archaeological sites, they survive purely as a collection of metal objects suspended in the plough soil and topsoil – which is exactly from where detectorists collect their material (though buried features such as graves may also be present on battlefields).

The Scottish law as it applies to ownership of objects recovered by metal detectorists differs markedly from that of England. In England, the 1996 *Treasure Act* (www.opsi. gov.uk/ACTS/acts1996/1996024.htm) states that metal objects are the property of the landowner unless prior ownership can be established or the object is regarded as 'Treasure', in which case it can be claimed by the Crown. For the purposes of law, 'Treasure' is defined as any object that is made from no less than 10 per cent precious metal, is at least 300 years old, or is part of a group of at least ten coins which are at least 300 years old. Anything classified as 'Treasure' immediately becomes the property of the Crown, though finders/landowners are usually reimbursed to the market value of the object (it is normal for metal detectorists working, with permission, on land owned by somebody else, to split the reward paid for any Treasure found with the landowner).

Under Scottish law (www.treasuretrovescotland.co.uk), the Crown has claim over any object, whether of metal or not, thought to be of historic significance, where the original owner cannot be traced. There is also no 300-year limit to Scottish finds, so, for instance, musket balls from Culloden dating to 1746 would be regarded as 'Treasure Trove' and therefore may be claimed by the Crown; in England, in contrast, such finds would not be regarded as 'Treasure' and therefore would not be covered by any form of legislation.

Although on the face of it the legislation for Scotland may appear to be more sympathetic to battlefields, with the potential for encompassing sites dating all the way up to the modern era, not all metal detectorists submit their finds as Treasure Trove. Very few military artefacts were reported in the most recent Annual Report of Treasure Trove in Scotland (Anon 2007) and this may in part be due to the absence of a scheme like the PAS, although, as previously noted, battlefield finds do appear to be falling through the net in England. Additionally, it may be due to detectorists in Scotland being unaware of the law as it impacts on their activities and, here, education is an important issue. Some detectorists are, however, submitting their finds to museums and interesting material is regularly submitted to Stuart Campbell at the National Museum in Edinburgh by a small number of detectorists with a specific interest in military sites.

Aside from those detectorists specifically interested in military sites, battlefields hold an attraction to generalist metal detectorists because they promise metal objects, in the form of musket balls, buttons, buckles and so on dropped during the battle. Some idea of the scale of the problem can be gleaned from an article written by a detectorist for the magazine *Treasure Hunting* and published in January 2005. In his personal account of experiences on battlefields, the detectorist told of a visit to Killiecrankie (and similar visits to Culloden) in the late 1970s by no fewer than 50 detectorists (Smith 2005). The hundreds of musket balls and other objects dug up during the day trip were then reportedly presented to the landowner and have never been seen since (this event pre-dated the introduction of the Treasure Trove law in 2004).

Much more recently a metal detector rally was held on fields very close to the

Bannockburn site, but unfortunately no archaeologists were present and to the author's knowledge nothing related to the battle has been reported. As far as battlefields are concerned, metal detector rallies are perhaps the most worrying development to have appeared in recent years. At the heart of the rally is a financial transaction between the organisers, sometimes a metal detecting club but increasingly individuals who may act outside the codes of conduct set down by a growing number of clubs, and the landowner.

Detectorists attending the rally pay an entrance fee, usually for a weekend's detecting and perhaps also a camp site, and then this pot is divided between the organiser and the landowner (sometimes the pill is sweetened by a donation to charity). Given that these rallies can attract hundreds of detectorists over a weekend, even an entry fee as low as £5 per head clearly has the potential to make a considerable amount of money for the organisers. Rallies are by no means confined to battlefields but in recent years there have been events held at Marston Moor, in an area just outside the battlefield as defined by the English Heritage *Register*, and at Bannockburn: the latter threatens to become a regular event. At Marston Moor several archaeological officers from the PAS were present to record finds but it seems unlikely that even then all of the detectorists taking part reported their finds on the day (Sutherland *pers comm* 2006).

Although the majority of metal detectorists are law-abiding, there are those who deliberately flout the law. Areas of Culloden battlefield owned by the National Trust for Scotland, who place a blanket ban on metal detecting on their properties, are periodically visited by so-called 'nighthawks'. These are unscrupulous detectorists who raid archaeological sites, largely under cover of darkness, and leave nothing but empty holes in the fields to tell of their nocturnal activities.

The foregoing may have painted a partly negative view of metal detectorists, but in truth these enthusiasts have much to offer battlefield archaeology, having built up a unique set of skills after sometimes 20 years or more experience in the pursuit. Metal detector clubs have assisted on every battlefield project thus far to have taken place in Scotland, many of the members putting in days if not weeks of effort for no other reward than the pleasure which discovery brings. Notable here is the Northern Historical Search Society, which has carried out metal detector survey under archaeological supervision at Culloden over several seasons (Fig 16.2).

BATTLEFIELDS AS ARCHAEOLOGICAL SITES

The English Heritage *Register of Historic Battlefields* is intended to draw the attention of curatorial bodies, planning departments, county archaeologists, developers and others to 43 of the most important English battlefields (http://www.english-heritage.org.uk/server/ show/nav.1436). The *Register* entry for each site includes a map on which the boundaries of the battlefield, as defined by the panel responsible for drawing up the *Register*, are marked. The aim is that a site's presence within the *Register* will be enough to ensure that the implications of any planning application on it are taken into account during the planning process and suitable mitigation measures implemented. Over the past ten years

FIG 16.1: PLAN OF 2005 CULLODEN SURVEY, SHOWING 20M X 20M GRIDS AND
FINDS PLOTTED BY TOTAL STATION WITHIN – ALL FINDS BATTLEFIELD RELATED.

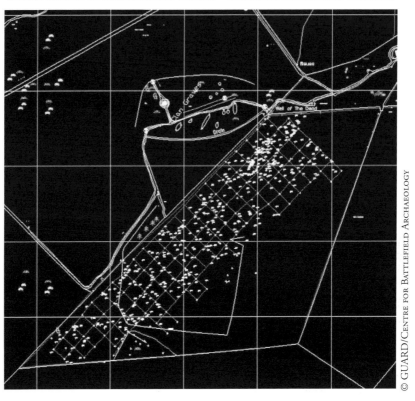

© GUARD/CENTRE FOR BATTLEFIELD ARCHAEOLOGY

or more a number of these sites have come under threat from various types of development, including roads (eg Newbury and Naseby), industrial complexes (eg Adwalton Moor) and housing (eg Tewkesbury and Stamford Bridge). While some of these threats have been blocked, including the proposal for quarry pits at Blore Heath, others, including the Newbury bypass, have gone ahead and impacted on battle sites. The *Register* has drawn criticism for lacking legislative teeth (eg Freeman 2001), and a site's presence on the non-statutory *Register* gives it no guarantee of protection in the face of development or metal detectorists who do not record their finds or submit them to the PAS. It is hoped that in the near future a similar Inventory of Scottish Battlefields, which will provide an important management tool, will be launched by Historic Scotland, but, like its English equivalent, it is unlikely to provide any added legal protection for battlefield sites, though hopefully this is something that could be worked towards.

The main problem with battlefields is that the vast majority of them include nothing in the way of upstanding monuments, and it is generally these to which current legal provision, in the form of scheduled ancient monument or listed building status, applies. Monuments such as standing stones, motte and bailey castles, Bronze Age barrows and even features invisible on the surface but traceable as cropmarks on aerial photographs clearly qualify for scheduling, which protects them from any form of unauthorised disturbance – including that by archaeologists. The same is not true for a collection of fields showing no obvious trace of the battle which may have taken place there. There are a few exceptions, of course: the clan cemetery at Culloden, which is marked by a number of mounds, is scheduled, as is the area of 'Spanish Hill' at Glenshiel, where in 1719 Spanish troops fighting on the Jacobite side erected a number of stone barricades which can still be seen today. There are also rare instances of battlefields enjoying preservation through the coincidence of unconnected monuments being present. At Prestonpans, the site of the first battle of the '45 Jacobite uprising, the core of the battle site is preserved as a Scheduled Ancient Monument because of the presence of two prehistoric or medieval ring works visible on aerial photographs. The protection of battlefields in England and Wales may be made more practicable through the recently proposed move to reform the designation of historic sites, including battlefields, and bring them more in line with designated conservation areas, but what this will mean in practical terms will have to await the enactment of these reforms as outlined in the white paper on the *Heritage Protection Bill* (a copy of which can be found at: www.culture.gov.uk).

Although the threats to battlefield sites clearly take a number of forms – for instance, in Scotland the planting of forestry in the 19th and 20th centuries has caused serious damage to a number of sites, including Culloden and Sheriffmuir – there can be little doubt that metal detecting ranks among these. One only has to scan the pages of *eBay* on the Internet to see the large numbers of battlefield finds, most clearly represented by musket balls, which have been put on sale without any recourse to reporting or recording. The danger is that these finds originate not only from well-known battlefields but also from less intensive engagements such as skirmishes, some of which may be otherwise invisible, as they do not appear in historic accounts. If this is the case then the loss of these finds means that we are being denied any knowledge of these smaller events. A much-needed assessment of the implications of the sale of artefacts on *eBay* and the use of metal detectors on battlefields in general is currently being carried out by Natasha Ferguson as part of her PhD research under the supervision of the author within the Centre for Battlefield Archaeology at the University of Glasgow.

Battlefield artefacts are highly collectable and this is not just a recent phenomenon, as soldiers have a long tradition of picking up souvenirs from the battlefields on which they fought. During the 1982 Falklands War, for instance, the classic American 1911 model .45 automatic pistol carried by Argentine troops was highly sought after by British troops (Lawrence and Lawrence 1988) – similarly, the German Luger was much prized during World War II. But this collectability is not limited to weapons, and as long ago as 1897 musket balls collected from the battlefield of Culloden were fetching as much as a pound a piece in auction (Pollard 2006a). Generally, though, musket balls do not fetch high prices on *eBay*, but artefacts associated with some campaigns do. For example, objects such as Martini Henry rifle shell cases recovered by detectorists operating illegally on Anglo-Zulu war sites in South Africa are highly regarded by militaria collectors in the UK and USA.

An embargo on metal detecting within the areas defined in the English *Register* and the forthcoming Scottish Inventory would provide some much-needed further protection to these fragile sites. What is probably required is some form of licensing scheme perhaps exclusively applicable to battlefields, which is quite different from a blanket ban on the use of metal detectors, which is unlikely to keep at bay those willing to break the law, as has been demonstrated in Ireland (Morgan and Shiels 2007). Nor is this the same as a blanket licensing scheme, though there are many who would like to see this.

A carefully thought-out licensing scheme (which now seems a distinct possibility as part of the *Heritage Protection Bill*) would in theory allow those detectorists interested in making a contribution to our archaeological knowledge to do so through the initiation of community-based projects carried out within the parameters of a research design vetted by the regional/county archaeologist or other curatorial body and involving archaeologists at the fieldwork level. Some idea of what can be achieved will hopefully become apparent in the discussion which follows. There is, however, no easy answer, as the licensing scheme proposed above would do little to protect battlefield sites not included on the *Register* and Inventory or the smaller skirmishes perhaps represented by some of the material on *eBay*. Nor would it protect areas associated with barracks, training grounds and camps, which have much potential to add to our knowledge of military activity away from the battlefield. In the light of these problems the best approach is undoubtedly one of education and collaboration within an environment of mutual respect, with archaeologists and detectorists having much to learn from one another. As ever, the situation is fraught with difficulty, but the author believes that he has gone some way to achieving a satisfactory balance in his own work and dealings with metal detectorists.

The truth of the matter is that much of the current archaeological research carried out on battlefields would not be possible without the skill and dedication of a growing number of metal detectorists who take part in these projects as unpaid volunteers (the author is probably the only archaeologist in the UK to have paid a group of detectorists to take part in a project, and on a par with archaeologists carrying out equivalent tasks).

The fact that the first archaeological investigation of a Scottish battlefield took place at Culloden in 2000 may give some idea of the nascent character of the sub-discipline as practised in the UK. Work on the site of the last pitched battle fought on what is, today, British soil has continued over several seasons and the site is now one of the most intensively investigated battlefields in the country, with the research programme, carried out under the auspices of the National Trust for Scotland, including topographic and geophysical survey, metal detector survey and excavation.

Metal detector survey has been central to the success of the Culloden project and in turn this would not have been possible without the efforts of a core team of detectorists drawn from the Highland Historical Research Group, based in Inverness. A rich assemblage of metal objects related to the battle, including musket balls, cannon shot, mortar shell fragments, pieces broken from muskets, buttons, buckles, personal possessions, such as a king's shilling and a pewter cross, and even a bayonet. But interesting as these objects are it is only when they are considered in relation to one another and to where they were

FIG 16.2: METAL DETECTORIST (SANDY SNELL) TAKING PART
IN MD SURVEY AT CULLODEN BATTLEFIELD.

©TONY POLLARD

found (their archaeological context) that they really begin to tell us something meaningful about the battle.

It has been established by metal detector survey that the location of the brutal hand-to-hand fighting between the Jacobite right and centre and the government regiments of Barrel and Munro took place further to the south than was previously thought. The point of contact, where Jacobite broadswords met government bayonets, has left a pattern of dropped objects which can be read like a signature etched into the landscape, and it is now up to us to learn how to read it. This is the only place on the battlefield where a large number of pistol balls was found, each of them having been fired at the close range at which these weapons were effective. There are also pieces of broken musket either shot away by a musket ball fired at close range (Fig 16.3) or smashed off by the stroke of a broadsword. Buckles and buttons have also been torn off in the struggle. It is here that musket balls were found in their greatest numbers, some of them mirroring the lines of men who fired them into the seething mass of the enemy (though more experimental work, including the test firing of period muskets, is required before we can make truly definitive statements about these distribution patterns). To an extent we can tell which were fired by the Jacobites and which by the government troops, as the Jacobites used French muskets with a slightly smaller calibre than the government issue 'Brown Bess' musket. This is not to say, however, that every 'Brown Bess' bullet was fired by a government redcoat as large numbers of these weapons had been captured by the Jacobites after earlier victories at the Battles of Prestonpans and Falkirk. Some of these bullets have been dropped without being fired and some missed their targets, but others have been distorted through their contact with a human body and it is a sobering experience to handle and study one of these and think that it may well have killed another human being.

METAL DETECTING AND THE PLANNING PROCESS – MITIGATION

Prior to the successful use of metal detectors on battlefield sites such as Culloden, their use as a survey tool was almost entirely unheard of in Scotland. Over the past five years, however, a clear indication of a change of attitude is reflected by the recommendation of such surveys by planning departments and regional archaeologists as part of the archaeological briefs prepared during the planning control process in accordance with national Planning Policy Guideline (PPG) 16.

Recent examples include the implementation by the East Lothian Council Archaeology Service of a metal detector survey prior to development on the site of the Battle of Pinkie (1547). The survey was carried out by a local metal detector club working under the supervision of the council archaeologist Biddy Simpson and the finds are currently undergoing analysis. The work was not executed on behalf of the developer as planning permission had already been granted by the authority but the initiative shown by Simpson is certainly deserving of praise.

Metal detector survey was carried out as a requirement of the pre-planning process in the case of several developments in the vicinity of Bannockburn, where the battle of 1314 has yet to throw up any definitive archaeological evidence. The most recent phase of this work was carried out in accordance with a brief prepared by Stirling Council's archaeologist, Lorna Main, by the Scottish Artefact Recovery Group working under the supervision of GUARD (Glasgow University Archaeological Research Division). Once again, no evidence for the medieval battle was recovered but some of the finds may relate to Jacobite activity associated with the siege of Stirling Castle in 1746, and accord with evidence recovered from previous projects in the area (Pollard 2008).

Further evidence of a change in attitude is reflected in the recent survey of the battlefield of Sheriffmuir, from the 1715 Jacobite uprising, in what is among the first relatively large-scale investigations of a battlefield carried out as part of the planning control process. In this case the development in question is the Beauly to Denny overhead powerline, the proposed route of which is to pass across part of what is traditionally regarded as the battlefield. The author was engaged by the developer to execute a survey which aimed to accurately locate the site of the battle for the first time and provide information which could be used to inform the routing of the powerline. Metal detector survey, once again carried out by members of the Northern Historical Research Group, succeeded in locating peripheral evidence for the battle, which quickly broke down into a running fight, but also established that the point at which the two sides originally encountered one another had long since been overwhelmed by a forestry plantation (Pollard 2006b).

Methodologies

As with other forms of disciplined survey designed to cover relatively large expanses of landscape, such as field-walking and geophysics, metal detector survey has developed its own methodologies and since 2000 the author has spent some time refining what has proved to be a cost effective and straightforward technique which allows for both sampling of large sites and intensive recovery, all with accurate recording of finds locations. It is not the only methodology available but it has been adopted in some form or other by several of the Scottish planning authorities discussed above.

When left to their own devices, many metal detectorists will operate in a fairly methodical manner, working fields in straight lines from one end to another – though experienced detectorists will at times target likely looking areas such as spurs of higher ground or those adjacent to known areas of past activity. Some detectorists will even go so far as to peg out lines to ensure an even coverage of the ground – those prepared to go to these lengths are among those most likely to make some record of the location of their finds, even it is nothing more than a field reference. Such basic levels of recording are very useful but there is something of a conceptual leap from simply recording a rough location in a field to giving that object what archaeologists would call a finds number and using this to identify both the object, by placing it in a marked bag, and the location, by associating the find number with the findspot on the map.

The author has had some success in pointing out the importance of this system to detectorists and it has proved most worthwhile in the case of John Pettet, who for a number of years had been collecting musket balls from the Sedgemoor battle site. While he had always recorded finds locations on large-scale field maps (by pacing out locations from field edges) – he did not in those early days assign each find an individual number. Pettet now represents a very good example of how a solo detectorist working remotely but under archaeological guidance can execute work of a high standard, while his presence on the ground also ensures that the impact of potentially less scrupulous detectorists is minimised as the area is generally regarded as his 'territory'. The hundreds of finds made by Pettet are currently undergoing analysis and when complete his work will make an invaluable contribution to the field.

It is vital, however, that we know not only where finds have come from but also where the blank areas are. The easiest way to ensure this is to apply a grid across the survey area. The author uses a series of 20m x 20m squares, the corners marked by bamboo canes. When working with a group of detectorists each person is assigned their own square, which is then swept along regular transects; though these are rarely laid out, a line can be used to ensure regular transects. The average width of transects across the square is around 1.5m – the equivalent of a side-to-side sweep of the machine. In order to enhance recovery levels the square will ideally be swept twice, first in one direction and then perpendicular to this. This double sweep will not only ensure that as close to 100 per cent coverage as possible is achieved within the square but also increase the chances of detecting objects which lie at awkward angles (there are a number of factors which can influence an object's detectability, including size, metal type, angle of rest in soil, moisture levels, soil type, depth and so on).

When beginning a survey, which, following on from a firm foundation of map and documentary research, is undoubtedly the best way to locate sites of battle (Pollard 2008), a narrow transect can be a useful starting point. Usually just one square wide, these transects are a very useful prospection tool and are an efficient way of locating concentrations of battle debris across wide expanses of the landscape. Once concentrations are located then the transect can be broadened out to cover a larger area. (It is important that bias in the data is not created through focusing only on areas where finds are clearly to be made – as noted above, genuine gaps in artefact scatters are as important as the scatters themselves.)

When a buried object is detected the spot is marked with a surveyor's pin flag and the sweep continued. Only once the entire square has been swept, a process which will usually leave behind it a healthy crop of flags, will the signals be excavated. This is best done by the detectorist rather than an archaeologist unfamiliar with detecting as further use of the detector or a small 'mole' may be required to pinpoint and extract the find (the author has himself spent interminably long periods trying to locate objects in holes which became ever larger as the search continued). Indeed, it is preferable to have a metal detector survey carried out by a group of hardened hobbyists rather than archaeologists new to the metal detector as there is no substitute for experience which may amount, as noted above, to 20 years or more interest in the hobby. There are battlefield archaeologists who insist on using archaeologists for the task but the number of finds recovered under these circumstances, to the author's eyes at least, in some cases appears to be well below those that would be expected. Despite what some archaeologists may think, detecting is a skill which can only be acquired with practice and the author still finds it more satisfying to watch an experienced detectorist at work rather than struggling with the task himself.

Once the finds are excavated, usually from within the topsoil (many detectors will not penetrate much beyond the average depth of topsoil, which is between 30 and 50cm), the find is placed in a bag and pinned to the ground at the findspot with the pin flag. Ideally the find is then dealt with by a designated Finds Officer who will mark an individual finds number and the grid square number on the bag and also make a record of this in the finds book. Experience has shown that a sketch plan of the grid with finds roughly spotted on can be a useful safety net should there be a technical error with the electronic recording which follows. It is at this stage that finds which are clearly scrap – in the form of ring pulls, tinfoil, pieces of harrow, modern coins etc, can be discarded (these should be removed from the site to be disposed of responsibly and not just reburied). If there is any doubt then finds should be retained for closer analysis in the lab – and ideally X-ray should be used in the case of more problematic pieces, such as the rusted lump of iron described by Hutton. During the *Two Men in a Trench* project at Bannockburn it was suggested that a rusted piece of iron may have been a war hammer, though this type of weapon became popular after the 1314 battle. It was therefore a cause of some amusement when the resulting X-ray revealed a modern adjustable clamp such as those used by plumbers to secure two pipes together.

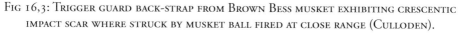

FIG 16,3: TRIGGER GUARD BACK-STRAP FROM BROWN BESS MUSKET EXHIBITING CRESCENTIC
IMPACT SCAR WHERE STRUCK BY MUSKET BALL FIRED AT CLOSE RANGE (CULLODEN).

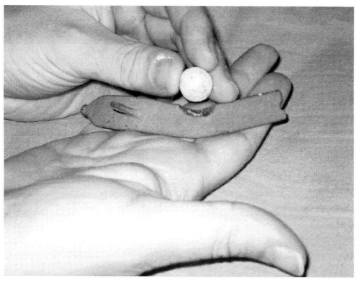

© TONY POLLARD.

Once the bags are marked, the findspot is then recorded using a Total Station (Fig 16.4), with the base of the prismatic staff held over the centre of the excavation hole (the unique finds number will prefix the resulting coordinates). Only then is the bag uplifted and the flag removed. There is currently some debate as to the best means of recording locational information. If at all possible a Total Station or a sub-centimetre GPS system is used for maximum levels of accuracy. Others, however, prefer handheld GPS systems like those used by hill walkers. These devices are certainly easy to use and relatively cheap but there are questions as to whether they are accurate enough. The levels of accuracy achieved can vary from 5m to over 20m, depending on the geographical location of the site. These parameters can also vary across the same site and in any case the error is not consistent.

Some practitioners would argue that, owing to the lack of secure stratification in the plough soil, which by its very nature has been subject to disturbance and the artefact therefore to movement, pin-point levels of accuracy are not required. Experience would, however, suggest that inferences can be made from find locations recorded with pin-point accuracy (Fig 1). At Culloden, for instance, the debris relating to the hand-to-hand fighting on the government left covers a limited area but within this the relative locations of pieces of broken musket and musket balls fired at close range have much to tell us about the position of the troops and the nature of the combat (Pollard 2006a).

Equally, though, it would be naïve to suggest that finds are always recovered from exactly the same place at which they were dropped, as the formation processes related to the archaeological record are complex (Schiffer 1987). However, studies of the movement

FIG 16.4: TOTAL STATION BEING USED TO PLOT FINDS DURING CULLODEN SURVEY.

© TONY POLLARD

of artefacts in the plough soil have suggested that within that horizon the movement of an object tends to be vertical rather than lateral (Haselgrove 1985). More studies specific to battlefield debris are certainly required but it seems unlikely that small objects such as musket balls, which are in any case spherical and therefore unlikely to catch on the plough blade, will tend not to have moved great distances as a result of ploughing.

The above notwithstanding, current research projects using handheld GPS recording techniques, including Towton (Sutherland 2002) and Edgehill (Foard 2005), are undoubtedly producing meaningful results and the system seems well suited to the sampling of very large expanses of landscape, as has been the case with both of these projects. But if these handheld GPS units are regarded as adequate, it is also true that more basic manual techniques of recording may also be applicable to battlefield sites. The author has on at least one occasion been forced to use old-fashioned manual recording techniques. Initially this required the setting out of the survey grid using tapes to position the canes at the corners of the 20m squares (which in any case is usual practice as tapes are quicker to use at this stage than the Total Station – the location of each cane is later surveyed in using the Total Station). The position of the grid was then marked on a map by taking measurements with tapes from field corners, gates, buildings etc. With the survey grid located within the landscape, finds from each of the squares could then be plotted on to the overall plan using tape off-sets across each square. This later process undoubtedly takes more time, but in reality is probably more accurate than using the handheld GPS systems with their unpredictable margins of error.

At Sedgemoor, Pettet has not used a grid but sweeps methodically across fields and uses tapes and pacing to plot his finds in relation to field boundaries. This may sound very basic, and indeed it is, but it produces results which are certainly no less accurate than the handheld GPS system. What is hopefully clear is that effective metal detector survey need not rely on high-tech equipment. The important thing is that the need to record individual finds locations is recognised and an appropriate methodology put in place to do so.

Although metal detector survey is now being adopted as a standard evaluation technique by a number of planning department archaeologists in Scotland, the methodologies followed in the field are not always satisfactory. Discussion with metal detector volunteers on a recent project made it clear that on at least one pre-planning project finds were recorded only to the survey square from which they were recovered, rather than to their exact location. This appears to be a hangover from field-walking methodologies, where surface finds are bagged by square or transect. This technique may be adequate for surveys designed to locate stratified sites in the subsoil through the presence of unstratified finds in the vicinity but for sites such as battlefields, where the finds in the topsoil are, at least in one sense, the site, then this approach is wholly inadequate.

Battlefield debris – the artefact assemblage

Battlefield sites may contain a wide range of related artefacts but the musket ball is a useful exemplar as battles post-dating the introduction of firearms, with handguns becoming relatively common place by the mid–16th century, are far easier to identify through metal detector survey than those pre-dating this time (battles such as Pinkie, fought in 1547, represent an important turning point as both firearms and the bow were used in combination). There are two major reasons for this. The first is that objects deposited during earlier battles are perhaps less likely to survive in the ground, as more time has passed between then and now than is the case with the firearm era conflicts. It is a misconception that all metal objects will survive in the ground for as long as they remain undisturbed, though this fact should not be used as an excuse for indiscriminate collection. All metal objects suffer from decay, with iron usually more subject to this than non-ferrous metals such as copper alloys – Hutton's 'rust of time'. Recent studies carried out at Glasgow University (Wilson and Hall 2008) have even established that lead musket balls, which are generally regarded as almost indestructible, suffer from shrinkage to varying degrees depending on the chemistry of the soil they inhabit. Given that the majority of weapons from medieval and earlier battles (post-Bronze Age) are likely to have been made from iron there is less likelihood of them surviving in the soil (again this depends to a degree on the chemistry of the soil). This may be one reason (but see below) why signature objects (ie those clearly indicative of fighting) such as arrowheads are very rare finds (an obvious exception being Towton, but this is a late medieval battle – 1461 – and in any case relatively few of these have been recovered during around ten years of metal detecting across the site).

Non-ferrous objects are certainly more likely to survive from these earlier battles and at Towton a large assemblage of copper alloy buckles, armour fittings and so on have been recovered (Fiorato *et al* 1996; Sutherland 2002). These are just the sort of objects which may be torn from the person during the hand-to-hand struggles of combat and in the later period are added to by buttons, coins, musket fittings and other items. It is unfortunate, however, that these non-ferrous objects are those most likely to have been collected from fields by detectorists over the last 20 or 30 years. Most detectorists will ignore ferrous signals as these are not as likely to be as interesting, or indeed as valuable, as non-ferrous objects, which include silver and gold. Prior to carrying out the metal detector survey of the Shrewsbury battlefield as part of the *Two Men in a Trench* project, the author was shown several bags full of buckles, strap ends, purse bars and the like which had been collected from the site over the years by just two detectorists (needless to say not many of these objects were recovered during the project). To their credit, the pair had made some effort to make a basic record of the location of their finds and document their work – though this information remains outside the public domain.

The second reason is that the weapons used in earlier battles, such as swords, axes, spears and so on, are more than likely to have been collected up after the fighting for reuse. This scavenging would also impact severely on the number of iron arrowheads left to become part of the archaeological record. Unless they are snapped or hit their target, arrows are likely to stick in the ground and with their feather flights uppermost resemble so many flowers to be harvested once the battle is over. The musket ball, on the other hand is small, and therefore less likely to be collected after the battle, though this has probably happened on some occasions. They can obviously be melted down for remoulding but might also be reusable in their already used state, as forensic tests have shown that lead balls are capable of passing through various obstructions, including the human body, without suffering much in the way of distortion (Fig 16.5), though this does obviously occur. Musket balls are also much easier to manufacture than the arrow, which included a variety of raw materials in its make-up.

The tendency of hobbyist detectorists to discriminate against ferrous objects (something which modern metal detectors have long been capable of doing) has also been adopted as a sampling methodology by some battlefield archaeologists. At Edgehill, the recovery of non-ferrous objects such as musket balls was given priority over ferrous objects, which were screened out of the survey (Foard *pers comm* 2007). There were two reasons for this: first, musket balls and also lead cannon shot were the most indicative objects on the site; and second, and perhaps most importantly, ignoring iron objects speeded up the survey. Despite the problems of iron decay many of the metal objects on the average site, battlefield or not, will be made from iron. Most of these will not be relevant, but instead represent modern detritus deposited on the site over the last 200 years or so. Therefore, given the temporal and financial constraints which impinge on all archaeological projects, such discrimination may be a viable option. There are, however, a number of good reasons why iron objects should be recovered along with the non-ferrous assemblage.

Fig 16.5: Musket ball after passing through replica Jacobite shield (targe), block of ballistic and recovered from sand bag – fired from a musket at about 25 yards.

© Tony Pollard

Even on sites characterised by musket balls and other forms of lead missiles, iron objects may provide an important further insight into the battlefield and the fighting it represents. One of these potentially important classes of object is horseshoes. Although horseshoes do not necessarily relate to battle, as horses are a not uncommon feature of rural life right up to the present day, they may relate to the activity of cavalry. The author has always made it a policy to collect all horseshoes recovered from surveys, even when they are obviously modern. Having by now carried out metal detector surveys on around a dozen British battlefield sites, we are in a position to discriminate between what could be described as normal background levels of equestrian activity, created by plough horses, recreational riding and hunts, for example, and pronounced peaks in quantities which may be indicative of cavalry and battle.

One result of the collection of horseshoes has been a reassessment of the typology of 18th- and 19th-century horseshoes, with comparative studies suggesting that types previously regarded as 19th century (Sparkes 1976) appear to date back as far as the early 18th century (Pollard 2006b). Cavalry activity has been recognised at Sedgemoor (1685), where almost 50 horseshoes of the 17th-century 'keyhole' type were recovered during the metal detector survey of quite a limited area of the battlefield (Pollard and Oliver 2003). Survey at Sheriffmuir (1715) resulted in the recovery of a similar number of horseshoes, at least some of which are suggestive of cavalry activity (Pollard 2006b). This interpretation was bolstered by the discovery of two iron snaffle bits – harness parts

– which would not normally break or go unrecovered during 'civilian' use (it is probably no coincidence that the only other site to include a snaffle bit was Sedgemoor). Both battles were fought on at least partly wet ground and it may be the mud which pulled so many shoes off the horses' hooves.

Although obvious evidence for cavalry action has not been recovered from Culloden, some notable iron artefacts have vindicated the use of 'all metals' survey. These finds included a fragment of socket bayonet (Fig 16.6), which appears to be of a French type and therefore likely to have been used by a Jacobite rather than a government soldier. Perhaps even more unexpected were several fragments of mortar shell, two of which were found not far to the front of the government line, on the left where the Jacobite charge struck home. Prior to their discovery the use of mortars on this part of the battlefield was unknown, although a map by artillery officer Jasper Jones drawn immediately after the battle does show three mortars engaged forward of the government right. Closer examination of eyewitness accounts following this discovery unearthed a reference to 'Royals' being brought forward to assist in halting the Jacobite charge – Royals are in fact Coehorn mortars with 5.5-inch calibre – exactly the size of the spheres represented by the heavy iron fragments (Pollard 2006a).

Metal detector survey on battlefields not only results in the recovery of artefacts which can be compared with finds from other sites, including those recovered from more traditional excavations, but also objects for which we have few known parallels. Again, Culloden has provided an example in the form of a Celtic-style round bossed cross cast from pewter, recovered not too far in front of the Jacobite front line (Fig 16.7). There seems little doubt that this object, which is very reminiscent of the standing stone crosses

FIG 16.6: FRAGMENT FROM SOCKET BAYONET RECOVERED FROM CULLODEN.

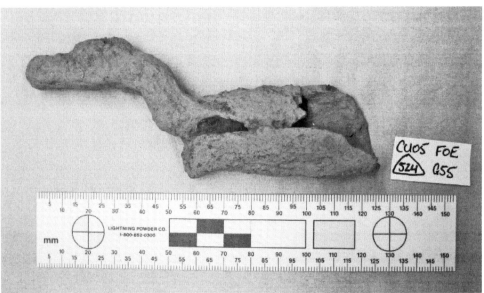

© TONY POLLARD

FIG 16.7: JACOBITE PEWTER CROSS FROM CULLODEN.

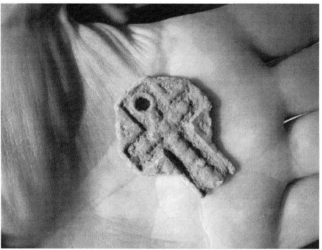

© TONY POLLARD

found in the Western Isles and the west coast of Scotland, was at one point suspended around the neck of a Jacobite soldier. Though the search continues, no direct parallel for this object has been identified in museum collections or within excavation reports. What the apparent uniqueness of the object may suggest is that the metal detector survey of battlefields not only results in the recovery of assemblages directly related to battle but also objects which have by and large escaped entry into the archaeological record elsewhere. Even more common types of artefact, such as buttons, of which numerous types have been recovered from post-medieval battle sites, are now appearing in much greater numbers than on excavated sites and it is quite apparent that we require more basic work on the dating and typology of these everyday artefacts (above and beyond the useful reference guides provided for metal detectorists, eg Bailey 2004) – and this much needed research is now being largely driven by the investigation of battlefields.

Further evidence of the important role the metal detector can play is provided by coins recovered from the battle sites of Culloden, Sheriffmuir and from fields close to the site of Fort George, built not far from Culloden in the 1750s. Coins are not an unusual find on battlefields, but those in question do not represent anything as mundane as lost spending money. They are silver shillings from William III and date to around 1696, though establishing a date is not straightforward as the coins are heavily worn. Despite, or perhaps because of, this poor condition, it is suggested that they are examples of the proverbial 'king's shilling' taken by soldiers on recruitment. The reverse side of the Sheriffmuir example is worn entirely flat and the Culloden piece not far behind. What this rubbing away of surface features tells us is that the coins were kept as lucky pieces by soldiers and probably rubbed during periods of stress or boredom. Again, metal detected finds seem to provide an insight into elements of material culture not apparent in assemblages recovered from traditional excavations, though in the UK this is partly due to the relative rarity of excavations on 17th-, 18th- and 19th-century military sites such as barracks, forts and camps (though all of these types of site are subject to metal detector activity).

CONCLUSION

Metal detector survey has undoubtedly proved its worth within the framework of research and commercially based archaeology, more than earning itself a place alongside geophysical survey and field-walking as a tool for prospection and evaluation and, in the case of battlefields, as a method of investigation on a par with the excavation of more traditional types of archaeological sites.

In Scotland and elsewhere in the UK, metal detector survey is working its way into the archaeological mainstream, most obviously but not exclusively in relation to battlefield sites. There is, however, a clear need for a standardisation of methodologies and a recognition that these surveys cannot be rushed if they are to produce a truly representative sample of the metal material in the topsoil. Recording techniques do not necessarily require expensive equipment, but due care and attention needs to be paid to the levels of recording. Far from setting themselves up in conflict with metal detectorists, archaeologists need to draw them into the fold and engender an atmosphere of collaboration, an accommodation which the author is the first to admit will not always be easily accomplished.

Further to the above, it is obvious that more research is required into the various elements of material culture recovered through the use of metal detectors. These include everything from the straightforward recognition of artefacts which may seem obscure or without obvious parallel and experimental work such as the ballistics tests using period firearms, like those currently ongoing at the Centre for Battlefield Archaeology, University of Glasgow. Additionally, we need to understand more about the plough horizon as an archaeological context, how soil chemistry impacts on artefacts and how agricultural regimes, including ploughing and the use of agrichemicals, can impact on the patterning and character of recovered assemblages. Only with this further research will we begin to more fully understand the historical events represented by these important assemblages.

ACKNOWLEDGEMENTS

Thanks to Richard Brand, Len Pentecost-Ingram, Sandy Snell, Eric Soanes, Gavin Eastwood and the other members of the Highland Historical Search Society who continue to put so much time and effort into Culloden and other sites and in doing so have made an important contribution to battlefield archaeology, and to Jon Pettet, whose dedication stands as an example to all. Barry Seger has been very helpful in sharing the results of his own work at Sedgemoor. I would like to thank Natasha Ferguson, Glenn Foard and Tim Sutherland for sharing their thoughts on metal detecting and battlefields.

BIBLIOGRAPHY

Bailey, G, 2004 *Buttons and Fasteners, 500 BC–AD 1840*, Greenlight Publishing, Witham, Essex

DCMS (Department for Culture, Media and Sport), 2008 *Draft Heritage Protection Bill*, available online at http://www.culture.gov.uk/reference_library/publications/5075.aspx (8 August 2008)

Fiorato, V, Boyslton, A, and Knüsel, C (eds), 2000 *Blood Red Roses: the archaeology of a mass grave from the Battle of Towton, AD 1461*, Oxbow, Oxford

Foard, G, 2005 *History from the Field: the Edgehill Battlefield survey* (interim report), available at http://www.battlefieldstrust.com/media/558.pdf (5 June 2008)

Freeman, P W M, 2001 Issues Concerning the Archaeology of Battlefields, in *Fields of Conflict: progress and prospect in battlefield archaeology*, P W M Freeman and A Pollard (eds), BAR International Series 958, 1–10

Hall, A J, Ellam, R, Wilson, L, Pollard, T, and Ferguson, N, 2008 *Corrosion studies and lead isotope analyses of musket balls from Scottish battlefield sites*, poster presentation at ISA 2008: metals and metallurgical ceramics (technology and provenance), 12–16 May, Siena

Haselgrove, C, 1985 Inference from ploughsoil artefact samples, in *Archaeology from the Ploughsoil: studies in the collection and interpretation of field survey data*, C Haselgrove, M Millett and I Smith (eds), Dept of Archaeology and Prehistory, University of Sheffield, 7–31

Hutton, W, 1813 *The Battle of Bosworth Field* (1999 reprint of 2nd edition, first published 1788), Tempus, Stroud

Lawrence, J, and Lawrence, R, 1988 *When the Fighting is Over: a personal story of the Battle for Tumbledown and its aftermath*, Bloomsbury, London

Morgan, H, and Shiels, D, 2007 *Irish Early Modern Military Maps*, paper given at Approaches to Conflict Archaeology Conference, Aughrim, Ireland, 24–25 March 2007

Pollard, T, 2006a *Culloden Battlefield: report on the archaeological investigation*, GUARD report 1981, University of Glasgow

— 2006b *Sheriffmuir Battlefield*, GUARD Data Structure Report 2214, University of Glasgow

— 2008 Dissecting 17th and 18th century battlefields: three case studies from the Jacobite Rebellions in Scotland, in *Method and Topic in the Historical Archaeology of Military Sites*, L Babits, C Grier, D Orr and D Scott (eds), University of Florida Press, Gainesville, Florida

Pollard, T, and Oliver, N, 2002 *Two Men in a Trench: battlefield archaeology, the key to unlocking the past*, Penguin/Michael Joseph, London

— 2003 *Two Men in a Trench II: discovering the secrets of British battlefields*, Michael Joseph/Penguin, London

Schiffer, M, 1987 *Formation Processes of the Archaeological Record*, University of New Mexico Press, Albuquerque

Scott, D, 2006 *Shot and Shell Tell the Tale: the rise of battlefield and conflict archaeology – a short retrospective*, paper given at the Fields of Conflict Conference IV, Leeds, 29 September 2006

Scott, D S, Fox, R A, Connor, M A, and Harmon, D, 1989 *Archaeological Perspectives on the Battle of Little Bighorn*, University of Oklahoma Press, Norman, Oklahoma

Smith, T, 2005 Detector Surveys of Battlefield Sites, *Treasure Hunting*, January, 56–58

Sparkes, I G, 1976 *Old Horseshoes*, Shire Album 19, Princes Risborough

Sutherland, T, 2002 *The Towton Battlefield Archaeological Survey Web Site*, available at http://mysite.wanadoo-members.co.uk/TowtonBattlefield/index.html (6 June 2008)

— 2005 The Battle of Agincourt: An Alternative Location? *Journal of Conflict Archaeology* 1 (1), 244–63

17

The Portable Antiquities Scheme and Education

Ceinwen Paynton

The Portable Antiquities Scheme (PAS) is the largest community archaeology project in England and Wales and its educational strategy and delivery is as exciting and unique as the community outreach that its Finds Liaison Officers (FLOs) carry out. The PAS is reaching out to learners of all ages and from all backgrounds, especially those that have, traditionally, felt socially excluded from the heritage sector. By taking the finds and the archaeologists out to learners, whether physically or virtually via the PAS's education microsite (www.pastexplorers.org.uk), the PAS aims to excite and involve everyone with an interest in our shared past.

When people think of the PAS, they think about a project that is all about archaeological small finds. That is only part of the story. Since its inception in 1997, the beating heart of the Scheme has been education. The finds do take centre stage and they are rewriting what we know about the past, as described in earlier chapters here, but the real stars of the show are the people that find, identify and interpret them. These people, who are learning about our past together, are what make the PAS work.

The PAS has been a huge success and is now the largest archaeological outreach project that this country has ever seen. Thirty-six Finds Liaison Officers work with their local communities to record finds, disseminate good archaeological practice and make archaeology accessible to all. They are supported by 6 Finds Advisers, 6 central unit support staff, 42 part-time Finds Assistants and 83 volunteers (although they do not all assist or volunteer at the same time). This team represents a consortium of over 60 partners and covers nearly all of the country. More than 10,000 people have worked with the PAS and more than 235,000 archaeological finds have been recorded, representing an immense change in attitudes around public involvement in archaeology, on the part of both professional archaeologists and amateurs. Portable antiquities are small pieces of other people's lives that are as diverse and varied as their finders. They have an enormous potential to inspire us to learn about the past through the objects that people made, used and lost. Artefact-based learning which has a local focus gives those people handling these objects a way of touching the past from where they live.

'Learning' is taken to be the interaction of a person with their surroundings and how that changes how they see the world. The Campaign for Learning defines it as:

a process of active engagement with experience. It is what people do when they want to make sense of the world. It may involve the deepening or development of skills, knowledge, understanding, awareness, values, ideas and feelings, or an increase in the capacity to reflect. Effective learning leads to change, development and the desire to learn more. (Campaign for Learning definition adapted by MLA 2004)

It is this 'learning' that is the topic of this chapter.

The educational strategy underlying the PAS has always been to raise awareness among finders regarding the learning potential of archaeological finds in their context and to facilitate further research. This has been done primarily by increasing opportunities for active public involvement in archaeology through encouraging finders not only to record what they have discovered, but also to gain access to archaeologists and information about good practice; first aid for finds, basic conservation and findspot recording. This has taken some time, longer in some parts of the country than in others, and has depended upon many factors: the history of cooperation between professionals and amateurs; the nature of the archaeology and the topography in the region; the length of time that an FLO has been established. The second step has then been to develop from this a way of unlocking some of the enormous learning potential that these local partnerships offer.

PAS AND ADULT LEARNERS

In more recent times, PAS has reached out to learners of all ages, but during the first few years of the PAS, before it was fully rolled out across the country, the educational work of the project was mainly concerned with adult learners. These people were the PAS's original target audience, people who were finding archaeology and archaeological objects but had often felt excluded from the heritage world and did not come into regular contact with heritage professionals or visit museums.

At this time, FLOs were often told by finders that they had been actively discouraged from 'doing' archaeology, being involved in fieldwork or enrolling on courses, because they were metal detector users. They felt that many in the heritage world were hostile to them because they disagreed with the use of metal detectors *per se*. Many professional archaeologists had experienced sites being raided illegally and had not come into contact with *bona fide* detectorists, only the rogue element in the hobby that were breaking the law. Consequently, many archaeologists believed all detectorists to be irresponsible treasure hunters at best, crooks at worst, and either way to be destroyers of archaeological context.

The fact that there was such a stand-off, and had been since the beginnings of metal detecting as a hobby in the 1970s, in turn reinforced feelings of exclusion that many hobbyists felt. Anecdotally, I have heard many detectorists say that a major motivating factor for 'getting into' metal detecting was because they were interested in history, as well as the thrill of discovery, but had not been able to do this academically because they had been told that they were not 'academic enough' to read archaeology or ancient history at university, or because life had taken a different path for them. For many finders, this was the first time that anyone from the archaeological community had gone to their clubs and meetings or asked them what motivated them or what they thought.

By asking potential learners what they wanted and what had stopped them from learning in the past (Paynton 2002), the PAS realised that what was needed was friendly, accessible archaeologists to act as both a conduit for information and a catalyst for learning. Research done in 2000 and followed up in 2004 (Chitty and Edwards 2004) showed that the finders of portable antiquities like learning through the PAS because it does all of the things that they are looking for: it takes the learning opportunities out to the metal detecting clubs and society meetings and by using the FLO as a learning facilitator, learning is personal, relevant and responsive to people's needs. When questioned about their learning needs in 2003, finders told the PAS that they wanted an individual learner-centred approach whereby learning is incorporated into other activities. They do not want formal learning scenarios or to be archaeologists. They want to know enough to satiate their thirst for knowledge and allow them to be more skilful at their hobby and then, if they are ready or have the inclination, possibly progress on to other areas of archaeology. Those finders that told us about learner progression said that what they wanted to do next was a practical course in excavation techniques, remote sensing and finds processing, something along the lines of practical courses like the old HND in Field Archaeology previously offered by Bournemouth University.

With this in mind, a series of ten regional Conservation Days were held during 2005–6 by the PAS in conjunction with York Archaeological Trust. They took place in Aylesbury, Cardiff, Colchester, Exeter, Leicester, Liverpool, Singleton, Taunton and York. The venues were varied and the programme at each event varied too, although all offered practical conservation advice for finders. Events were tailored to regional interests and specialisms: so, for example, the event held at the Weald and Downland Open Air Museum near Chichester included sessions on Anglo-Saxon brooches, horse furniture and archaeological work being undertaken in the region, as well as the chance to go 'behind the scenes' and see ancient technology experts giving demonstrations.

The regional events have been reinforced and accompanied by a series of free, friendly advice notes dealing with questions such as how to record and lift finds on site, how to store and display finds and why cleaning is not a good idea, so that people unable to attend in person can still access information about good conservation practice (PAS 2005).

Special events like the Conservation Days have been in addition to the Finds Days, lectures, history fairs, local society and community group evenings and other outreach sessions that the FLOs go to and talk at. In the year 2003–4, 13,390 people were involved in learning in this way.

Feedback was collected from those attending and was very positive, with finders wanting more of the same and especially liking being given access to the conservation labs and having techniques such as radiography, X-ray fluorescence and airbrasion explained and demonstrated.

17.1: 'GOOD LEARNING' (TOUR OF CONSERVATION LABS). FINDERS 'HAVING A GO' AT CONSERVATION AT DONCASTER MUSEUM'S LAB. 'EXCELLENT HANDS ON…CONSERVATION' (QUOTES FROM ATTENDEES AT THE CONSERVATION DAY HELD IN YORK ON SATURDAY 9 NOVEMBER 2005).

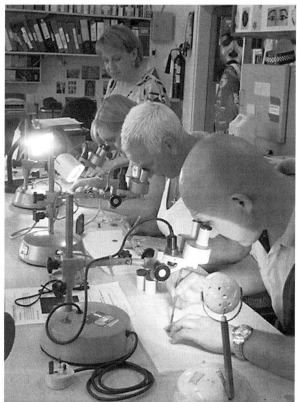

So, it can be seen that, since 1997, things have moved on. Recording finds with the local FLO has become normalised within the hobby of metal detecting, thanks in huge part to the tireless work of many people within the hobby and the governing bodies of the two main metal detecting organisations, the National Council for Metal Detecting (NCMD) and the Federation of Independent Detectorists (FID).

PAS AND YOUNG LEARNERS

As the project has grown, it has become apparent to everyone involved that the scope for learning through portable antiquities is much, much wider than the core audience of finders. In 2004, an education plan was developed in order to build upon what had already been achieved (Paynton 2004) and make sure that the whole community would benefit from the data being gathered and networks being established.

Anyone, no matter what their background, age or learning style can enjoy

17.2: NORTH LINCOLNSHIRE FLO LISA STAVES WORKING WITH CHILDREN AT SPRINGWOOD PRIMARY SCHOOL.

© PORTABLE ANTIQUITIES SCHEME

experiencing an archaeological object and use it to fire their imagination, and none more so than children. Long term, teaching children about the historic environment is key to its protection, preservation and to society's wider understanding of where we have come from. By developing educational resources to support what is already being taught in schools, academia can be linked with the wider world and the experience of young learners enriched. The most effective way of doing this is to not only go and visit schools wherever possible, with handling collections of finds, but also to create learning and teaching resources within the framework of the National Curriculum at Key Stage 2, where all pupils are taught history.

FLOs do get involved in educational outreach when they are invited to schools but it is quite a balancing act; FLOs do this in addition to their finds recording and outreach to groups of finders. They also try not to duplicate the work done by, or become competition to, colleagues working in museums or archaeological units.

For example, Lisa Staves, FLO for North Lincolnshire, along with Anna Marshall, FLO for South and West Yorkshire, and Rose Nicholson, Archaeology Assistant at North Lincolnshire Museums Service, spent a day with the pupils of Springwood Primary School, South Yorkshire, where a whole day of activities revolving around artefacts got the children thinking about history, talking about citizenship issues around who owns the past and why museums collect, and also some real finds identification and data handling. The kids loved it, especially the most hands-on and interactive activities like the finds handling and 'skeleton game', an activity that introduces and then explores topics including reversible and irreversible changes of materials, survival of materials, soil chemistry and the science of decay, as well as exploring how we feel about excavating finds and human remains.

A prescriptive, uniform, national education and outreach strategy is not possible because every region is different. Each has differing development levels in terms of the museum education provision offered, the way that archaeology is 'done' there and other factors, such as how museum school loans services work. The educational priorities for the Renaissance in the Regions Hubs, the number of heritage professionals working there and the sheer size of some regions also change the way that this outreach has to be done. When FLOs do go to schools the response has been brilliant, but the nature of the PAS and the cultural sector in England and Wales has necessitated another way of letting people access their portable past.

Resources are needed that can be available to all and that work in lessons, in school. To do this, we had to make sure that they were free and, more importantly, usable for teachers, without the need for any extra people or books to be brought in to the classroom. This makes the resources democratic and inclusive. This is a completely different strategy to the one adopted with adult learners because such a prescriptive educational framework already exists for this group.

The PAS decided to develop resources for these learners too, making the project's educational strategy a twin-pronged one. The first stage in this was research: seeing what resources were out there, what resources teachers liked and used and then working out how to build resources that used the artefacts as a starting point.

After a lot of talking to people both inside and outside the heritage and wider cultural sectors, observing, asking questions and investigating teaching methods and technologies, the PAS has developed a website devoted to these resources and to younger learners called PASt explorers (playing on the project being known as the PAS); this is a fun, interactive digital resource for Key Stage 2 (primary-school-aged children) history, history & ICT, geography & ICT and STEM (science, technology, engineering and maths). On this site, young learners (and their parents, carers and teachers) can explore the virtual Anglo-Saxon village of West Mucking, have a go at virtual fieldwork and get information about archaeological techniques and chronologies, and there is also a virtual staffroom for teachers with lesson plans, examples of children's work and support materials.

> I'm in Year 4 and for our history ICT lesson our teacher Mrs Sherriff showed us West Mucking. I liked the first part because I learned that you had to wash raw wool before you can spin it, I also liked the second part because the metal detector didn't find everything and you also had to use the boots as well. (Year 4 pupil, St Mary's C E Primary)

The site was developed by the PAS and the Education and Multimedia Unit at the British Museum, and several specialists from the worlds of archaeology and education advised on content. For example, it was important that the information presented was as up-to-date in terms of archaeological finds and theory as possible. Many 'historical' or interactive sites that are aimed at the Key Stage 2 age group would horrify archaeologists

17.3: Pictured: the two characters that guide young learners through PASt explorers.

17.4: Jarren and Sophie, both Year 5 pupils at Henry Moore Primary School in Castleford explore the PAS's virtual Anglo-Saxon village of West Mucking!

with their content, which is often poorly researched or hopelessly out of date. Several teachers and several children aged 7–11 helped us to test it and they liked it because it did not rely too much on text, it did not look like any other websites – so looked as new and innovative as it actually was – and the children were given real, serious information about things that actually interested them. For example, a very popular part of the site was that in which archaeological good practice was presented in exciting ways, with, for example, concepts behind conservation being explained through the Pack Your Bag interactive game.

PASt explorers was launched in late 2005, and at the time of writing, the lesson plans have been downloaded hundreds of times. If that equates to 168 classes using them then it can be extrapolated that more than 4000 children have benefited from this archaeology in their classrooms, and this does not include factoring in the physical outreach from FLOs going into the classroom or coordinating fieldwork with children. Can you imagine how much more exciting our lessons would have been at school if we had been shown real artefacts or wandered around a virtual Anglo-Saxon village or used evidence from long-lost lives to learn about maths or science?

> The discovery section of the computer program seemed to excite the children. They appeared eager to find the different objects. (History & QTS NQT)

> I truly loved the resource and used it as a historical simulation for the children. (Year 4 class teacher)

> The website is clear, informative, great for teachers and young pupils – you are onto a winner! (Specialist Inspector for Humanities)

The feedback from the teachers, Local Education Authority Advisers and Initial Teacher Training centres that we have been working with has been very positive and the next step is to build on this and develop more resources for Key Stage 2 before extending this to Key Stages 3 and 4.

With the success that the PAS has had with both informal adult learners and formal young learners, an obvious next step would be to use elements of both of these strategies to make archaeology more accessible to the groups that fall between these, such as teenage learners and children wanting to learn out of school hours. These are the areas that we will be developing next. Already, FLOs are reporting back on GCSE sessions that they have delivered and several are involved in after-school or out-of-school-hours learning like the Young Archaeologists' Clubs. The Education Coordinator has been working with colleagues from other heritage organisations, LEAs and schools to test sessions for Key Stage 3 and 4 learners. The PAS has been busy adding content aimed at these groups to the PASt explorers website and is always keen to have reciprocal links or content from other organisations: these can all be browsed at: www.pastexplorers.org.uk.

If the thousands of finds recovered every year in this country by a dedicated band of ordinary members of the community who carry out this work free of charge are not recorded, we will lose the archaeological information that they hold and their secrets will be irrevocably lost. Hopefully, this will not be the case and we will continue to learn about our shared past through archaeological finds, together.

In conclusion, while there is sometimes a tendency to validate archaeological projects by saying that something is 'educational', this really is the case with the PAS. Since the very beginning of the project, it has had as its aims education, awareness-raising, research and dissemination of knowledge and this is what we are still trying to achieve. There is a lot to do but the end result will be to change the places where archaeology, outreach and education overlap and maybe even change the way that we do and see archaeology in Britain. We are learning just as much from the finders and learners that work with us as they are from us. Given enough time, continued funding and cooperative working, we will make the way that both professionals and amateurs approach archaeology more democratic, more inclusive and more relevant to more people.

We have come from small beginnings and, in the scheme of things, the PAS is still a new project but for those of us working in the middle of all of this, it feels like the heritage world is changing and we are entering a whole new age of information and participation. I would like to think that the people who use the PAS feel this way too and that they are being included, inspired and most importantly helped to learn the things that they want to learn by the PAS.

BIBLIOGRAPHY

Chitty, G, and Edwards, R, 2004 *Review of the Portable Antiquities Scheme*, Hawkshead Archaeology and Conservation, MLA

Edwards, R, 2006 *Portable Antiquities Scheme User Survey 2006*, Arboretum Archaeological Consultancy

MLA, 2004 Introduction, *Inspiring Learning for All*, available at http://www.inspiringlearningforall.gov.uk/introduction/what_do_we_mean/what_do_we_mean/default.aspx (23 April 2008)

Paynton, C, 2002 Public perception and 'pop archaeology': a survey of current attitudes toward televised archaeology in Britain, *The SAA Archaeological Record*, March, 33–44

— 2004 *The Portable Antiquities Scheme Education Plan, a research assessment and strategic planning document for the HLF in three parts* (discussion and strategy document, appendices of evidence, project management and budgetary forward plans), publ. internally, PAS/MLA

PAS (Portable Antiquities Scheme), 2005 *Conservation Advice Notes*, available at http://www.finds.org.uk/conservation/ (23 April 2008)

Author Biographies

Peter V Addyman

Peter Addyman, a retired archaeologist whose career spanned the period when metal detecting became an issue in British archaeology, maintained an interest in the subject since watching as a child the use of military mine detectors on an archaeological site. Initially a lecturer in archaeology at Belfast and Southampton Universities, from 1972 to 2002 he was Director of York Archaeological Trust. A protagonist of the 1970s STOP campaign against metal detecting, he was President of the Council for British Archaeology in the 1990s and chairman for 10 years of the Portable Antiquities Working Group and the Standing Conference on Portable Antiquities, when Britain's present policies on metal detecting emerged.

Trevor Austin

In addition to his role as General Secretary of the National Council for Metal Detecting, Trevor Austin is also personnel manager for a group of Shell petrol stations in and around West Yorkshire. He has been metal detecting since the late 1980s, a hobby which began as a fascination for historical items and grew from there. Trevor joined the NCMD in 1987 and became Assistant General Secretary in 1994. In 1997 he was elected General Secretary, a position which he still holds. Trevor is also a member of the Treasure Validation Committee, a post which he thoroughly enjoys; he is currently in the third year of a four-year term.

Elize Becker

Elize Becker obtained her qualifications as an anthropologist and archaeologist at the University of Pretoria (RSA) and commenced with research studies related to Socio-Economic Activities at an Informal Pottery Production Village located at Mukondeni, Venda (Limpopo Province, RSA). Elize was employed as a Heritage Officer (Senior Archaeologist) at Amafa–aKwaZulu–Natali, where her duties included, among other things, the planning, organisation, management and control of heritage resources, being responsible for the administration of all legal processes related to the enforcement of the Provincial Heritage Resources Act (Kwazulu–Natal RSA). Her responsibility to protect battlefield areas against development threats resulted in an interest in the legal and controlled application of metal detectors as part of archaeological excavation.

ROGER BLAND

Roger Bland is Head of the Department of Portable Antiquities & Treasure at the British Museum. From 1994 and 2002 he worked for the Culture Department on the *Treasure Act* and established the Portable Antiquities Scheme. Before that he was a curator of Roman Coins in the Department of Coins & Medals at the British Museum, working on coin hoards such as the Cunetio hoard of some 55,000 3rd-century coins and the great late Roman Treasure from Hoxne.

DOT BOUGHTON

Dot Boughton completed her MSt and MPhil in Anglo-Saxon Archaeology at Oxford before researching British late Bronze/early Iron Age metalwork. She is currently working for the Portable Antiquities Scheme as Lancashire/Cumbria FLO. When she is not recording finds for the Scheme, she writes post-excavation specialist reports for smaller metalwork assemblages (late Bronze Age metalwork) and lectures at the University of Central Lancashire in Preston (late Roman and early medieval archaeology, Bronze and early Iron Age metalwork).

JOHN CORNELISON

John E Cornelison Jr. is an archaeologist at the US National Park Service, Southeast Archeological Center. Mr Cornelison received his graduate education at the University of Southern Mississippi. He has worked extensively with metal detecting volunteers on battlefield sites in the southern United States, focusing primarily on the American Revolutionary and Civil Wars. He is also well versed in computer applications of archaeology, such as geographical information systems.

DECLAN HURL

Declan P Hurl is an archaeologist who, at the time of writing, was with the Environment and Heritage Service, an agency in the Department of the Environment for Northern Ireland. Although his degree is in social anthropology, he has worked on many archaeological excavations and post-excavation programmes, and achieved a Certificate in Field Archaeology from Oxford. He also successfully undertook training as an HSE-qualified diver in Fort William. He has directed, and published articles on, a range of excavations, has participated in underwater projects and has liaised with metal detector users, divers and other discoverers of archaeological artefacts. He has worked as a consultant on proposed legislation and departmental agreements. He has since taken up a post with the RSK Group plc, an environmental consultancy.

ZBIGNIEW KOBYLIŃSKI

Zbigniew Kobyliński, dr habil., is professor at the Cardinal Stefan Wyszyński University and at the Institute of Archaeology and Ethnology of the Polish Academy of Sciences. He is an archaeologist who between 1995 and 1999 was deputy to the Commissioner General for Historical Monuments. Since 1997 he has taught archaeological heritage management at the University and conducts research on such subjects as the non-destructive methods of archaeological prospection, preventative conservation of archaeological sites, and public attitudes towards archaeological heritage. He is currently a member of the Executive Board of the European Association of Archaeologists, president of the Scientific Society of Polish Archaeologists, and editor of the journal *Archaeologia Polona*. In Poland Zbigniew has published a book on theoretical backgrounds for the conservation of archaeological heritage, as well as several papers on various aspects of archaeological heritage management, and has edited ten volumes of collected papers on the protection and conservation of archaeological heritage, among them a volume on the problem of metal detector users.

MARK LODWICK

Mark Lodwick has worked since 2004 on coordinating the Portable Antiquities Scheme in Wales, based at Amgueddfa Cymru – National Museum Wales – in Cardiff. Some significant discoveries made by metal detector users have resulted in developing research projects in conjunction with National Museum Wales. The projects have benefited from innovative educational packages, community engagement and responses from creative individuals, ensuring that archaeological discoveries receive an enhanced public and academic engagement.

JOHN NAYLOR

John Naylor is the Portable Antiquities Scheme's National Finds Adviser for Early Medieval and Later Coinage based at the Ashmolean Museum, Oxford. From 2004 to 2007 he worked with Julian Richards on the 'Anglo-Saxon Landscape and Economy' project at the University of York, prior to which he studied at the University of Durham culminating in a PhD focusing on patterns of regional trade in pre-Viking Anglo-Saxon England.

CEINWEN PAYNTON

Ceinwen read archaeology and anthropology at Girton College, Cambridge, after being hooked on archaeology from about the age of eight. She then went on to do postgraduate studies in landscape archaeology and then in education and worked as an FLO on the Portable Antiquities Scheme for five years. Subsequently she worked in TV, being the resident finds specialist for *Time Team*, and has recently appeared in a number of television programmes. A specialist in public archaeology and tackling exclusion, Ceinwen is very keen to promote museums as unique places and cultural learning foci within communities.

She is passionate about taking the museum and museum people out into the community, which is why she went to work on the PAS as their National Learning Coordinator. Since the time of writing, Ceinwen has left the PAS to take up the position of Principal Keeper for Leeds' brand-new £26 million City Museum.

TONY POLLARD

Tony Pollard PhD is Director of the Centre for Battlefield Archaeology at the University of Glasgow. In 2000 he co-organised and hosted *Fields of Conflict*, the first international conference on battlefield archaeology, which is still held every two years. He was co-presenter of the BBC television series *Two Men in a Trench*, which brought battlefield archaeology to a worldwide audience. He has carried out battlefield projects in the UK, Europe, Africa and South America and has published widely on this and other aspects of archaeology.

JULIAN RICHARDS

Julian Richards is a Professor in Archaeology at the University of York. His research interests focus on Anglo-Saxon and Viking England and on computer applications in archaeology. Since 1996 he has been Director of the Archaeology Data Service and the e-journal *Internet Archaeology*. He has directed excavations of the Viking cemetery and Heath Wood, Ingleby, and has worked with metal detector users on the discovery and excavation of Anglo-Scandinavian settlements in the Yorkshire Wolds since 1993, including Cottam, Cowlam and Burdale. From 2004 to 2007 he directed an AHRC-funded research project on Anglo-Saxon Landscape and Economy: Using Portable Antiquities to Study Anglo-Saxon and Viking England.

ALAN SAVILLE

Alan Saville is Senior Curator (Earliest Prehistory) in the Department of Archaeology at National Museums Scotland, Edinburgh, where he has worked since 1989. He is also Head of the Treasure Trove Unit, which is based at the National Museums, and has overseen the development of the Scottish Treasure Trove systems since 1995. In an honorary capacity he has served as President of the Council for Scottish Archaeology, Treasurer and Vice-President of the Society of Antiquaries of Scotland, and as a member of the Ancient Monuments Board for Scotland. He is currently Editor of the *European Journal of Archaeology* and a member of the Executive Board of the European Association of Archaeologists.

FAYE SIMPSON

Faye Simpson is a community archaeologist who has worked for the Portable Antiquities Scheme as an FLO and has directed community archaeology projects for the Museum of London. Faye is currently the Exeter Graduate Fellow in Community Archaeology within the Department of Archaeology at the University of Exeter. For her Graduate

Fellowship, Faye is a project assistant for the X-Arch community archaeology project (2006–2009) and a doctoral candidate researching the efficacy and social context of community archaeology in the UK. She is a long-term contributor to the Channel Four *Time Team* television series.

GEORGE SMITH

Dr George S Smith is currently the Associate Director at the Southeast Archeological Center in Tallahassee, Florida, USA. The Center undertakes many projects through partnerships with metal detecting groups who assist archaeological staff in locating metal artefacts associated with various military engagements throughout US history. Dr Smith has served on various Society for American Archaeology (SAA) committees as well as on the Board of Directors and received the 2007 SAA award for Excellence in Cultural Resource Management. He co-edited *Protecting the Past, Teaching Archaeology in the 21st Century* and *Cultural Heritage Management, Policies, and Issues in Global Perspective.*

PETER SPENCER

Until recently, Peter Spencer was a member of the panel of approved tutors in the School of Continuing Education at the University of Leeds and a part-time lecturer for Bradford College, but he no longer does any teaching work. He now acts as a freelance consultant and writer on coins and antiquities and is a member of the panel of commercial advisers to the Treasure Valuation Committee. His experience and involvement in metal detecting has proved that pre-conceived expectations in relation to patterns of coin finds can be wrong and his chapter attempts to explain the reasons for this.

PIOTR SZPANOWSKI

Piotr Szpanowski is an archaeologist who graduated from the Institute of Archaeology, University of Warsaw (1996) and the Academy of Heritage – Krakow International Cultural Centre (2003). Between 1997 and 2002 he worked as a specialist in the Department for the Protection of Archaeological Monuments in the Office of the Commissioner General for Historical Monuments. In 2002 he worked in the Wilanow Palace Museum in Warsaw, and since that time he has been involved mainly in the management of the Museum's historical and natural resources. As co-writer of Zbigniew Kobyliński's chapter, Piotr provided support through his contacts within the provincial offices for the protection of monuments. He has also attempted to compare the state of knowledge on metal detecting in Poland from the second half of 1990 (as described by him in articles published at that time) with the present situation.

SUZIE THOMAS

Suzie Thomas completed her PhD at Newcastle University in 2009, which investigated the relationships between archaeologists and metal-detector users in England and Wales.

She has since worked for the Council for British Archaeology and University of Glasgow, and is currently lecturer in museum studies at the University of Helsinki.

PHILIPPA WALTON

Philippa Walton studied Anglo-Saxon, Norse and Celtic and Classics at Cambridge University before training as a finds specialist at both Oxford Archaeology and the Ashmolean Museum. Following the nationwide expansion of the Portable Antiquities Scheme in 2003, she took up post as the FLO for the North East. While working in Newcastle, she developed a particular interest in Roman finds and riverine votive deposits, in part stimulated by the recording of a large archaeological assemblage from the bed of the River Tees at Piercebridge, County Durham. In 2005, she left the North East to become the FLO for Cambridgeshire. She is now studying the Portable Antiquities Scheme Roman coin data as part of a collaborative AHRC PhD based at the Institute of Archaeology, University College, London, and the British Museum.

Index

Entries in **bold** refer to the illustrations